T0213096

Lecture Notes of the Institute for Computer Sciences, Social Informatics and Telecommunications Engineering

206

Editorial Board

Ozgur Akan
Middle East Technical University, Ankara, Turkey

Paolo Bellavista
University of Bologna, Bologna, Italy

Jiannong Cao
Hong Kong Polytechnic University, Hong Kong, Hong Kong

Geoffrey Coulson
Lancaster University, Lancaster, UK

Falko Dressler
University of Erlangen, Erlangen, Germany

Domenico Ferrari
Università Cattolica Piacenza, Piacenza, Italy

Mario Gerla
UCLA, Los Angeles, USA

Hisashi Kobayashi
Princeton University, Princeton, USA

Sergio Palazzo
University of Catania, Catania, Italy

Sartaj Sahni
University of Florida, Florida, USA

Xuemin Sherman Shen
University of Waterloo, Waterloo, Canada

Mircea Stan
University of Virginia, Charlottesville, USA

Jia Xiaohua
City University of Hong Kong, Kowloon, Hong Kong

Albert Y. Zomaya
University of Sydney, Sydney, Australia

More information about this series at http://www.springer.com/series/8197

Fatna Belqasmi · Hamid Harroud
Max Agueh · Rachida Dssouli
Faouzi Kamoun (Eds.)

Emerging Technologies for Developing Countries

First International EAI Conference, AFRICATEK 2017
Marrakech, Morocco, March 27–28, 2017
Proceedings

Springer

Editors
Fatna Belqasmi
Zayed University
Abu Dhabi
United Arab Emirates

Hamid Harroud
Al Akhawayn University
Ifrane
Morocco

Max Agueh
LACSC - ECE
Paris
France

Rachida Dssouli
CIISE
Montreal
Canada

Faouzi Kamoun
ESPRIT
Tunis
Tunisia

ISSN 1867-8211   ISSN 1867-822X (electronic)
Lecture Notes of the Institute for Computer Sciences, Social Informatics
and Telecommunications Engineering
ISBN 978-3-319-67836-8   ISBN 978-3-319-67837-5 (eBook)
https://doi.org/10.1007/978-3-319-67837-5

Library of Congress Control Number: 2017956082

© ICST Institute for Computer Sciences, Social Informatics and Telecommunications Engineering 2018
This work is subject to copyright. All rights are reserved by the Publisher, whether the whole or part of the material is concerned, specifically the rights of translation, reprinting, reuse of illustrations, recitation, broadcasting, reproduction on microfilms or in any other physical way, and transmission or information storage and retrieval, electronic adaptation, computer software, or by similar or dissimilar methodology now known or hereafter developed.
The use of general descriptive names, registered names, trademarks, service marks, etc. in this publication does not imply, even in the absence of a specific statement, that such names are exempt from the relevant protective laws and regulations and therefore free for general use.
The publisher, the authors and the editors are safe to assume that the advice and information in this book are believed to be true and accurate at the date of publication. Neither the publisher nor the authors or the editors give a warranty, express or implied, with respect to the material contained herein or for any errors or omissions that may have been made. The publisher remains neutral with regard to jurisdictional claims in published maps and institutional affiliations.

Printed on acid-free paper

This Springer imprint is published by Springer Nature
The registered company is Springer International Publishing AG
The registered company address is: Gewerbestrasse 11, 6330 Cham, Switzerland

Preface

AFRICATEK 2017 was the first edition of the EAI International Conference on Emerging Technologies for Developing Countries. It focuses on the use of new technologies (e.g., cloud computing, IoT, data analytics, green computing, etc.) in developing countries. Building innovative solutions and services based on cutting-edge technologies is very challenging in developing countries for several reasons. The limited IT infrastructure and Internet penetration are two of the key hindering barriers. The goal of this conference is to bring together researchers and practitioners from academia and industry to share their results and ideas on how to benefit the developing world from the advances of technologies despite the existing limitations.

AFRICATEK 2017 received 41 submission, including full papers, short papers, invited papers, and posters. Of these submissions, 22 were accepted as full papers. The authors are from several countries and institutions, including Morocco, Algeria, Tunisia, South Africa, Benin, UAE, Japan, Pakistan, Belgium, Portugal, Italy, France, Canada, and the USA. Some contributions were also joint works between several institutions and countries.

The accepted papers cover several topics related to emerging technologies and their use in developing countries in particular, and in rural areas in general. These topics span different infrastructures, technologies and paradigms, and application areas. Examples of targeted infrastructures are wireless sensor networks, vehicular area networks, mobile networks, and the cloud. The technologies and paradigms used include virtualization, cloud computing, Internet of Things, data analytics, knowledge management, Web services, software engineering, and artificial neural networks. The application areas covered span e-services and mobile-based applications (e.g., e-health, e-learning, e-commerce, and e-collaboration), smart energy, disaster management, language-based applications (e.g., speech recognition), and security.

We would like to express our gratitude and thanks to the many people who contributed to the organization of this first edition. Without their support and dedicated efforts, this would not have been possible. Special thanks go to the Organizing Committee members and to all the persons who voluntarily put much effort in creating, planning, advertising, and organizing the event. Many thanks to the authors who contributed their work to the conference; to the Technical Program Committee chairs and committee members, who dedicated their time to thoroughly review the submitted papers and share their comments to enhance the technical quality of the program; and to our valuable keynote and tutorial speakers, who enriched the program with their contribution.

Special thanks also go to the Kingdom of Morocco for its openness to promote advanced technologies in developing countries. We are also grateful to the EAI support throughout the process and to our sponsors and supporters.

August 2017

Fatna Belqasmi
Max Agueh
Hamid Harroud

Organization

Steering Committee

Imrich Chlamtac   Create-Net, Italy
Fatna Belqasmi   CTI, Zayed University, UAE

Organizing Committee

General Chair

Fatna Belqasmi   CTI, Zayed University, UAE

General Co-chairs

Hamid Harroud   Al Akhawayn University, Morocco
Max Agueh   ECE Paris, Graduate School of Engineering, France

TPC Chair and Co-chair

Faouzi Kamoun   Esprit School of Enginnering, Tunisia
Rachida Dssouli   Concordia University, Canada

Sponsorship and Exhibit Chair

Ahmed Legrouri   Al Akhawayn University, Morocco

Local Chair

Zahi Jarir   Cadi Ayyad University, Morocco

Workshops Chair

Marco Zennaro   Telecommunications, ICT for Development Laboratory, Italy

Publicity and Social Media Chair

Cherif Belfekih   Al Akhawayn University, Morocco

Publications Chair

Farhi Marir   Zayed University, UAE

Web Chair

Taoufiq Abdelouhab   Al Akhawayn University, Morocco

Posters and PhD Track Chair

Muthoni Masinde   Central University of Technology, South Africa

Panels Chair

Farhi Marir   Zayed University, UAE

Demos Chair

Thar B. Shamsa   Liverpool John Moores University, UK

Tutorials Chairs

Omar Al Fandi   College of Technological Innovation, Zayed University,
                                    UAE
John Beachboard   College of Technological Innovation, Zayed University,
                                    UAE

Conference Manager

Lenka Oravska   European Alliance for Innovation

Technical Program Committee

Slimane Bah	Ecole Mohammadia d'Ingénieurs (EMI), Rabat, Morocco
Mohammed Boulmalf	International University of Rabat (IUR), Rabat, Morocco
Abdellah Boulouz	Ibn Zohr University, Agadir, Morocco
Ernesto Damiani	Università degli Studi di, Milano, Italy
Abdeslam Ennouaary	Ecole des Télécomsmunications et des Technologies de l'Information (INPT), Rabat, Morocco
Mohammed Erradi	Ecole Nationale Superieure d'Informatique et d'Analyse des Systèmes (ENSIAS), Rabat, Morocco
Mohammed Essaaidi	Ecole Nationale Superieure d'Informatique et d'Analyse des Systèmes (ENSIAS), Rabat, Morocco
Eugene C. Ezin	University of Abomey Calavi, Republic of Benin
Michael Gerndt	Technische Universität München (TUM), Germany
Mehdi Kaddouri	Université Mohamed Premier-Oujda, Morocco
Mohammed Ouzzif	ESTC, University Hassan II, Morocco
Adel Serhani	UAE University, UAE
Rabeb Mizouni	Khalifa University, UAE
Sofiene Tahar	Concordia University, Canada
Pierre de Saqui-Sannes	ISAE SUPAERO, Institut Supérieur de l'Aéronautique et de l'Espace, France
Fatima Zahra Errounda	Concordia University, Montreal, Canada
Ilham Amezzane	Université Ibn Tofail, Morocco
Zakaria Maamar	Zayed University, UAE
Aurel Randolph	Ecole Polytechnique, Montreal, Canada

Ahmed Dooguy Kora   ESMT, Dakar, Senegal
Vincent Oria   NJIT, USA
Radouane Mrabet   ENSIAS, University Mohammed V, Morocco
Jamal Bentahar   Concordia University, Canada
Taha Ridene   ENSTA ParisTech, France
Alemayehu Desta   Université Paris-Est Marne-la-Vallée (UPEM), France
Asad Khattak   Zayed University, UAE
Hénoc Soude   Institut de Mathematiques et de Science Physique
            (IMSP/UAC), Benin
Jean-Francois Diouris   Université de Nantes, France
Tounwendyam Frederic   Université de Koudougou, Burkina Faso
    Ouedraogo
Tubaishat Abdallah   Zayed University, UAE
Boudriga Nourredine   University of Carthage, Tunisia
Mezrioui Abdellatif   INPT, Morocco
Belkasmi Mostafa   ENSIAS, Morocco
Bakhouya Mohamed   International University of Rabat (IUR), Rabat, Morocco
Eleanna Kafaeza   Zayed University, UAE
May El Barachi   University of Wollongong in Dubai, UAE

Contents

WSNs, VANs and Mobile Networks

Seamless WSN Connectivity Using Diverse Wireless Links 3
    Omar Alfandi, Jagadeesha RB, and John Beachboard

Mixed Method: An Aggregated Method for Handover Decision
in Heterogeneous Wireless Networks 12
    Saida Driouache, Najib Naja, and Abdellah Jamali

Analysis of the Impact of Cognitive Vehicular Network Environment
on Spectrum Sensing 22
    Amina Riyahi, Marouane Sebgui, Slimane Bah, and Belhaj Elgraini

High Availability of Charging and Billing in Vehicular Ad Hoc Network . . . 33
    Mohamed Darqaoui, Slimane Bah, and Marouane sebgui

IoT and Cloud Computing

Developing the IoT to Support the Health Sector: A Case Study
from Kikwit, DR Congo 45
    Piers W. Lawrence, Trisha M. Phippard, Gowri Sankar Ramachandran,
    and Danny Hughes

Designing a Framework for Smart IoT Adaptations 57
    Asmaa Achtaich, Nissrine Souissi, Raul Mazo, Camille Salinesi,
    and Ounsa Roudies

ABAC Based Online Collaborations in the Cloud 67
    Mohamed Amine Madani, Mohammed Erradi, and Yahya Benkaouz

Smart Energy and Disaster Management

Evaluating Query Energy Consumption in Document Stores 79
    Duarte Duarte and Orlando Belo

Joint Energy Demand Prediction and Control 89
    Mehdi Merai and Jia Yuan Yu

Big Data, Data Analytics, and Knowledge Management

Trust Assessment-Based Multiple Linear Regression for Processing Big
Data Over Diverse Clouds 99
  *Hadeel El-Kassabi, Mohamed Adel Serhani, Chafik Bouhaddioui,
  and Rachida Dssouli*

Opinions Sandbox: Turning Emotions on Topics into Actionable Analytics ... 110
  Feras Al-Obeidat, Eleanna Kafeza, and Bruce Spencer

E-Healthcare Knowledge Creation Platform Using Action Research 120
  May Al Taei, Eleanna Kafeza, and Omar Alfandi

Web Services and Software Engineering

Framework for Dynamic Web Services Composition Guided
by Live Testing 129
  Mounia Elqortobi, Jamal Bentahar, and Rachida Dssouli

Modernization of Legacy Software Tests to Model-Driven Testing 140
  Nader Kesserwan, Rachida Dssouli, and Jamal Bentahar

Mobile-Based Applications

Porting the Pay with a (Group) Selfie (PGS) Payment System
to Crypto Currency 159
  *Ernesto Damiani, Perpetus Jacques Houngbo, Joël T. Hounsou,
  Rasool Asal, Stelvio Cimato, Fulvio Frati, Dina Shehada,
  and Chan Yeob Yeun*

Security

Cloud Digital Forensics Evaluation and Crimes Detection 171
  Raja Jabir and Omar Alfandi

Detecting Malware Domains: A Cyber-Threat Alarm System 181
  *Khalifa AlRoum, Abdulhakim Alolama, Rami Kamel, May El Barachi,
  and Monther Aldwairi*

Intrusion Detection Using Unsupervised Approach 192
  Jai Puneet Singh and Nizar Bouguila

Short Papers

Cloud Computing and Virtualization in Developing Countries 205
  Yness Boukhris

Analysis and Effect of Feature Selection Over Smartphone-Based Dataset
for Human Activity Recognition   214
    Ilham Amezzane, Youssef Fakhri, Mohammed El Aroussi,
    and Mohamed Bakhouya

Empowering Graduates for Knowledge Economies
in Developing Countries   220
    Maurice Danaher, Kevin Shoepp, Ashley Ater Kranov,
    and Julie Bauld Wallace

Designing an Electronic Health Security System Framework
for Authentication with Wi-Fi, Smartphone and 3D Face
Recognition Technology   226
    Lesole Kalake and Chika Yoshida

Posters

Investigating TOE Factors Affecting the Adoption of a Cloud-Based
EMR System in the Free-State, South Africa   233
    Nomabhongo Masana and Gerald Maina Muriithi

Author Index   239

WSNs, VANs and Mobile Networks

Seamless WSN Connectivity Using Diverse Wireless Links

Omar Alfandi[1(✉)], Jagadeesha RB[2], and John Beachboard[1]

[1] Zayed University, Abu Dhabi, United Arab Emirates
{omar.alfandi,john.beachboard}@zu.ac.ae
[2] National Institute of Technology, New Delhi, India
jagadeesha_rb@yahoo.com

Abstract. Data transfer using wireless sensor networks (WSN) is bound by its limited coverage range. In order to communicate data beyond the coverage capability of a WSN link and make it pervasive, the authors here propose a method of information handover using heterogeneous wireless links for sensor-based data transmission. They draw on connectivity, one of the main features of a pervasive network. In the handover method proposed here, the WSN link is part of a wireless module which integrates various heterogeneous wireless links. All these wireless links are combined and coordinated using media independent handover functions (MIH) in accordance with the 802.21 Standard. As wireless modules have multiple wireless links, each module can communicate with the others using any one of the active links. When these wireless modules consisting of multiple links move beyond the communication range of the WSN link to maintain continuous connectivity the MIH in the module triggers the other wireless links to hand over the service with the help of access points in the surrounding area. The concept is discussed here in the context of a smart home application which transfers the sensed information continuously to a remotely located controlling station using the existing wireless infrastructure.

Keywords: IEEE 802.21 · WSN · MIH · Pervasive

1 Introduction

The wireless sensor network has become a prevalent network due to its simplicity of protocol stacking, network formation, durability, and suitability to a wide range of common applications involving unattended monitoring compared to the other wireless standards. When the WSN nodes are deployed to monitor an activity and to transfer the monitored data directly to a remote controlling station, the data transfer is possible as long as the nodes are in communication range of each other. However, as they move out of the physical range, communication gets interrupted.

As a solution to this problem, one can adopt various network topologies though each has its own capabilities, and an ideal solution may not be plausible. A strategy involving the Internet of Things (IoT) may be the best solution with modifications to the existing internet system. Nowadays, it is common to find wireless communication devices enabled with several wireless standards to facilitate communication with similar devices.

© ICST Institute for Computer Sciences, Social Informatics and Telecommunications Engineering 2018
F. Belqasmi et al. (Eds.): AFRICATEK 2017, LNICST 206, pp. 3–11, 2018.
https://doi.org/10.1007/978-3-319-67837-5_1

For example, a mobile phone equipped with 3G, GPRS, Wi-Fi, or Bluetooth facility can communicate data through any device which has any one of these standards.

The current wireless environment motivates development of a method of achieving seamless connectivity between wireless sensor network nodes using other wireless standards. This paper proposes a method for integrating wireless standards into a single module and communicating in a coordinated manner. In this proposal, the IEEE 802.21 media independent handover functions are used as a platform in which wireless standards of varying types coexist and hand over the data between similar wireless modules. The IEEE 802.21-2008 is a standard [1] to provide handover facility between 802 and non-802 devices such as IEEE 802.11, IEEE 802.16, and 3G cellular networks. It consists of a set of functions called media independent handover functions which form the core regulating the overall functionality of such a stack. The media independent handover (MIH) function comprises an event, command, and information services to monitor network parameters and to regulate, validate and gather information for efficient communication between any two nodes.

In this proposal, the communication capabilities of the ordinary IEEE 802.15.4 based WSN node are extended using this feature of media independent handover functions.

According to this model, a wireless node consists of multiple wireless standards like IEEE 802.11 (Wi-Fi), IEEE 802.16 (Wi-Max), and 3G cellular interface, along with the IEEE 802.15.4 (WSN) which is called a combined wireless node (mobile node) as shown in Fig. 1. The MIH functions direct the overall interaction between them and enable other wireless links to perform a handover whenever a node moves out of range. Such an enabled link, with the assistance of its home network, transfers the data to the destination.

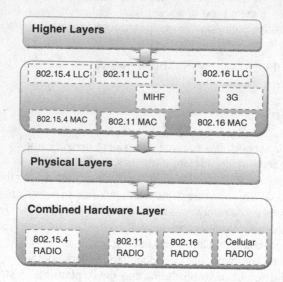

Fig. 1. Mobile node architecture

2 Literature Review

The handover feature of MIH has appeared in several previous works. Kim, Moon and Cho [2] discussed a handover method between Wi-Fi and Wi-Max links using a prospective candidate for handover. Introducing a new framework for MIH, as in the works of Lim and Kim [3] as well as Ali-Yahiya and Bullot [4] provides faster handover between 802 links. The cross-layer design for the stack in Vulpe, Obreja and Barbu [5] provides handover between the 802 and cellular networks. In this example, the new network selection policy engines and mobile node architecture are discussed. The Qualnet simulation [6] for mobile node handover deals only with limited parameters. For efficient handover, an information server and a new architecture and prototype are evaluated in Fratu, Popovici and Halunga [7]. Their results show optimum processing time in handover and vary based on the application. To collect the handover information from the information servers effectively, center node architecture is proposed in Andrei, Popovici and Fratu [8]; this system collects information from all servers to update the network as in Popovici, Fratu and Halunga [9]. Handover techniques are similarly analyzed in RB [10], Chukwu [11], and Fallon and Murphy [12].

Until now, MIH features have been used to provide handover between 802 or cellular networks. In this paper, the MIH is used to trigger the handover process whenever the WSN node is about to lose connectivity with the destination to continue the data transfer. In this case a wireless node (the MN) is a portable wireless unit with a stack consisting of multiple wireless links and MIH.

3 Specifications

3.1 Technical Aspects

The technical aspects of this work mainly involve the development of architecture to support handover between the WSN (802.15.4) and other wireless links by having them all reside within the same module. The wireless module that integrates all the wireless links and MIH and coordinates them is called a combined wireless module or mobile node (MN). The media independent handover functions can provide three set of services: event, command, and information services. The event services deal with reporting of events related to the change in link behavior, link status such as link up or down, or any changes in the link parameters of the communication link.

Media independent command services are generated by any higher layer which enables them to control the lower layers (PHY, DLL) to set up the network connectivity based on the reported parameters of the event services. In this way, command services enable the user to select the best network for the task.

As the IEEE 802.21 standard does not specify the handover service for WSN, the architecture has an internal partition to separate the communication traffic of other wireless links from the WSN link. The MIH service has another important terminal called the Information Server which maintains the database of all the wireless nodes to share with the access points. Information from all the networks operating within a physical region including their network type, address information, and services offered will be stored in the server to make it available during the time of handover.

The combined wireless module (MN) proposed here has an architecture that consists of a union of heterogeneous radio links such as 802.11, 802.16, 3G cellular, or 802.15.4 on the same board as integrated hardware as depicted in Fig. 1. The data link layer consists of link-specific MAC and LLC along with MIH functions. The MIH functions are used to regulate and coordinate between these wireless links for information transfer. The higher layers are defined according to the user's preference.

As per this protocol for data transfer, initially the nodes communicate via WSN link (802.15.4) for sensor-based data transfer. Meanwhile, the MIH within a module continuously monitors the link status using its service functions. If any of them moves out of its limited coverage range, the data communication will be interrupted. During such a situation, in order to have continued connectivity between the modules, the application in conjunction with the MIH functions in the module trigger the handover process by enabling the other wireless links like 802.11, 802.16 or 3G because they offer a better coverage range than the WSN link and attempt to resume connectivity with the destination.

In order to achieve this, the information about all the network links must be dynamically maintained in a central database called the information server (IS) located such that it must be reachable from any one of the wireless links in a module at any time. The proposal therefore emphasizes the need for an improved network formation procedure rather than the one described by IEEE in January 2009 [1].

The proposed network formation method suggests using the wireless module to transfer all its network parameters and link specifications to the coordinator as soon as it joins the WSN coordinator or the access point. The coordinator transfers this information to the information server. Additionally, the server periodically transmits the status of all the wireless modules to indicate the network status. This enables all the network elements to recognize each other, as there is a good chance in a dynamic network that some of the nodes may become inactive in the due course of network formation. The periodicity of this transmission can be configured based on the required quality of service. The transmission of this information is made in a link-independent manner to enable all modules to receive via any link. As a result, all the nodes will confirm connectivity to any particular access point. This process eliminates the need to search for a potential candidate to perform the handover as the link goes down. When compared to the existing method of MIH handover as described in IEEE [1], the proposed method also proves to be power efficient due to the reduced number of communication steps.

3.2 Technical Aspects

We will now describe the technical aspects of this proposal using the example of a smart home to automate the process of monitoring the various events in the home such as variations in temperature, pressure, and humidity conditions using WSN-enabled sensors and reporting data to a remote monitoring station. In such a scenario both integrated wireless modules are equipped with multiple link technologies. If a user wants to access the sensor-monitored data while traveling in a car with a controlling station, communication is not possible beyond a certain range of the WSN link. Nevertheless, to facilitate user access to the data continuously, we exploit wireless links operating near the home where sensor-based data is generated and link to the user's new location where data is collected. As a link goes down due to the user's movement, the MIH within the module continuously monitors the link status. As the node transmits its link details to the server and they are received, the network information from the information server will be continuously updated. As a result, as soon as the signal strength goes below a certain threshold, the MIH triggers the handover by enabling the IEEE 802.11 link which joins the appropriate access point and tries to serve the node. If the node is beyond the coverage range of this link, a higher order link is enabled to perform the data transfer. The selection of the link in this proposal is made as in the order 802.11, 802.16, 3G.

Figure 2 depicts a scenario in which the sensor data from the home must be transferred to the controlling station using a WSN link. As the collecting mobile node (MN) moves away from the coverage range, in order to have continued connectivity, the surrounding wireless infrastructure is utilized. The newly enabled link associates with the homogeneous point of service (its access point) and communicates the data without interruption. Each node has distributed data in its architecture to exchange the data collected from various links. As an example, whenever the WSN link goes down to the threshold, the 802.11 link of the same wireless module gets enabled by the MIH and associated with the 802.11 access points present in the surroundings and then transfers the data to the controlling station. Thus, data communication continues uninterrupted. In case the node is not reachable through the 802.11 link, the node can enable other links with higher coverage range like Wi-Max or cellular and try the same procedure. This quicker handover is made possible by the proposed network formation method.

The network information server is located at a place where all the nodes can conveniently reach it by any one of its active links. The information server has access to the Internet backbone; thus any link like Wi-Fi, Wi-Max, or cellular that can access the

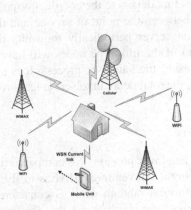

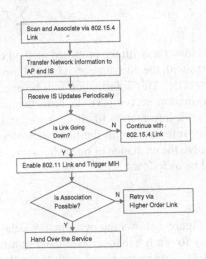

Fig. 3. Flow chart for implementation of network formation

Fig. 2. Smart home scenario

Internet will be able to access the information server. Figure 3 shows the sequence of the network formation handover scheme.

4   Analysis of Handover Delay

In this section, we investigated the delay involved in the handover of information between the links. The handover delay as per the 802.21 based handover process is due to a series of message exchanges between the initiating node, its point of service/access point, the information server and the prospective candidate network [1]. This is necessary to acquire the network parameters essential to knowing about the future point of service. Each of these messages has a fixed length. Whenever a node finds the signal strength falling below the threshold, it triggers the handover process by transmitting a packet to collect the list of possible links in the surrounding area to which it can connect. When the message reaches the receiver, it sends the acknowledgment; in this way multiple packets are exchanged between multiple network elements [12]. Here we analyze the delay involved in performing the handoff as per the 802.21 handover procedure.

A node starts to transfer the data at an initial time T_{init}. The data generation time T_{gen} depends on the amount of data to be transmitted and the data transfer rate of the link. The transmitted data reaches the receiver after a certain propagation delay T_{pron} When this data reaches the receiver it sends an acknowledgement after turnaround time T_{TA}. Thus the total delay involved in sending a part of the handover process takes

$$T_{init} + T_{gen} + T_{pro} + T_{TA}$$

Performing handover after N message transmissions (assuming acknowledgments are received within the short interval) is therefore expressed as follows:

$$T_N = T_{init} + \sum_{i=0}^{N-1} T_{gen}(i) + T_{pro}(i) + T_{TA}(i)$$

However, with the proposed method of network formation, as soon as a node associates with the coordinator, it has to transfer all its link details to the coordinator/point of service. This information will be exchanged between the point of service and the information server (IS). In turn, the information server periodically transmits the network information to all the nodes independent of the link. The nodes will have a ready reference to all the link parameters as a result; the handover process does not involve the exchange of query information. Thus, the total delay involved in handover will be as follows:

$$T_{pro} + T_{gen} + T_{TA}$$

Figure 4 shows the performance delay in the handover process. We compared the delay for each handover command transmission in the conventional MIH as in IEEE 802.21 and the proposed method. In this simulation, a random delay is considered between each command transmission for both cases. The graph shows that the delay increases for each command transmission in the conventional method, whereas delay is held almost constant in the proposed method.

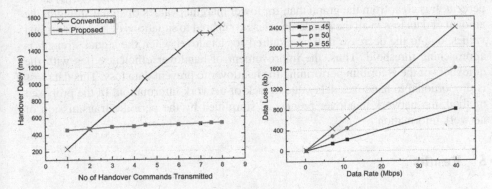

Fig. 4. Comparison of handover delays   **Fig. 5.** Data loss for several wireless standards

If multiple nodes request handover at a common access point, the total time needed to process all the requests will be the sum of the handover duration for the individual nodes. But in the case of handover by the method proposed here, which precedes proper network formation, there will not be any need to request the access point because the network information will be periodically updated by the information server. As a result of this the total delay in processing the handover requests of 'N' number of nodes will be the same as the duration of a single node.

Similarly, by considering the buffer capacity of each of the wireless transceivers, the amount of time involved to transmit a data packet requires transmission attempts based on data buffer size.

In the case of the proposed handover scheme, the number of transmissions required to perform the handover is lesser, which leads to minimum power consumption. Yet another parameter investigated here is the amount of data loss that occurs in different wireless standards due to delay in handover. The key factor to initiate the handover process is signal strength falling below the minimum threshold level. Once the signal falls below the threshold level, the service is terminated. However, in this case, we considered a margin signal strength 'P' above the minimum threshold level of the signal. Below the threshold, the received data is no longer useful as the BER is unacceptable.

In such a case, the time spent receiving the signal between these two events without performing the handover results in unnecessary power consumption without contribution to valid data reception. If P_{Thr} is the minimum threshold of signal strength and P is the marginal signal strength above the threshold, then for different wireless networks offering various data rates (WSN 250 kbps, Wi-Fi 11 Mbps, Wi-Max 40 Mbps, 3G 7.2 Mbps), the amount of data loss in a conventional MIH handover can be calculated as follows:

$$Data\ loss = \frac{P - P_{Thr}}{Total\ time\ spent} * Data\ Rate$$

The parameter Total Time Spent is the total duration of data communication. As shown in Fig. 5 the simulation is done for different wireless standards by considering their data rate and various margin values 'P' by considering the threshold (P_{Thr}) as 40 percent. It is clear from the graph that, for lower marginal values of signal strength, the amount of data loss in all the standards is less compared to situations of higher marginal values, due to the decrease in time required for handover when the signal strength is approaching threshold. Thus, the improvement of handover efficiency lies with the quickness of the algorithm performing the handover to prevent data loss. This data loss is proportional to handover delay due to lack of network information. In the proposed method, the network handover process is simplified by the periodic transmission of network information.

5   Results

As indicated in Table 1, the conventional method of handover using the media independent handover functions as in IEEE 2009 [1] would require more handover time due to the need to exchange several commands between access point, mobile node and IS.

Table 1. Handover performance

Handover Method	Parameter	Performance
Conventional	Handover time	$T_N = \sum_{i=0}^{N-1} T_{pro}(i) + T_{gen}(i) + T_{TA}(i)$
	Handover time at access point due to N nodes	$N * T_N$
	Handover command TX time	N*(Data_ in_one Command / Buffer size)
Proposed	Handover time	$T_N = T_{pro} + T_{gen} + T_{TA}$
	Handover time at access point due to N nodes	T_N
	Handover command TX time	Data_in_one Command /Buffer size

Thus, the total time is the sum of the transmission time for all commands. In the proposed handover, the nodes have the network information and, as a result, require a single command transmission time. Because of this the time to serve multiple nodes at the access point is the same as the handover time, whereas in the conventional method it is additive. Similarly, due to the need to transmit multiple commands in the conventional method, time to transmit the handover command for the same sized data packets and buffer is higher.

6   Conclusion

The proposed scheme of handover services for wireless sensor networks using multiple wireless links and media independent handover functions is a novel method as it addresses the integration of wireless modules within an MIH based stack.

It works efficiently due to the concept of a new network formation method. The efficiency of the handover with the proposed network formation method is reflected in reduced handoff delay when compared to conventional MIH-based handover methods. The proposed method eliminates the burden at the access points during multiple handover requests as information from the information server is periodically transmitted and the wireless modules acquire enough information to manage the handover with a minimum number of transmissions. The number of periodic transmissions can be configured by considering the required quality of service.

This scheme also reduces use of power by reducing time and reduces data loss by reducing handover delay.

References

1. IEEE 802.21-2008, IEEE Standard for Local and Metropolitan Area Networks Media Independent Handover Services (2009)
2. Kim, M., Moon, T.-W., Cho, S.-J.: A study on IEEE 802.21 MIH frameworks in heterogeneous wireless networks. In: Proceedings of ICACT (2009)
3. Lim, W.-S., Kim, D.-W.: Implementation and performance study of IEEE 802.21 in integrated IEEE 802.11/802.16e networks. Comput. Commun. 32 134–143 (2009). Elsevier
4. Ali-Yahiya, T., Bullot, T.: A cross-layer based autonomic architecture for mobility and QoS supports in 4G networks. In: Proceedings of IEEE CCNC 2008, pp. 79–83 (2008)
5. Vulpe, A., Obreja, Ş.G., Barbu, O.-E.: QualNet implementation for mobility management in a MIH enabled system. In: IEEE (2010)
6. Mateus, A., Marinheiro, R.N.: A media independent information service integration architecture for media independent handover. In: Ninth International Conference on Networks (2010)
7. Fratu, O., Popovici, E.C., Halunga, S.V.: Media independent vertical handover in hybrid networks – from standard to implementation. In: 3rd International Symposium on Applied Sciences in Biomedical and Communication Technologies (ISABEL) (2010)
8. Andrei, V., Popovici, E.C., Fratu, O.: Solution for Implementing IEEE 802.21 Media Independent Information Service (2008)
9. Popovici, E.C., Fratu, O., Halunga, S.V.: An IEEE 802.21-based approach of designing interoperability modules for vertical handover in wireless. In: Proceedings of International Conference on Wireless VITAE 2009, Aalborg, Denmark, May 17–19 (2009)
10. Jagadeesha, R.B., Soft handover scheme for WSN nodes using media independent handover functions. Netw. Complex Syst. 1(2) (2011)
11. Chukwu, M.: Personalized mobile monitor for assisted Heath Living. In: IEEE International Workshop on Consumer e-Heath Platform, Services and Applications, pp. 18–22 (2011)
12. Fallon, E., Murphy, J.: Towards a media independent handover approach to heterogeneous network mobility. In: ISSC (2007)

Mixed Method: An Aggregated Method for Handover Decision in Heterogeneous Wireless Networks

Saida Driouache[1]([⊠]), Najib Naja[1], and Abdellah Jamali[1,2]

[1] STRS Laboratory, INPT, Rabat, Morocco
{driouache,naja}@inpt.ac.ma, abdellah.jamali@uhp.ac.ma
[2] IR2M Laboratory, FST, Hassan 1st University, Settat, Morocco

Abstract. The next generation of wireless networks is marked by a variety of access networks. A mobile user desires to run a service seamlessly regardless of his access network. This makes the continuity of service during handover and QoS relevant issues to deal with. In this context, Media Independent Handover (MIH) standard was developed to facilitate the interworking between IEEE and non-IEEE Access technologies. This paper suggests an aggregated method for the best access network selection. This method combines Technique for Order Preference by Similarity to Ideal Solution (TOPSIS) and VIse Kriterijumska Optimizacija kompromisno Resenja (VIKOR) decision algorithms together with Shannon entropy to assign handover criteria weights. Entropy is an adequate tool to weigh up the handover criteria. Compared with TOPSIS and VIKOR, mixed method performs better in terms of handovers number, packet loss rate, end to end delay, and throughput. Simulations are realized within the scope of MIH using NS3 simulator.

Keywords: Heterogeneous networks · Seamless handover · QoS

1 Introduction

The unification of Heterogeneous wireless Networks (HetNets) affords better QoS. Vertical Handover (VH) happens when a user switches his access network. This mechanism is divided into three phases: The first phase is the network discovery when the Mobile Terminal (MT) recognizes all the available access networks. The second phase is the handover decision, when the MT selects its target network. The third phase is the handover execution, when MT switches to the elected network. Seamless handover [1] allows mobile users to be always connected to the best network. It involves decision making criteria and algorithms. To be always best connected, the handover should start at the suitable time and select the adequate target network. The IEEE organization participates in the provision of interoperability and seamless VH via a standard called MIH [2]. MIH serves to connect IEEE and non-IEEE technologies, and establish handover via a set of protocols and mechanisms.

© ICST Institute for Computer Sciences, Social Informatics and Telecommunications Engineering 2018
F. Belqasmi et al. (Eds.): AFRICATEK 2017, LNICST 206, pp. 12–21, 2018.
https://doi.org/10.1007/978-3-319-67837-5_2

To choose a network that meets user needs is a challenge, because some criteria may conflict with each other. The network selection turns into a Multi-Criteria Decision Making (MCDM) problem [3]. This paper proposes an approach, which combines two MCDM methods: TOPSIS and VIKOR. It employs the ranking results of TOPSIS [4,5] and VIKOR [6,7], to re-rank the available access networks. We also propose Shannon entropy to calculate the objective weights of handover criteria. Number and latency of handovers, packet loss rate, end to end delay, and throughput, are measured to evaluate QoS and network performance. Results of the suggested method are compared with those of TOPSIS and VIKOR. Simulations are performed in an IEEE 802.11, IEEE 802.16, and LTE system. The rest of the paper is arranged as follows: Sect. 2 reviews the related work, Sect. 3 introduces MCDM methods. The suggested decision making method is introduced in Sect. 4. Section 5 evaluates the proposed method. Conclusions are given in Sect. 6.

2 Related Work

In the literature, various VH algorithms [8] have been proposed. Radio Signal Strength (RSS) based algorithms [9] employ RSS value and other metrics (cost, bandwidth, power consumption, etc.). They afford low handover latency but a low to medium throughput. Other algorithms determine a cost function for every candidate network [10]. Mainly, cost function algorithms offer the same throughput level as RSS algorithms. Also, delays are higher because of the information collection and cost function computing complexity. Fuzzy logic and artificial neural networks [11], are extensively used in the literature to make handover decisions [12]. The use of these complex algorithms is required by the complexity of handover decisions and wireless networks dynamic conditions. The context-aware [9] handovers depend on informations related to the MT, network, and other contextual factors. MCDM methods integrate informations in a problem decision matrix to select the best from among the possible choices. Some of them have been suggested to make handover decisions [2,4,5,8,10]. MCDM algorithms afford high throughput [5]. However, their complexity raises the handover delay. This is also true for more complex methods like artificial intelligence and context-aware methods. In [4], the author analyses two MCDM approaches: TOPSIS and Simple Additive Weighting (SAW). For many considered criteria, TOPSIS performance is decent. VIKOR, TOPSIS, PROMETHEE (Preference Ranking Organization METHod for Enrichment of Evaluations) and Analytic Hierarchy Process (AHP) [14] are used to seek the most appropriate target network for the MT [7,14]. Authors in [15] found out that the final ranking of the possible network choices differ across MCDM methods. Authors [17] introduced a comparison of SAW, TOPSIS and VIKOR. They noticed the identical ranking of TOPSIS and SAW which is different from VIKOR ranking. They assumed that both TOPSIS and VIKOR are appropriate to give results not far from reality. Authors [16,20] presented a comparative study of TOPSIS and VIKOR. These algorithms adopt different normalization and aggregation methods.

Researchers noticed that in many cases, every MCDM approach gives a different result. To fix this problem, some aggregation methods have been suggested [13]. A decision problem is solved with many MCDM methods. Then, an aggregation of applied methods results gives the final decision. The reason why researchers try aggregation methods for decision making is to improve selection confidence of MCDM methods.

3   MCDM Methods

Handover decision making can be treated as an MCDM problem where there are n candidate networks, and m performance criteria. Rows and columns of the decision matrix present the alternatives A_1 ... A_n and criteria C_1 ... C_m, respectively. a_{ij} defines the quantity of alternative A_i against criterion C_j. Weights w_1 ...w_m have to be positive and designated to all criteria. They define the criterion importance to the decision making.

3.1   TOPSIS

TOPSIS is one of the extensively adopted classical MCDM tools. It is based on the following idea: the best alternative is assumed to have the shortest distance from the positive ideal solution and the longest distance from the negative ideal solution. Appropriately, TOPSIS is a reliable method for risk-avoidance as the decision makers may want a decision that not only augments the profits but also prevents risks. TOPSIS steps are:

step 1: decision matrix normalization

$$p_{ij} = (\frac{a_{ij}}{\sqrt{\sum_{i=1}^{n} a_{ij}^2}}) \tag{1}$$

step 2: weights are multiplied to the normalized matrix as follows

$$v_{ij} = w_j p_{ij} \tag{2}$$

step 3: positive ideal solution is $A^+ = (v_1^+, ..., v_j^+, ..., v_m^+)$, where v_j^+ is the best value of the jth attribute over all the available alternatives. Negative ideal solution is $A^- = (v_1^-, ..., v_j^-, ..., v_m^-)$, where v_j^- is the worst value of the jth attribute over all the available alternatives. They are computed as follows:

$$A^+ = \{(max_i v_{ij} | j \in J), (min_i v_{ij} | j \in J\prime) | i = 1, 2, ..., n\}$$
$$A^- = \{(min_i v_{ij} | j \in J), (max_i v_{ij} | j \in J\prime) | i = 1, 2, ..., n\} \tag{3}$$

$J\{1, 2, ..., m\}$ and $J\prime\{1, 2, ..., m\}$ are the sets of criteria which need to be maximized and minimized, respectively.

step 4: the normalized euclidean distance between alternatives and ideal solutions is applied

$$d_i^+ = \sqrt{\sum_{j=1}^{m} \left(v_{ij} - v_j^+\right)^2} \quad and \quad d_i^- = \sqrt{\sum_{j=1}^{m} \left(v_{ij} - v_j^-\right)^2} \tag{4}$$

step 5: the relative closeness C_i to the ideal solution is computed

$$C_i = \frac{d_i^-}{d_i^- + d_i^+} \tag{5}$$

The best ranked alternative is the one with the maximum value of C_i.

3.2   VIKOR

VIKOR [20] was created to provide compromise solutions to optimization problems that include conflicting criteria with different units. The compromise ranking of alternatives is accomplished by comparing the measure of closeness to the ideal solution. Any exclusion or inclusion of an alternative could affect VIKOR ranking results. In VIKOR algorithm ν is the strategy weight of the maximum group utility, usually it takes the value 0.5, whereas $1 - \nu$ is the weight of the individual regret. VIKOR aggregate function is always close to the best solution, while in TOPSIS it must be distant from the worst solution even if it is not very close to the ideal solution. This makes VIKOR adequate for obtaining maximum profit. The VIKOR procedure is described below:

step 1: determination of aspired (f_j^+) and tolerable (f_j^-) levels of benefit and cost criteria, respectively where $j = 1, 2, ..., m$

$$\begin{aligned} f_j^+ = \max_i a_{ij}, \quad f_j^- = \min_i a_{ij} \\ f_j^+ = \min_i a_{ij}, \quad f_j^- = \max_i a_{ij} \end{aligned} \tag{6}$$

step 2: calculation of utility S_i and regret R_i using the following where $j = 1, 2, ...m$

$$S_i = \sum_{j=1}^{m} w_j \frac{f_j^+ - f_{ij}}{f_j^+ - f_j^-} \qquad R_i = \max_j \left(w_j \frac{f_j^+ - f_{ij}}{f_j^+ - f_j^-} \right) \tag{7}$$

step 3: The index Q_i is calculated. S_{min} and R_{min} are the minimum values of S_i and R_i, respectively. S_{max} and R_{max} are their maximum values, respectively.

$$Q_i = \nu \frac{S_i - S_{min}}{S_{max} - S_{min}} + (1 - \nu) \frac{R_i - R_{max}}{R_{min} - R_{max}} \tag{8}$$

Q_i, S_i, and R_i, are three ranking lists. The alternatives are arranged in a descending order in accordance with Q_i values. They are also arranged in accordance with S_i and R_i values separately. The best ranked alternative A_1 is the one with the minimum value of Q_i. A_1 is the compromise solution if:

Condition 1: $Q(A_2) - Q(A_1) \geq (1/(n-1))$, where A_2 is the second best alternative ranked by Q_i.

Condition 2: A_1 must be also best ranked alternative by S and/or R.

If one of the conditions is not fulfilled, a group of compromise solutions is proposed: A_1 and A_2 if only condition 2 is not satisfied. $A_1, A_2, ..., A_m$ if condition 1 is not satisfied. A_m is defined by the relation $Q(A_m) - Q(A_1) \leq (1/(n-1))$.

4 Mixed Method for Vertical Handover Decision Making

apparently, different decision making methods give different results in accordance with their hypotheses. Since seamless VH decision making is very critical, it is better to employ more than one method. To overcome this problem, we present an aggregate method named mixed or Rank Average method. As it implies other methods results and details, mixed method is capable of being perfect for access network selection. It ranks alternatives based on the average of implied approaches rankings. The ranking $R_{mixed}(i)$ of the ith candidate network is acquired as follow, where k is the number of implied MCDM methods:

$$R_{mixed}(i) = \frac{\sum\limits_{k} R_k(i)}{k} \tag{9}$$

This average ranking is invaluable because it is capable of adding the respective powers of each implied method. In our scenario, TOPSIS and VIKOR rank the alternatives. Then mixed method computes the average of their results for all alternatives. We choose TOPSIS and VIKOR for three reasons: (1) Each of them is advantageous and efficient for handover decision making. (2) They employ different aggregation and normalization functions. So, they give distant results for the same decision problem. For example, a selected alternative as the best by TOPSIS may be considered as the worse by VIKOR. (3) Mixed method can take advantage from their complementary powers regardless of their differences, and make efficient handover decisions.

We employed entropy [18,19] to compute the appropriate weight of each criterion. Entropy has the benefits of computational simplicity and efficiency. It determines the weights through the following steps:

step 1: normalization of the decision matrix using Eq. (1), in order to eliminate the criteria units.

step 2: calculation of the entropy value for each criterion, where k is the *Boltzmann's* constant

$$E_j = -k \sum_{i=1}^{n} p_{ij} \ln p_{ij} \quad where \quad k = \frac{1}{\ln n} \tag{10}$$

step 3: extraction of objective criteria weights

$$w_j = \frac{1 - E_j}{\sum_{j=1}^{m}(1 - E_j)} \tag{11}$$

5   Performance Evaluation and Results

In this section, we assess and compare mixed method, TOPSIS, and VIKOR through some important performance metrics: throughput, end to end delay, packet loss rate, and handover decision delay. [21]. We added MIH module to NS3 under which we have run simulations. We have considered WiFi, LTE, and WiMAX HetNets. Two MTs are equipped with three network devices of every access technology, and an MIH interface. MIH is needed to establish a list of local interfaces, obtain states and control the behaviour of these interfaces. MTs are initially connected to Wifi1 network while they are running real time applications: Voice over Internet Protocol (VoIP), and video streaming.

- MT1 starts to run a VoIP application while moving with a constant speed equal to 1 m/s. The VoIP application uses a G.729 codec, with 8,5 Kbps data rate and 60 B packet size.
- MT2 starts to run a video streaming application while moving with a constant speed equal to 1 m/s. The video streaming application sends MPEG4 stream using H.263 codec, with 16 Kbps bit rate.

mixed method, TOPSIS, and VIKOR are implemented in the MTs. Table 1 shows the list of simulation parameters. The measurements are taken every 10 s.

5.1   Throughput

Throughput figures among important QoS statistics. In our context, it is the number of bits received successfully by the MT divided by the difference between the last packet reception time and the first packet transmission time. The results in Fig. 1 shows that the three methods maximize the throughput. Mixed method is able to enhance the transmission throughput of real-time services. It offers a bit higher throughput than TOPSIS and VIKOR.

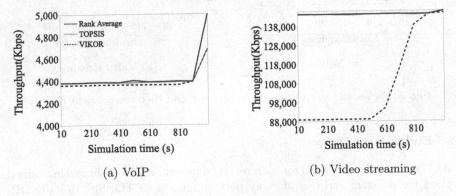

(a) VoIP   (b) Video streaming

Fig. 1. MTs throughput

Table 1. Simulation parameters

Simulation parameters	Values
IEEE802.11 frequency bandwidth	5 GHz
IEEE802.11 transmission radius	100 m
IEEE802.11 data rate	20 Mbps
IEEE802.16 frequency bandwidth	5G Hz
IEEE802.16 transmission radius	600 m
IEEE802.16 channel bandwidth	10 MHz
Propagation model	COST231_PROPAGATION
IEEE802.16 modulation and coding	OFDM QAM16_12
MAC/IEEE802.16 UCD interval	10 s
MAC/IEEE802.16 DCD interval	10 s
LTE uplink bandwidth	25 resource blocks
LTE downlink bandwidth	25 resource blocks
LTE link data rate	10 Gbps
LTE channel bandwidth	5 MHz
Maximum transmission Power	30.0 dBm
LTE path loss model	Friis propagation
LTE transmission radius	2000 m
Mobility model	constant-position

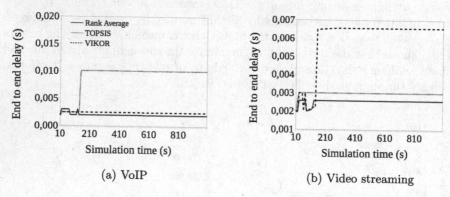

(a) VoIP   (b) Video streaming

Fig. 2. Packet end to end delay between MT and its correspondent node

5.2 End to End Delay

End to end delay is computed for each received packet. Figure 2 shows that mixed method has a better end to end delay performance than TOPSIS and VIKOR. Since real-time flows such as VoIP and video streaming are very sensitive to delay. We can say that decreased delay is a potential benefit of mixed method.

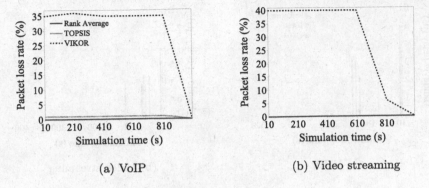

(a) VoIP

(b) Video streaming

Fig. 3. Packet loss rate

5.3   Packet Loss Rate

To achieve seamless VH in HetNets, it is essential to guarantee service continuity and QoS, which means low latency and packet loss rate during handover. Figure 3 shows that the three evaluated approaches guarantee low packet loss rate. Furthermore, mixed method assures null packet loss. This enhances the QoS for real-time-services.

5.4   Handover Delay

Handover delay is the time taken by the MT to make a decision and select the best access network. Every time we employ mixed method, TOPSIS, or VIKOR. We monitor the MN for 1000 s to get the number of handovers, and measure decision delay for each handover event. Figure 4 shows the obtained results. The number of handovers executed by VIKOR is higher compared to TOPSIS and Rank Average. For VoIP at 10s, the three evaluated methods executed a handover, but mixed method has handover delay greater than TOPSIS and VIKOR. This is because mixed method waits for the ranking results of TOPSIS and VIKOR to compute their average for every alternative. Even if the proposed VH approach requires more delay to decide a handover, it can accomplish better performance than conventional TOPSIS and VIKOR, with respect to end to end delay, packet loss rate, and throughput.

Ping-pong effect is the unnecessary handover to the neighbouring access point that returns to the original network after a very short interval of time. This unnecessary back and forth handover engenders heavy processing and switching loads. For example, mixed method compared to VIKOR reduces the number of unnecessary handovers. Hence, resources are saved and the number of dropped calls is reduced, thereby the VH QoS is improved. Since, mixed method and TOPSIS have less total number of handovers compared to VIKOR, the ping-pong effect is decreased.

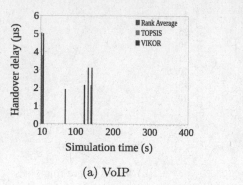
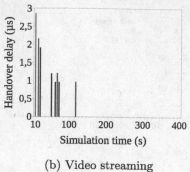

(a) VoIP   (b) Video streaming

Fig. 4. VH decision delay

6 Conclusions

In this paper, we used mixed method as a VH decision making method in which two powerful but different ranking methods were implied: TOPSIS, and VIKOR. Mixed method is useful to determine which method is close to perfect VH decision, and which one is not. Performance of the three compared methods were assessed under NS3 simulator within MIH scope. The employed criteria are throughput, end to end delay, handover decision delay, and packet loss rate. Mixed method has the best performance in accordance with simulation results, except for decision delay. It can reduce the number of unnecessary handovers, ping-pong effects, end to end delay, packet loss rate, and improve throughput. So, mixed method has the ability to add the powers of applied methods (TOPSIS and VIKOR), and find a compromise between their proposed solutions despite their differences.

References

1. Sagar, E.L., Bhadla, M.: A survey of handover mechanism with mobility management in femtocell & macrocell for lte. cell **4**(11) (2015)
2. Ali, T., Saquib, M.: Analysis of an instantaneous packet loss based VH algorithm for heterogeneous wireless networks. IEEE Trans. Mob. Comput. **13**(5), 992–1006 (2014)
3. Sasirekha, V., Chandrasekar, C., Ilangkumaran, M.: Heterogeneous wireless network vertical handoff decision using hybrid multi-criteria decision-making technique. Int. J. Comput. Sci. Eng. **10**(3), 263–280 (2015)
4. Lahby, M., Cherkaoui, L., Adib, A.: An enhanced-topsis based network selection technique for next generation wireless networks. In: 2013 20th International Conference on Telecommunications (ICT), pp. 1–5. IEEE (2013)
5. Bisio, I., Delucchi, S., Lavagetto, F., Marchese, M.: Performance comparison of network selection algorithms in the framework of the 802.21 standard. J. Netw. **10**(1), 51–59 (2015)

6. Gul, M., Celik, E., Aydin, N., Gumus, A.T., Guneri, A.F.: A state of the art literature review of vikor and its fuzzy extensions on applications. Appl. Soft Comput. **46**, 60–89 (2016)
7. Baghla, S., Bansal, S.: Effect of normalization techniques in vikor method for network selection in HetNets. In: 2014 IEEE International Conference on Computational Intelligence and Computing Research (ICCIC), pp. 1–6. IEEE (2014)
8. Bhute, H.A., Karde, P., Thakare, V.: AVH decision approaches in next generation wireless networks: a survey. Int. J. Mob. Netw. Commun. Telemat. (IJMNCT) **4** (2014)
9. Bhute, H.A., Karde, P., Thakare, V.: Vertical handover decision strategies in heterogeneous wireless networks. In: International Conference on Recent Trends in Information, Telecommunication and Computing, ITC. Citeseer (2014)
10. Madaan, J., Kashyap, I.: An overview of vertical handoff decision algorithm. Int. J. Comput. Appl. **111**(3), 0975–8887 (2015)
11. Geetika, K.B.: Handover management in HetNets. Int. J. Sci. Eng. Res. **4**(4) (2013)
12. Munoz, P., Laselva, D., Barco, R., Mogensen, P.: Dynamic traffic steering based on fuzzy q-learning approach in a multi-rat multi-layer wireless network. Comput. Netw. **71**, 100–116 (2014)
13. Rao, R.V.: Multiple attribute decision making in the manufacturing environment. In: Decision Making in Manufacturing Environment Using Graph Theory and Fuzzy Multiple Attribute Decision Making Methods, pp. 1–5. Springer, London (2013)
14. Preethi, G., Chandrasekar, C.: A network selection algorithm based on ahp-ow a methods. In: Wireless and Mobile Networking Conference (WMNC), 2013 6th Joint IFIP, pp. 1–4. IEEE (2013)
15. Agrawal, A., Jeyakumar, A., Pareek, N.: Comparison between vertical handoff algorithms for heterogeneous wireless networks. In: 2016 International Conference on Communication and Signal Processing (ICCSP), pp. 1370–1373. IEEE (2016)
16. Zhang, N., Wei, G.: Extension of vikor method for decision making problem based on hesitant fuzzy set. Appl. Math. Model. **37**(7), 4938–4947 (2013)
17. Aguilar-Gonzalez, R., Cardenas-Juarez, M., Pineda-Rico, U., Arce, A., Latva-aho, M., Stevens-Navarro, E.: Reducing spectrum handoffs and energy switching consumption of madm-based decisions in cognitive radio networks. Mob. Inf. Syst. **2016** (2016)
18. Jiang, W., Shen, P., Liu, F., Fang, X.: An interactive group decision making approach based on satisfaction degree. In: Zhang, Z., Shen, Z.M., Zhang, J., Zhang, R. (eds.) LISS 2014, pp. 1249–1254. Springer, Heidelberg (2015). doi:10.1007/978-3-662-43871-8_181
19. Zamri, N., Abdullah, L.: A new linguistic variable in interval type-2 fuzzy entropy weight of a decision making method. Proced. Comput. Sci. **24**, 42–53 (2013)
20. Dou, Y., Zhang, P., Jiang, J., Yang, K., Chen, Y.: Mcdm based on reciprocal judgment matrix: a comparative study of e-vikor and e-topsis algorithmic methods with interval numbers. Appl. Math. **8**(3), 1401–1411 (2014)
21. Wu, J., Cheng, B., Yuen, C., Shang, Y., Chen, J.: Distortion-aware concurrent multipath transfer for mobile video streaming in heterogeneous wireless networks. IEEE Trans. Mob. Comput. **14**(4), 688–701 (2015)

Analysis of the Impact of Cognitive Vehicular Network Environment on Spectrum Sensing

Amina Riyahi[✉], Marouane Sebgui, Slimane Bah, and Belhaj Elgraini

LEC Laboratory Ecole Mohammedia D'Ingénieurs, University Mohammed V in Rabat,
Rabat, Morocco
aminariyahi@research.emi.ac.ma, {sebgui,bah,elgraini}@emi.ac.ma

Abstract. The Cognitive Vehicular Network (CVN) has emerged as a promising solution providing additional resources and allowing spectrum efficiency. However, vehicular networks are highly challenging for spectrum sensing due to speed, mobility and dynamic topology. Furthermore, these parameters depend on the CVNs' environment such as highway, urban or suburban. Therefore, solutions targeting CVNs should take into consideration these characteristics. As a first step towards an appropriate spectrum sensing solution for CVNs, we first, provide a comprehensive classification of existing spectrum sensing techniques for CVNs. Second, we discuss, for each class, the impact of the vehicular environment effects such as traffic density, speed and fading on the spectrum sensing and data fusion techniques. Finally we derive a set of requirements for CVN's spectrum sensing that takes into consideration specific characteristics of CVN environments.

Keywords: Cognitive radio · CVNs · Spectrum sensing · Data fusion

1 Introduction

Recently, Vehicular Ad hoc Network (VANET) [1] has attracted a lot of interest from industries and research institutions, particularly with increasing number of vehicles on the road especially in urban area. VANET is a special kind of Mobile Ad hoc Networks MANETs that are applied to vehicular context. They provide Vehicle to Vehicle (V2 V) and vehicles to infrastructures (V2I) communications. On the opposite of MANET, in VANET the movements of vehicles are predictable due to the road topology. Besides, the high mobility leads to a higher probability of network partitions, and the end to end connectivity is not guaranteed [1]. The VANET applications can be classified into two categories: safety applications which provide the drivers with early warnings to prevent the accidents from happening, this represent the higher priority traffic, and user applications which provide road users with Network accessibility which represent traffic with less priority. Growing usage of applications such as exchanging multimedia information with high data in car-entertainment leads to overcrowding of the band and thereby giving rise to communication inefficiency for safety applications [1]. Furthermore, the 10 MHz reserved in the IEEE 802.11p standard as a common control channel is likely to suffer from large data contention, especially during peaks of road traffic [2], which might not provide sufficient spectrum for reliable exchange of safety applications. To alleviate this

© ICST Institute for Computer Sciences, Social Informatics and Telecommunications Engineering 2018
F. Belqasmi et al. (Eds.): AFRICATEK 2017, LNICST 206, pp. 22–32, 2018.
https://doi.org/10.1007/978-3-319-67837-5_3

problem Cognitive Radio (CR) technology has been proposed [2]. The main role of CR is to allow the unlicensed users (a.k.a Secondary Vehicular Users: SVUs) to identify spectrum holes and exploit them without interfering with the licensed users (a.k.a Primary Users: PUs). This makes the spectrum sensing (SS) a crucial function in CR networks. Even if spectrum sensing in CR networks is well studied, however the research solutions proposed in static CR networks may not be directly applicable to CVNs due to high dynamic networking environment.

The works in [3–5] provide comprehensive surveys about spectrum sensing in CVNs. The authors in [3] review the existing studies related to SS in CVNs and provide the open issues in this area. In [4, 5], the authors provide an overview of distributed and centralized cooperative SS for CVNs and review some challenges and open issues in CVNs. In this paper, we provide an overview of spectrum sensing mechanisms and we propose a classification for existing CVN schemes. In fact, four classes are presented: centralized, distributed, partially centralized and integrated schemes. Indeed, the main characteristic that influences the spectrum sensing mechanisms used in CVNs is the changeable topology of vehicular environment which may be urban, suburban or highway area. The common features of these vehicular environments are the vehicles speed, fading and traffic density. But, the effect of these features differs from vehicular environment to another. Therefore, we analyze for each class the impact of the characteristics of each vehicular environment including speed, fading and traffic density on the SS techniques and data fusion techniques used to combine the reported or shared sensing results for making a cooperative decision. This analysis allowed us to derive the main spectrum sensing requirements in CVNs. The rest of this paper is structured as follows: in Sect. 2, we present background information on CVNs and we present the most used spectrum sensing techniques. In Sect. 3, we classify the existing CVNs sensing schemes. In Sect. 4, we analyze the environment effects on the sensing mechanisms used by these classes and we derive the corresponding spectrum sensing requirements for each environment. Finally, we draw final conclusions in Sect. 5.

2 Background on CVNs and Spectrum Sensing

2.1 Cognitive Vehicular Networks

The CVNs are composed of vehicles equipped with the CR system, allowing SVUs to change their transmitter parameters based on interactions with the environment in which they operate. Similarly to the traditional CR, The execution of CVNs is defined by a cycle which is composed by four phases: observation, analysis, reasoning and act [6]. Observation consists of sensing and gathering the information (e.g. modulation types, noise, and transmission power) from its surrounding area in order to identify the best available spectrum hole. In analysis phase, after sensing, some parameters have to be estimated (e.g. interference level, path loss and channel capacity). In reasoning phase, the best spectrum band is chosen for the current transmission considering the QoS requirement. The optimal reconfiguration is finally done in Act phase. But, the main novel characteristic that differentiates CVNs from the traditional CR is the nature of SVUs mobility. In one hand, due to road topology and usage of navigational systems, the vehicles can predict the future position and then it can know in advance the spectrum resources available on its path. On the other hand, the mobility increases spatial diversity in the observations taken on the different locations. This may influence the sensing performance. Furthermore, fast speed increases the number of collected samples which improves the sensing performance and requires less cooperation from other SVUs [7]. But, when the high fading (i.e. correlated shadowing) and the presence of obstacles are taken into account, the correlated samples affect the performance [8]. Besides, with faster speed the SVUs will have a higher probability to miss detect the PUs, because the PU will be outside the sensing range of SVU very quickly [9]. In addition, another parameter which can affect particularly the cooperation is the traffic density; the road topology becomes congested with dense traffic which declines the speed and the vehicles tend to be closer to each others, this decreases the performance due to correlation [8]. Thus, the main features of vehicular environment which influence the sensing are speed, fading, traffic density and the obstacles. These parameters vary according to the area type (i.e. urban, suburban, or highway).

The urban area is characterized by high fading, and dense traffic with low speed (around 50 km/h). The main features of suburban area are light traffic with medium speed, surrounded by some buildings which give rise to fading. The highway area is characterized with few surrounding structures which decline the fading effect, and vehicles can exceed 120 km/h [10].

2.2 Spectrum Sensing Techniques

The Spectrum Sensing (SS) techniques are divided into two types local SS (performed individually) and Cooperative Spectrum Sensing (CSS) [11]. Depending on the availability of the knowledge about the Primary Users (PUs), the local SS techniques can be classified into two main classes: informed and blind SS techniques [12].

2.2.1 The Local Informed Sensing Techniques

These techniques require the prior knowledge about PU's features such as sine wave carriers, hopping sequences, pulse trains, repeating spreading, modulation type etc. [12]. In addition they are robust to noise uncertainties, but their implementation is complex. In the informed techniques, we mention Matched Filtering Detection (MFD) [12] and Cyclostationary Detection (CD) [12]. The MFD could achieve the higher sensing accuracy with less sensing time, whereas sensing accuracy in CD requires long sensing time and it is not capable to differentiate the PUs from the secondary users.

2.2.2 The Local Blind Sensing Techniques

The blind techniques don't require any information about the primary signal. Among these techniques: Energy Detection (ED) [12], Eigenvalue-based Detection (EBD) [12] and the Compressed Sensing (CS) [11]. They present the advantage of requiring less sensing time. Even if the ED is the most popular technique due to its simplicity, it is the worst performer technique, especially in the case of noise uncertainty. The EBD deals well with noise uncertainty than the ED, while the CS facilitates wideband SS, and reduces the channel switching overhead of narrowband SS. However the CS incurs additional hardware cost and computational complexity [11].

2.2.3   Cooperative Spectrum Sensing

The Cooperative Spectrum Sensing (CSS) has been proposed in [11] and [13] to improve the performance of SS under fading environment conditions which is especially in the case of vehicular channels characterized by a strong fading. The key concept of CSS is to exploit spatial diversity among observations made about the status of channel by multiple SVUs [11]. The process of CSS requires the use of some techniques such as: local observations using individual sensing techniques, cooperation models, eventually a user selection technique can be used, reporting, and data fusion [11]. However the gain of CSS is limited by cooperation overhead which includes: sensing delay, shadowing, energy efficiency, mobility and security [11].

Table 1. Summary of SS techniques

	Blind SS techniques			Informed SS techniques	
	ED	EBD	CS	CD	MFD
Sensing time	short	medium	short	long	short
Performance	low	high	high	high	high

3   Classification of the Spectrum Sensing Schemes in CVNs

In literature, CVNs are usually based on the cooperative spectrum sensing, but can also integrate a geo-localization database to assist the traditional SS. Hence, in this section, we classify these spectrum sensing schemes in CVNs into four classes: centralized, distributed, partially centralized and integrated. And we identify the SS and fusion techniques used in these classes (Table 2).

3.1   Centralized CVN Schemes

In centralized CVN schemes, a central node act as fusion center (FC) that controls the process of cooperation. In the case of V2I a fixed node such as RSU (Road Side Unit) or BS (Base Station) acts as a FC [14, 15]. But, having a fixed FC may not be always possible in the case of CVNs. Thus, some works focus on a clustering strategy where the vehicles are selected to act as a FC cluster head [16, 17]. The cooperation process is defined as follow: Firstly, the SVUs sense the channels selected independently by the FC using Compressed Sensing (CS) in [14], Eigenvalue-Based Detection (EBD) in [15] and Energy Detection (ED) in [17]. The FC combines the local sensing received from SVUs for making a final decision by using the data fusion techniques such as Hard Fusion (HF) [14, 17], Soft Fusion (SF) [15] or Hidden Markov Model (HMM) [16]. Using SF at FC provides better sensing accuracy than HF [11], because the SVUs report to FC the entire local sensing samples. However it incurs control channel overheads in terms of time and energy consumption especially with large number of cooperating

SVUs. While, the HF requires much less control channel because the SVUs report to FC one decision bit (0 or 1), the performance can be decreased. While, the HMM is used to speed up the detection of PUs by indicating to FC the observations' number that should be received before making the fusion [16]. Once the final decision is made, the FC broadcasts it to SVUs.

3.2 Distributed CVN Schemes

Works in [18–20] focus on using decentralized CVN architectures where SVUs are cooperating in a distributed way. In [18], a distributed scheme based on the belief propagation algorithm is proposed specifically for highway, where each SVU senses the spectrum independently. Then, each vehicle combines its own belief with information received from other neighbors and a final decision can be generated after several iterations. In [19] the road topology is taken into account, where the highway road is divided into equal short segments which can be recognized with a unique identifier. Periodically, each SVU senses the spectrum, stores the results in its internal memory and share it later to inform others vehicles about spectrum holes in their future segments. This framework is further enhanced in [20] by an experimental study. The measurements are undertaken from moving vehicle travelling under different urban conditions and vehicular speeds. And then, a cooperative spectrum management framework is proposed, where the correlated shadowing is taken into consideration. Data fusion in [19, 20] is based on a weighted algorithm.

3.3 Partially Centralized CVN Schemes

The partially centralized CVN schemes [21, 22] are composed of two sensing levels. The first level is fast sensing (generally energy detection) performed by a central node [21] or by a set of selected nodes using cooperation [22]. In the second level, the requesting vehicles (RVs) rescan the list of holes received from coordinators using fine sensing such as cyclostationary detection [21, 22]. This may reduce the overhead of identifying all holes. Besides, the RVs use the sensed holes without seeking permissions from the coordinator. This scheme is then a partially unshackle master/slave sensing relationship between FC and SVUs.

3.4 Integrated CVN Schemes

In CR the integrated concept is based on the use of a geo-localization database. This later is described in [23] as a spectral map of available channels in a given geographical area, that can be provided to secondary users according to their location. However, its implementation may not be suitable for CVNs when road traffic is congested which leads to many vehicles trying to query the database. Thus, to mitigate the problems above, the use of database is combined with traditional sensing [24, 25]. In [24], in each segment of the highway, the vehicles should dynamically select their role (Mode I, Mode II or Sensing-only) according to the traffic load. In low traffic, vehicles choose the mode II to access the spectrum database through an internet connection. In mode I the vehicles get informed from vehicles on mode II. While in high traffic, the vehicles perform Sensing-only and cooperate to detect PUs. In [25], a BS is directly connected to a TV white space and database similarly to [24], the vehicles should dynamically select their role but this time according to the traffic load and the coverage of BSs.

Table 2. Summary of classification of CVN schemes

Classes	Ref.	Coordinator nodes	Sensing technique	Data fusion algorithm	Road Topology
Centralized	[14]	Base station	Compressed sensing	Hard fusion	Highway
	[15]	Base station	Eigenvalue-based detection	Soft fusion	Not specified
	[16]	vehicle	Not specified	Hidden markov model	Not specified
	[17]	Three vehicles	Energy detection	Hard fusion	Highway/ Suburban
Distributed	[18]	Coordination is not needed	Not specified	Belief algorithm	Highway
	[19]		Energy detection	Weighted algorithm	Highway
	[20]		Energy detection	Weighted algorithm	Urban
Partially centralized	[21]	RSU or vehicle	– Energy detection at coordinator – Fine sensing at RVs[a]	Data fusion is not needed	Highway
	[22]	Three vehicles	– Cooperation among coordinators – Fine sensing at RVs[a]	Hard fusion (Majority rule)	Highway/ Suburban
Integrated	[24]	Coordination is not needed	Dynamic detection: Mode I, Mode II or	Data fusion is not needed	Highway
	[25]		Sensing-only (local or cooperative detection)	Hard fusion (Majority rule)	Not specified

[a]RVs: Requesting Vehicles

4 Derived Requirements of Spectrum Sensing in CVNs

As seen in previous section each area has its own features including speed of vehicles, traffic density, and the surrounding obstacles. In fact, the spectrum sensing accuracy depends on the vehicle's speed, traffic density and the channel fading. To the best of our knowledge, the conditions of the surrounding area are not taken into account in literature. In this section, we first analyze the impact of the vehicular environment (i.e. highway, Suburban and Urban), especially the effect of traffic density, mobility and fading, on both spectrum sensing and fusion techniques for each class. Second, we derive the corresponding spectrum sensing requirements for each environment.

4.1   The Impact of CVN Environment on the Local Spectrum Sensing

The detection techniques for local spectrum sensing include cyclostationary detection (CD), matched filtering detection (MFD), energy detection (ED), compressed detection (CS) and eigenvalue-based detection (EBD). Each of these techniques has its pros and cons in terms of sensing time and performance as shown in Table 1. Thus, the choice of the appropriate SS according to the environment properties is very important.

In highway context, high speed requires fast detection (ED, CS and MFD). However, ED could be used for open space but with high fading, it is better to use the fast and accurate detection (CS or MFD). In suburban context, the speed is light which can affect the sensing performance, and fading effect is more challenging than highway context. Thus, in these cases the fast and accurate detection (CS or MFD) is favored. Whilst in urban context, the fast detection is not necessary due to low speed, but the accurate detection (EBD, CS, MFD or CD) is required due to strong fading.

4.2   The Impact of CVN Environment on Data Fusion of the Centralized Schemes

Generally, the cooperative spectrum sensing schemes are a composition of local SS and data fusion. As previously mentioned, each fusion technique in centralized schemes such as soft fusion (SF), hard fusion (HF) or hidden Markov model (HMM), has its pros and cons in terms of delay and overhead. Thus, we have to carefully choose the appropriate fusion techniques according to the environment properties.

In highway context, the data fusion such as HF and HMM present the advantage of fast fusion, but due to low density, sometimes there will not be enough vehicles to cooperate for sensing, thus the SF is preferred. In suburban context, the traffic density effect is challenging than highway context. Thus, it is better to use fast fusion. While in urban context, the fast fusion is vital due to high traffic.

4.3   The Impact of CVN Environment on Data Fusion of the Distributed Schemes

The data fusion techniques which may be used in distributed schemes are belief algorithms and weighted algorithms. In belief algorithm, the data from different cooperating vehicles is merged considering the spatial and temporal correlation of different observations hence the performance of this algorithm will be affected by fading (i.e. correlated shadowing). Furthermore, belief procedure is rather time consuming when larger number of SVUs participate in the process. While in weighted algorithm, the data is merged using weights and only if the correlation between the sensing samples of two vehicles are below a given threshold. Besides, the performance of weighted algorithm degrades under low density.

In highway context with open space, belief algorithm performs well under low density. But, if fading is considering this algorithm is not preferred. In both suburban and urban contexts, the data fusion techniques are affected by dense traffic and fading.

Hence in this case, it is better to use the selection of cooperating nodes (i.e. correlation selection) either to reduce the number of cooperating SVUs and to select the uncorrelated SVUs. Generally, for both urban and suburban contexts, belief algorithm may not be suitable due to fading and high traffic density. While, weighted algorithm is required because it performs well under dense traffic.

4.4   The Impact of CVN Environment on the Partially Centralized Schemes

As mentioned in Sect. 3, in the partially centralized, the first level (i.e. fast sensing) is based on the local sensing at the coordinator or at a subset of selected coordinators. At second level (i.e. fine sensing), it is possible to use cyclostationary detection (CD) or eigenvalue-based detection (EBD).

In highway context, to speed up the detection at first level it is required to use fast detection or both fast and accurate detection according to fading effect. While in the case of cooperation at first level, it is possible to use fast fusion. At second level, it is better to use EBD because sensing time of EBD is less than CD. In suburban and urban context, it is favored to use at first level the cooperation among the coordinators to alleviate the problem of hidden PU due to presence of obstacles. At second level, it is required to use EBD in the suburban context because the effect of speed is considered, while in the urban context it is possible to use CD and EBD.

4.5   The Impact of CVN Environment on the Integrated Schemes

For integrated schemes, an optimal ratio between querying the spectrum database and sensing according to the traffic density and BSs coverage is required. In dense traffic the SVUs perform in sensing-only mode (local SS or cooperative sensing). The accuracy in this mode is also important; hence the choice of the appropriate sensing and fusion techniques depends on the environment requirements as mentioned above in Subsects. 4.1, 4.2 and 4.3. Generally, in highways, it is preferred to use mode I and mode II due to low traffic density. While in suburban and urban context, it is possible to use sensing-only mode due to high traffic density. However, as mentioned above, due to the hidden PU issue it is better to use cooperative spectrum sensing (CSS) at sensing-only mode.

4.6   Summary of Spectrum Sensing Requirements in CVNs

The main constraints in urban and suburban context are hidden PU, strong fading and dense traffic. The hidden PU issue requires CSS among SVUs, but due to fading and dense traffic a correlation selection is very important. The cooperation in highway context is affected by fast speed and low density, thus the accurate SS techniques with short sensing time at local SS are required such as matched filtering detection (MFD) or compressed detection (CS). The fusion techniques in CSS (centralized or distributed) should be adequate with the surrounding environment. For example, soft fusion (SF) and belief algorithm are favored in low traffic, while, hard fusion and weighted algorithm are required in dense traffic. In contrast, we can observe that these requirements are not always respected in literature, as in [14] where the CS with hard fusion (HF) is considered for highway. Hence the effect of low density is not taken into account by using HF. In [17], the energy detection (ED) with HF is considered applicable for both highway and suburban, which could not be optimal since SF is preferred for highway and ED does not provide the required accuracy in urban context. Furthermore, the schemes in [15, 16] are considered applicable for all contexts, and in [16] the SS technique is not also specified.

Therefore, the real features of the surrounding area are not studied well in the literature either for centralized or distributed CVNs. Generally, it is important to use adequate SS and fusion techniques according to the properties of the surrounding environment. Furthermore the restricted and predictable mobility is not addressed for improving the SS accuracy (Table 3).

Table 3. Summary of spectrum sensing requirements in CVNs

Classes	Context		
	Highway	Suburban	Urban
Centralized	Fast and/or accurate local detection with soft fusion	Fast and accurate local detection with fast fusion	Accurate detection and fast data fusion.
Distributed	Fast and/or accurate local detection with belief algorithm	– Fast and accurate local detection – Weighted algorithm	– Accurate local detection – Weighted algorithm with correlation selection
Partially centralized	– First level:local SS or CSS – Second level: EBD	– First level: CSS (fast local detection with fast fusion) – Second level: EBD	– First level: CSS (fast local detection with fast fusion). – Second level: EBD or CD
Integrated	Mode I and Mode II	Sensing-only mode (CSS)	Sensing-only mode (CSS)

5 Conclusion

In this paper, we have analyzed the impact of environment effects (traffic density, speed and fading) on spectrum sensing and fusion techniques applied in CVNs. And then, we have derived the main spectrum sensing requirements in CVNs. This analysis enabled us to conclude that the real effects of vehicular environment are not studied well in literature for CVNs, this motivate further research needed for practical implementation. Thus, our discussions on the environmental effects on CVNs are needed to be grounded in established empirical studies as a part of future directions pertaining to CVNs. In our future work, we will be interested in spectrum sensing in urban context. Firstly, because the spectrum sensing in urban context is not studied well and secondly there are many challenging constraints in urban context such as high traffic, high fading and the PU's hidden problem. However, exploiting advantageously the predictable mobility may enhance the spectrum sensing performance.

References

1. Toor, Y., Muhlethaler, P., Laouiti, A., De La Fortelle, A.: Vehicle ad hoc networks: Applications and related technical issues. IEEE Commun. Surv. Tutor. **10**(3), 74–88 (2008)
2. Ghandour, A.J., Fawaz, K., Artail, H.: Data delivery guarantees in congested Vehicular ad hoc networks using cognitive networks. IEEE IWCMC **2011**, 871–876 (2011)
3. Abeywardana, R.C., Sowerby, K.W., Berber, S.M.: Spectrum sensing in cognitive radio enabled vehicular ad hoc networks: a review. In: IEEE ICIAfS, pp. 1–6 (2014)
4. Ahmed, A.A., Alkheir, A.A., Said, D., Mouftah, H.T.: Cooperative spectrum sensing for cognitive vehicular ad hoc networks: an overview and open research issues. CCECE **2016**, 1–4 (2016)
5. Chembe, C., Noor, R.M., Ahmedy, I., Oche, M., Kunda, D., Liu, C.H.: Spectrum sensing in cognitive vehicular network: state-of-Art, challenges and open issues. Comput. Commun. **97**, 15–30 (2017)
6. Singh, K.D., Rawat, P., Bonnin, J.M.: Cognitive radio for vehicular ad hoc networks (CR-VANETs): approaches and challenges. EURASIP J. Comm. Netw. **2014**, 49 (2014)
7. Min, A.W., Shin, K.G.: Impact of mobility on spectrum sensing in cognitive radio networks. CoRoNet@MobiCom 2009, pp. 13–18 (2009)
8. Zhu, S., Guo, C., Feng, C., Liu, X.: Performance analysis of cooperative spectrum sensing in cognitive vehicular networks with dense traffic. VTC Spring **2016**, 1–6 (2016)
9. Zhao, Y., Paul, P., Xin, C., Song, M.: Performance analysis of spectrum sensing with mobile SUs in cognitive radio networks. IEEE ICC **2014**, 2761–2766 (2014)
10. Mecklenbrauker, C., Karedal, J., Paier, A., Zemen, T., Czink, N.: Vehicular channel characterization and its implications for wireless system designs and performance. IEEE Trans. Veh. Technol. **99**(7), 1189–1212 (2011)
11. Akyildiz, I.F., Lo, B.F., Balakrishnan, R.: Cooperative spectrum sensing in cognitive radio networks: a survey. Phys. Commun. **4**(1), 40–62 (2011)
12. Axell, E., Leus, G., Larsson, E.G., Poor, H.V.: Spectrum sensing for cognitive radio: state-of-the-art and recent advances. IEEE Signal Process. Mag. **29**(3), 101–116 (2012)
13. Ghasemi, A., Sousa, E.S.: Collaborative spectrum sensing for opportunistic access in fading environments. In: First IEEE International Symposium on New Frontiers in Dynamic Spectrum Access Networks, pp. 131–136. USA (2005)
14. Duan, J.Q., Li, S., Ning, G.: Compressive spectrum sensing in centralized vehicular cognitive radio networks. Int. J. Future Gener. Comm. Netw. **6**, 1–12 (2013)
15. Souid, I., Chikha, H.B., Attia, R.: Blind spectrum sensing in cognitive vehicular ad hoc networks over nakagami-m fading channels. IEEE CISTEM **2014**, 1–5 (2014)
16. Brahmi, I.H., Djahel, S., Ghamri-Doudane, Y.: A hidden markov model based scheme for efficient and fast dissemination of safety messages in VANETs. In: IEEE GLOBECOM, pp. 177–182 (2012)
17. Abbassi, S.H., Qureshi, I.M., Abbasi, H., Alyaie, B.R.: History-based spectrum sensing in CR-VANETs. EURASIP J. Wirel. Comm. Netw. **2015**(1), 163 (2015)
18. Li, H., Irick, D.K.: Collaborative spectrum sensing in cognitive radio vehicular ad hoc networks: belief propagation on highway. VTC Spring **2010**, 1–5 (2010)
19. Di Felice, M., Chowdhury, K.R., Bononi, L.: Analyzing the potential of cooperative cognitive radio technology on inter-vehicle communication. Wirel. Days, 1–6 (2010)
20. Di Felice, M., Chowdhury, K.R., Bononi, L.: cooperative spectrum management in cognitive vehicular ad hoc networks. IEEE VNC **2011**, 47–54 (2011)
21. Wang, X.Y., Ho, P.H.: A novel sensing coordination framework for CR-VANETs. IEEE Trans. Veh. Technol. **59**(4), 1936–1948 (2010)

22. Abbassi, S.H., Qureshi, I.M., Alyaei, B.R., Abbasi, H., Sultan, K.: An efficient spectrum sensing mechanism for CR-VANETs. J. Basic Appl. Sci. Res. **3**, 12 (2013)
23. Pagadarai, S., Wyglinski, A.M., Vuyyuru, R.: Characterization of vacant UHF TV channels for vehicular dynamic spectrum access. IEEE VNC **2009**, 1–8 (2009)
24. Di Felice, M., Ghandhour, A.J., Artail, H., Bononi, L.: Integrating spectrum database and cooperative sensing for cognitive vehicular networks. IEEE VTC Fall **2013**, 1–7 (2013)
25. Doost-Mohammady, R., Chowdhury, K.R.: Design of spectrum database assisted cognitive radio vehicular networks. IEEE CrownCom **2012**, 1–5 (2012)

High Availability of Charging and Billing in Vehicular Ad Hoc Network

Mohamed Darqaoui(✉), Slimane Bah, and Marouane sebgui

Electrical and Communication Laboratory, Ecole Mohammadia d'Ingénieurs,
Mohamed V University in Rabat, Rabat, Morocco
darqaoui.med@gmail.com, {Slimane.bah,sebgui}@emi.ac.ma
http://www.emi.ac.ma/

Abstract. VANET (Vehicular Ad Hoc Network) is actually an important field for the development of a variety of services. In VANET charging and billing of services could not be enabled in the same way as in 3GPP networks and MANET (Mobile Ad Hoc Network) because of the characteristics of such network namely the high speed of nodes, frequent disconnection between nodes, rapidly changing topology and the large size of the network. The purpose of this work is to propose a flexible high level charging and billing scheme to allow a high availability of the charging and billing process in VANET.

Keywords: VANET · Charging · Billing · Prepaid · Online/Offline charging

1 Introduction

In recent years, the field of vehicular ad hoc network (VANET) has attracted a growing amount of interest. VANET [1] is a term associated with technologies (architecture, data, and protocols) developed and standardized under the umbrella work of intelligent transport systems (ITS) [2]. Standardization of ITS is done in various governmental and nongovernmental standard development organizations namely IEEE, ISO, ITU. VANET comprise vehicle-to-vehicle and vehicle-to-infrastructure communications based on wireless local area network technologies. Vehicular networking offers a wide variety of applications [3], including safety, non safety and infotainment applications. The abundance of VANET applications is a benefit for a wide range of parties: governments, vehicle manufacturers, operators and consumers. For the operators promoting their services in VANET a robust charging and billing architecture is needed. Although many works have been done in charging and billing in ad hoc environment, most of them does not addressed the high availability of charging and billing process when nodes move from VANET infrastructure to a pure infrastructureless VANET environment. Charging and billing process relies on an existing infrastructure which constitutes a severe limitation and raises a highly complex problem for which no satisfying solution exists.

© ICST Institute for Computer Sciences, Social Informatics and Telecommunications Engineering 2018
F. Belqasmi et al. (Eds.): AFRICATEK 2017, LNICST 206, pp. 33–42, 2018.
https://doi.org/10.1007/978-3-319-67837-5_4

To address this problem, we propose a scheme making the charging and billing control available even out of VANET infrastructure. We address this problem from two perspectives: First, when a vehicle under online charging and billing in VANET environment moves to an infrastructure-less environment; Second, when a vehicle under online charging in VANET moves to a different autonomous VANET domain or network.

This paper is structured as follows: Sect. 2 provides background information on vehicular networks and charging/billing systems in traditional mobile networks. Section 3, proposes requirements for billing and charging in VANETs and provides a critical overview of existing solutions. Section 4 proposes a hybrid charging and billing mechanism to take into consideration VANETs characteristics. We conclude our work in Sect. 5.

2   Background on VANET and Charging/Billing

2.1   Vehicular Ad Hoc Network

Ad hoc networks are communication networks that are formed in a more or less spontaneous way and comprise an arbitrary number of participating nodes. They typically comprise wireless communication terminals forming a wireless stand-alone network. Examples of such networks are mobile ad hoc network (MANET) [4] and vehicular ad hoc network (VANET). The current trend in ad hoc networks is vehicular ad hoc network. VANET is an emergent technology that receives, recently, the attention of the industry and research groups. It allows different deployment architectures in highways, urban and rural environments [5]. In VANET architecture, the communication can be either among nearby vehicles or/and between vehicles and roadside units leading to three possibilities: Vehicle-to-Vehicle (V2V) communication, Vehicle-to-Infrastructure (V2I) communication and Hybrid architecture (as shown in Fig. 1):

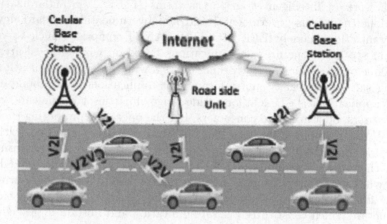

Fig. 1. VANET communication architecture

Vehicular ad hoc networks present some particular characteristics despite being a special case of classical mobile ad hoc networks namely the high speed of nodes, the rapidly changing topology, frequent disconnections between nodes [1] and in several cases the large size of the network. The particularities of VANET make it a very interspersing domain which deserves in the last years several studies addressing different aspects, such as: applications [6,7], communication [8], security [9,10], routing protocols [11–13], access [14] and cloud computing in VANETs [15–17].

Although researchers have achieved much great progress on VANETs study, there are still some challenges that need to be overcome and some issues that need to be further investigated (e.g., security, services.). Especially, one aspect that has not been tackled by research namely the charging and billing issue.

2.2   Charging and Billing

Charging is the process of collecting, evaluating and accounting a network resource usage [18]. This resource usage is related to an event that can be either a voice communication or an internet session or a value added service. Billing is the step that follows the charging operation, it consists of two mains steps: mediation step that collect, validate, filter correlate, aggregate and convert data to create data record called data Detailed Record (CDR) and rating step which is a process that puts a cost on a call or a service (monetary values). After the rating step bills are generated.

There exist two modes of charging: postpaid and prepaid. In postpaid mode a bill is generated in arrears periodically stating what was owed to the service provider by the customer. The subscriber is then expected to settle the bill (payment). In Prepaid mode of charging and billing, the customer pays a sum in advance. The paid amount is depreciated as telecoms services are consumed.

In mobile networks (GSM/UMTS/LTE) online and offline charging are two mechanisms used to charge subscribers for rendered services [18]. Offline charging is a mechanism that consists of a chain of logical functions, this chain end by generating charging information (CDR) related to a resource usage in the network which is then transferred to the billing system to generate the subscriber bill. In this scenario the charging process does not affect, in real time, the service rendered. Offline mode is used to charge a postpaid user. In the same fashion, the online charging information passes through a chain of logical functions. However, authorization for the network resource usage must be obtained by the network prior to resource usage to occur. The online mode is used to charge prepaid users.

3   Requirements and Critical Overview of Existing Solutions

3.1   Requirements

The charging and billing system in VANET must be different from the charging and billing process in other mobile networks. We identified main charging and billing requirements to be fulfilled by a charging and billing system in order to carry out its basic tasks in vehicular ad hoc network:

(a) The VANET charging/billing system should take into consideration the high speed of vehicles in terms of controlling the charging process and insuring its high availability.
(b) The VANET charging/billing system should be flexible. In fact, due to frequent disconnections, the charging solution needs to be aware of the underlying environment updates and adapt to the network topology changes.
(c) The VANET charging/billing system should allow the roaming of the charging function between different VANET providers. In fact, when a vehicle travels long distance it is not unusual to traverse different VANET infrastructures belonging to different domains. A service should be charged continuously and accurately in this context.

3.2   Related Work

To the best of our knowledge there is no solution dedicated to VANET environments for billing and charging issues. However, some research works have addressed this problem in peer-to-peer and MANET networks. Authors in [19] propose the MMAPPS (Market-Managed Peer-to-Peer Services) charging solution for peer-to-peer networks. The MMAPPS accounting and charging system addresses, mainly, the issue of accountability in peer-to-peer environments and associated problems.

The work [20] proposes a Secure Charging Protocol (SCP). SCP aims at answering the complex authentication, authorization, accounting and charging (AAAC) problem in MANET. It provides a view based on a different business model. This later has been adjusted to cope with technological changes. The work also addresses the improvements made to the SCP protocol in terms of Quality of Service (QoS) and User Interfaces.

The work in [21] proposes a solution for charging in MANET. The solution enables charging without any access to external networks. For example, when a communication is initiated by a mobile communication device within an ad hoc network, a small initiation fee is stored securely on the device, typically on a smart card. Transfer of the charging information may then occur more or less automatically and/or when the device reaches a coverage area of the operator network. When the network operators system receives the charging information from a communication device (i.e. when it comes into contact with the infrastructure) the corresponding account is updated and charged with the activities that have occurred since the last update.

3.3   Analysis and Discussion

Generally, the works discussed above provide a suitable charging and billing solution for peer-to-peer networks and ad hoc environment but did not meet the requirements highlighted previously. Specifically, the peer-to-peer architecture proposed in [18] does not consider mobility and then does not meet the requirement (a) and (b) in term of flexibility and high availability. The SCP protocol proposed in the work [19] has only addressed the security issue in charging process assuming an existing solution. As far as the work in [20] is concerned, it does not take into consideration the requirement (b) and (c). In fact, this work focus on updating the operator charging system with data collected during offline charging. The cooperation between the offline and online charging systems is not considered. Therefore, when a node roams from an environment with VANET infrastructure to an environment where the infrastructure of VANET is absent (i.e. no RSUs and no possible connection with external networks) the charging process is interrupted. Similarly, when the vehicle traverses different autonomous VANET systems the charging is interrupted or may not be possible to update the operator charging system. Therefore the high availability of charging and billing is not considered at all.

4 Proposed Solutions for High Availability Charging in VANET

The main goal of this work is to insure the high availability of charging and billing control in vehicular environment. First, we propose a high level mechanism to address the problem of a vehicle leaving the VANET infrastructure while it is under online charging and billing process. Then, we propose a high level mechanism for seamless charging between VANET and 3GPP domains. Both cases involve a context-aware charging and billing system. Both mechanisms rely on a context-aware charging and billing solution. Through this solution, the operator will be able to continuously control its resource usage in VANET and out of VANET. Indeed, the roadside units will be responsible for detecting if a vehicle is under VANET control or not using some protocol (e.g. heartbeat protocol) or when the Signal Noise Ratio (SNR) reaches some predefined thresholds. Following is the presentation of our proposed schemes.

4.1 Online to Offline Charging and Billing Roaming

In this scenario, vehicles establish a V2V session (e.g. direct voice call service between vehicles). We propose to equip the vehicles with a prepaid system such as smart card or virtual storage in the operating system running on the vehicle.

However, the charging of the call is carried out by the VANET online Charging and billing infrastructure (OCS), the RSU collects the charging data (V2I communication) and send them to billing domain BD (Fig. 2). The data charging are information related to the call such as start time, duration of the call and end time of the call.

Since the communication between vehicle A and B is Vehicle-to-Vehicle communication, the media channel is not controlled by the RSU. Therefore, when the two vehicles leave the VANET charging area (i.e. the zone covered by VANET infrastructure namely RSUs) to a non VANET charging area (i.e. area where

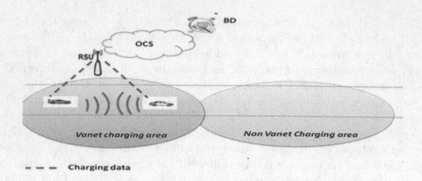

Fig. 2. Online charging based system

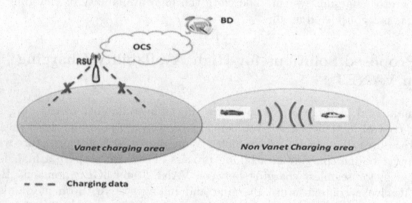

Fig. 3. Charging flow interruption

there is no VANET infrastructure and where VANET become a pure peer-to-peer mobile environment) the communication is not interrupted but the charging of the call is lost (Fig. 3).

From the VANET provider's business perspective, the scenario above present a crucial problem since the wireless resource (bandwidth) is used for free. To avoid this problem, we propose that the VANET provider implements an on-line context-aware charging and billing system (Context-aware OCS).

This system will collect several parameters in order to decide to switch automatically to the prepaid charging system implemented in the vehicle (e.g. smart card). We propose to use two parameters: the SNR (signal to Noise Ratio) between the RSUs and the vehicles, and/or GPS positions of RSU's zone edges. For the SNR, When the signal power reaches a predefined threshold the charging OCS system upload the charging profile to the prepaid system storage. As for the RSU edges GPS positions, the system (eventually the RSU) records the vehicles' GPS positions in each instant and compare them with a preconfigured table containing the GPS positions of RSU's zone edges. If the vehicle is near

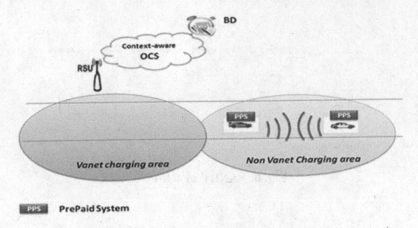

Fig. 4. Context-aware OCS and prepaid system

of these positions, the system switches the charging control to the prepaid by uploading the charging profile to the vehicles prepaid system.

The charging profile consist of subscription information namely, vehicle ID, owner of vehicle (subscriber), accounts, balances, services (voice, data, sms, video...), subscription time, expired time. The prepaid system is not necessarily a smart card it could be for example a virtual storage in an operating system implemented in the vehicle which stores the charging profile. Once the charging profile information is uploaded from the OCS to the vehicle's storage, the pre-paid system will have a real-time control on the call. Therefore, a credit, or an appropriate amount of credits, is deducted from the currently available credits (Fig. 4). Consequently the user will be denied to make any VANET communication when it runs out of credits.

4.2 VANET-Online Charging to Non-VANET Online Charging Roaming

Similarly, in this scenario the service charging is carried out by the VANET online Charging and billing infrastructure (OCS). But the vehicles A and B move from a VANET infrastructure domain to a non charging VANET domain but covered by external network such as 2G/3G or 4G, (Fig. 5). When vehicle A and vehicle B leave the VANET charging environment to 3GPP domain, the operator loses the charging and billing control. To avoid this, the OCS system and the vehicle should include context-aware functions.

For the OCS system, we propose to measure the signal power parameter between the RSU and the vehicle, and collect GPS positions of RSU's edges. For vehicles, we propose to measure the signal power parameter received from both RSU and Radio Access Network (RAN) node. Thus, when the vehicle reaches the RSUs edges, it measures and compares the signal power of RSU and RAN node, when the signal power of the RAN node is higher, then the charging control

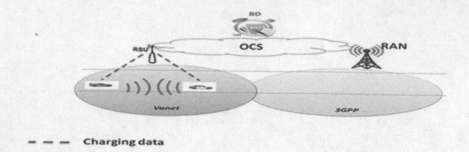

Fig. 5. VANET to 3GPP

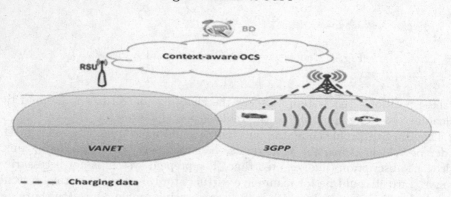

Fig. 6. VANET-to-3GPP charging roaming

is switched to the 3GPP network (Fig. 6). The charging switching is preceded by an authentication procedure of the vehicle in the visited 3GPP network. This authentication is, generally, performed by an authentication server of the operator such as Authentication, Authorization and Accounting server (AAA). Therefore the high availability of charging and billing is granted.

5   Conclusion

Vehicular ad-hoc network are a challenging environment especially for charging and billing. Nowadays many VANET research are addressing several aspects (e.g. access, routing and services). However, no works have been found in charging and billing systems. In this paper we showed that existing solutions mainly for MANET and peer-to-peer do not meet our proposed requirements and therefore are not suitable for VANET. Hence, we described two high level proposals for insuring the high availability of charging and billing in vehicular ad hoc environment especially when a vehicle moves from a VANET charging environment to a non-VANET charging one. In the next steps of our work we will detail our solution in term of, business model, architecture, functional entities, protocols, procedures and interfaces and in order to best enforce our solution a simulation of the work is also planned.

References

1. Zeadally, S., Hunt, R., Chen, Y.S., et al.: Telecommun. Syst. **50**, 217 (2012). doi:10. 1007/s11235-010-9400-5
2. Hartenstein, H., Laberteaux, K.: Intelligent Transport Systems, VANET Vehicular Applications and Inter-Networking Technologies (2010)
3. Vegni, A.M., Biagi, M., Cusani, R.: Smart vehicles, technologies and main applications in vehicular ad hoc networks, vehicular technologies - deployment and applications. In: Giordano, L.G. (ed.) InTech. doi:10.5772/55492, http://www. intechopen.com/books/vehicular-technologies-deployment-and-applications/ smart-vehicles-technologies-and-main-applications-in-vehicular-ad-hoc-networks
4. Al-Omari, S.A.K., Sumari, P.: An Overview of Mobile Ad Hoc Networks for the Existing Protocols and Applications. CoRR abs/1003.3565 (2010)
5. da Cunha, F.D., Boukerche, A., Villas, L., Viana, A.C., Loureiro, A.A.F.: Data communication in VANETs: a survey, challenges and applications. Research Report RR-8498, INRIA Saclay; INRIA (2014). <hal-00981126v4>
6. Hartenstein, H., Laberteaux, L.P.: A tutorial survey on vehicular ad hoc networks. IEEE Commun. Mag. **46**(6), 164–171 (2008)
7. Campolo, C., Molinaro, A., Scopigno, R.: Vehicular Ad Hoc Networks Standards, Solutions, and Research, 1st edn. Springer, Cham (2015)
8. Rawashdeh, Z.Y., Mahmud, S.M.: Communications in vehicular ad hoc networks, mobile ad-hoc networks: applications. In: Wang, X. (ed.) InTech. doi:10.5772/13399
9. Lin, X., Rongxing, L.: Vehicular Ad Hoc Network Security And Privacy, 1st edn., p. 216, 22 June 2015
10. Mejri, M.N., Ben-Othman, J., Hamdi, M.: Survey on VANET security challenges and possible cryptographic solutions. Veh. Commun. **1**, 53–66 (2014)
11. Lin, Y.-W., Chen, Y.-S., Lee, S.-L.: Routing protocols in vehicular ad hoc networks: a survey and future perspectives. J. Inf. Sci. Eng. **26**(3), 913–932 (2010)
12. Lee, K.C., Lee, U., Gerla, M.: Survey of routing protocols in vehicular ad hoc networks. In: Advances in Vehicular Ad-Hoc Networks: Developments and Challenges. IGI Global, October 2009
13. Benamar, M., Benamar, N., Singh, K.D., El Ouadghiri, D.: Recent study of routing protocols in VANET: survey and taxonomy. In: 1st International Workshop on Vehicular Networks and Telematics, WVNT, Marrakech, Morocco, 02–04 May (2013)
14. Sjöberg, K.: Medium Access Control for Vehicular Ad Hoc Networks. Chalmers University of Technology, Goteborg (2013)
15. Whaiduzzaman, M., Sookhak, M., Gani, A., Buyya, R.: A survey on vehicular cloud computing. J. Netw. Comput. Appl. doi:10.1016/j.jnca.2013.08.004
16. Lee, E., Lee, E.K., Gerla, M., Oh, S.Y.: Vehicular cloud networking: architecture and design principles. IEEE Commun. Mag. **52**(2), 148–155 (2014)
17. Nkenyereye, L., Park, Y., Rhee, K.H.: J. Wirel. Com. Netw. **2016**, 196 (2016). doi:10.1186/s13638-016-0687-0
18. 3GPP TS 32.240 v9.0.0:3rd: Generation Partnership Project; Technical Specification Group Services and System Aspects; Telecommunication Management; Charging Management; Charging Architecture and Principles (Release 9)

19. Kuhne, R., Huitema, G., Carle, G.: Charging and billing in modern communications networks a comprehensive survey of the state of the art and future requirements. IEEE Commun. Surv. Tutor. **14**(1), 170–192, First Quarter 2012
20. Girão, J., Lamparter, B., Westhoff, D., Aguiar, R.L., Barraca, J.P.: Implementing charging in mobile ad-hoc networks. Electrnica e Telecomunicaes **4**(1). ISSN 1645–0493, October 2004
21. Plymoth, A.N., Plymoth, B., Plymoth, A.: Charging In Ad Hoc Communication Networks, Sweden (2009)

IoT and Cloud Computing

Developing the IoT to Support the Health Sector: A Case Study from Kikwit, DR Congo

Piers W. Lawrence[1]([⊠]), Trisha M. Phippard[2], Gowri Sankar Ramachandran[1], and Danny Hughes[1]

[1] Department of Computer Science, KU Leuven, Leuven, Belgium
piers.lawrence@cs.kuleuven.be
[2] Institute for Anthropological Research in Africa, KU Leuven, Leuven, Belgium

Abstract. Effective implementation and evaluation of development projects depends on access to accurate, complete, and timely information about the outcomes of project implementation. We explore the proposition that next-generation ICTs offer solutions for development actors operating in decentralised and extremely low-power environments to improve data collection, monitoring, and project feedback. This paper describes the potential integration of novel distributed monitoring technologies and techniques within the health sector in developing countries, and in particular the use of Internet of Things (IoT) technologies for monitoring widely distributed projects in areas with little or no infrastructure. We discuss the application of an emerging low-power wide area networking technology, LoRa, which is ideally suited to resource-limited contexts due to its low cost, low power usage, and long range. We describe our experiences in implementing a pilot project carried out in Kikwit, DR Congo to develop a LoRa-based wireless network to track the temperature of blood products, ensuring their security and viability through a decentralised, low-power, and low-cost monitoring system.

Keywords: LoRaWAN · e-Health · ICT4D · IoT for development · Smart fridge · Cold chain

1 Introduction

The Internet of Things (IoT) uses tiny, low-cost devices equipped with sensors and low-power radios to build networks that are capable of sensing and controlling the physical world. In recent years, many IoT technologies have appeared on the market, enhancing quality of life and solving nontrivial problems. These technologies have emerged mainly in developed countries due to the widespread availability of and market for consumer goods and the existence of high levels of underlying networking, electrical, and basic service infrastructure supporting these technologies. Examples of these innovations include the development of IoT applications for hyper-connected "smart city" infrastructure, agricultural monitoring and control [1], and remote sensing and data collection to support personal health care, particularly in the domain of elder care [2].

© ICST Institute for Computer Sciences, Social Informatics and Telecommunications Engineering 2018
F. Belqasmi et al. (Eds.): AFRICATEK 2017, LNICST 206, pp. 45–56, 2018.
https://doi.org/10.1007/978-3-319-67837-5_5

However, IoT applications remain largely oriented toward high-income countries and consumer markets, and relatively little research has been conducted as to how emerging IoT technologies can be applied and tailored to developing country contexts. Yet, as others have argued [3,4], the IoT has the potential to benefit the development sector immensely, leveraging appropriate new technologies and techniques for monitoring widely distributed projects in areas with limited existing infrastructure. In these environments, emerging IoT technologies may hold tremendous potential to offer low-cost, low-power solutions to make service delivery and project monitoring 'smarter' (i.e. better informed through more efficient and effective monitoring).

Meaningful planning and responsible governance of development projects depends on access to accurate, complete, and timely information about the outcomes of project implementation. Key stakeholders engaged in development work often lack data about what is really happening 'on the ground', in part due to the inherent difficulties involved in Monitoring and Evaluation (M&E) in the face of large geographic distances, lack of infrastructure, and limited resources [5, pp. 71]. Quality M&E is critically important for responsive and responsible development project planning and implementation, as it provides a means to assess how precious human and material resources should be allocated, and to respond quickly to crisis situations or system failures. The lack of access to timely, reliable, and comprehensive data and feedback on project outcomes hinders the decision-making of development actors. In theory, the use of IoT technologies in this context could enable near real-time monitoring of projects, allowing stakeholders to more quickly study, refine, and optimise the execution of projects based on changing facts on the ground.

In the health sector in particular, near real-time monitoring and feedback is essential not only for saving lives but also for safeguarding essential supplies. In the past ten years, an abundance of literature has explored the emerging field of 'mHealth' and the uses of mobile technologies in the health sector in developing countries [6–9], but this has rarely been extended to explore the application of the next-generation of ICTs (such as IoT technologies) in developing countries.

To address this gap in the literature and explore the applicability of emerging IoT technologies in the health sector in development contexts, we conducted an exploratory pilot project in the Democratic Republic of Congo. This paper describes our experiences with our deployment of a LoRa Wide Area Network (LoRaWAN) for medical cold chain surveillance in an environment with unreliable electricity and a distributed health system. LoRa is a next-generation network technology that is ideally suited to resource-limited contexts due to its low cost, low power usage, and long range. This case study enabled us to test in practice the theoretical potential of IoT for real-time monitoring and feedback, to identify potential political and socio-cultural barriers to its effective local adoption, and to determine whether the economic and technological limitations of using this emerging technology in a developing country context are consistent with its application in highly developed countries.

Next we will describe the local context of our case study in the health sector in Kikwit, DR Congo, with its distributed health system and precarious access to power. The subsequent section describes the LoRa network and end devices used for monitoring blood supplies. Finally, we will offer some reflections on the lessons learned and future applications for this sort of IoT in the context of the health sector in developing countries and for development projects more broadly.

2   Project Context

Many sectors in DR Congo are currently confronted by insufficient capacity for effective and timely data collection and monitoring. Conflict and political instability have compounded the challenges of serving a population distributed over a vast geographic area with limited infrastructure [5]. Decentralised mechanisms for data collection and M&E are critically important in this context. This is particularly true for the health sector, due to the extensive reliance on donor funding and the distributed nature of both state health structures and donor-led health interventions [10].

Our pilot project is based in Kikwit, DR Congo, a representative example of a low-infrastructure environment. Kikwit is a secondary town in the interior of the country, located 525 km southeast of the capital, Kinshasa. The town was the site of a serious Ebola outbreak in 1995, which spurred an influx of biomedical technologies and expertise [11]. However, the town of about 1.2 million inhabitants spread throughout an area of 92 km^2 remains cut off from the electricity grid. The primary form of energy supply in Kikwit is thus provided by petrol-powered generators or solar panels. Although there have been some donor-supported initiatives to partially electrify critical locations (such as the general hospital) with more sophisticated solar systems, the vast majority of health centres do not have a regular electricity supply (a best-case scenario usually involves a generator running at most a few hours per day).

The state health infrastructure in DR Congo is decentralised, with a large number of provincial and district health offices involved in the distribution of essential medicines, vaccines, and blood products. The cold chain extends only to the district level, as community health facilities usually lack access to any electricity, and GSM coverage—although improving—is still lacking in many rural areas. The distances between health centres and the extremely degraded state of the roads compound the challenge of delivering essential medical supplies. The ability to monitor the integrity of the cold chain is vitally important for supply safety, as is the ability to coordinate supply levels and stock movements.

The second author conducted fourteen months of anthropological fieldwork in the health sector in Kikwit (since January 2015), which has revealed significant challenges associated with data collection, the urgent need for monitoring of projects, and the desire for new technologies to ease the strain on over-burdened and under-resourced organizations and individuals. In particular, local health institutions lack reliable, systematic, and cost-effective monitoring for medical supplies cooled by these often sporadic power sources. For example, the current approach to monitoring medical cold storage is time- and labour-intensive, based upon manual twice-daily temperature measurements with no electronic records. Furthermore, when temperature-controlled medical supplies such as blood, vaccines, and insulin leave the central office, their status is no longer monitored, introducing scope for unsafe use.

This location is thus an ideal site for the our LoRa case study because it features a large, decentralised population and health infrastructure without any reliable power source. Health facilities face serious challenges in ensuring the medical cold chain, and M&E is crippled by constant barriers to electricity and communication. Moreover, given the paramount importance of foreign donors in supporting both state and private health institutions in the region, local partners have a strong desire for improved monitoring capacity and any means of producing more reliable measurements and evaluation of project results and successes (in order to help secure future funding and support from these donors).

We conducted our initial pilot in collaboration with the Provincial Centre for Blood Transfusion (*Centre Provincial de Transfusion Sanguine*, or CPTS), the local body responsible for coordinating the collection, testing, and storage of blood and blood products. CPTS is centrally located in the Plateau neighbourhood of Kikwit, but it oversees and coordinates transfusion-related activities throughout the Bandundu region (a large territory encompassing 52 health zones across the former Bandundu province, now comprising the provinces of Kwilu, Kwango, and Mai-Ndombe). CPTS relies heavily on a network of fridges and cooler boxes (for the transportation and storage of blood products) and has expressed an interest in the monitoring capacities that IoT technologies could provide (e.g. to verify fridge temperature or stock levels of different blood types, or potentially even to identify individual donors by code or RFID tag). They are usually able to keep their blood stored at safe temperatures in a solar-powered fridge, the temperature of which is monitored manually and recorded twice daily. However, this system can on occasion break down, for example due to the large amount of dust in the air during the dry season, reducing the efficiency of the solar panels. From the CPTS central office, they distribute blood to smaller health zones where and when it is needed. When blood is distributed to the surrounding health centres, however, no temperature monitoring is carried out.

Although the initial pilot encompasses only the surveillance of temperature for blood products, we envisage this quite easily being extended to the monitoring of other aspects of the medical cold chain in Kikwit and the surrounding region, particularly for the transportation of vaccines and other temperature-sensitive medications. The central office of the health district, for example, has a critical need for monitoring the temperature of fridges for vaccines and other medications, and could benefit greatly from systematic monitoring technology (both in terms of efficiency and the security of ensuring cold chain integrity).

3   Project Implementation

In this section, we will describe our experience of rolling out a communication network and monitoring system suitable for development projects in DR Congo, and offer a technical description of the technology we have implemented.

3.1   Choice of Technology

The limited existing infrastructure and unreliable electricity access that characterised the local context, as described above, necessitated the use of networking infrastructure with the following key features:

- Low cost: network and devices should have low manufacturing costs and should not depend on a cellular connection so as to eliminate recurring network fees.
- Long range: given the wide geographic distribution of the local health system (as is the case for many sectors in developing countries), hardware should have an inherently long range and should support software for extensible mesh networking, enabling sequences of wireless devices to form arbitrarily large mesh networks.
- Low power: since power infrastructure is unreliable or absent and projects are often too widely distributed for manual battery changes as a feasible solution, operational power requirements should be very low and capable of running on locally available alternative solutions such as solar systems.

With these general goals in mind, we evaluated a number of emerging technologies that would enable the realisation of a robust wireless network serving the community in Kikwit. Numerous competing technologies have emerged on the market that realise Low Power Wide Area Networks (LPWANs) that do not depend on cellular network coverage. The most notable of these are the SigFox [12] and LoRa [1] radio technologies, both of which are already being employed to support IoT applications in Europe and North America. The two technologies differ significantly in their marketing models: SigFox requires users to subscribe to licensed network providers, whereas LoRa enables users to establish their own private network infrastructure. In the DR Congo, there is currently no established SigFox infrastructure [12] and the authors are not aware of any current plans to establish one in the near future. It is thus also likely that until SigFox networks are established in the developing world, it will remain an unsuitable technology to support such applications.

In contrast to SigFox, the LoRa radio technology enables users to establish their own network infrastructure using any one of the numerous gateways or concentrators available on the market at low prices (ranging from €100 to €1200). Such gateways offer an effective range of over 15 km and offer end device battery lives of more than 10 years with messages sent daily. Furthermore, the range of the network can be arbitrarily extended by building a 'mesh' of networks wherein each node serves as a router, as described below. This technology thus fulfills our three essential criteria (low cost, long range, low power) outlined above.

These features make the LoRa radio technology ideally suited to widely distributed monitoring where there is little or no existing infrastructure.

3.2   Gateway Infrastructure

For our pilot implementation, we installed LoRa-based network infrastructure at the CPTS office in Kikwit, as shown in Fig. 1. This was an ideal location to place the networking infrastructure as it covered a large majority of the most important health facilities in Kikwit (marked with a cross symbol) and enables the monitoring of all of the frequently used schools and churches where the CPTS carries out blood collection drives.

We installed a Multitech® Conduit MTCDT-H5 gateway [13] equipped with a LoRa mCard to provide the base station at the CPTS offices. This was equipped with a Taoglas® 5dBi antenna [14] mounted on the antenna pole of the building at approximately 5 m above the ground level.

To enable the gateway to operate continuously without the need to draw on the sporadic energy sources available at the CPTS offices, we also installed an independent solar system. The continuous power consumption of the gateway was found to be approximately 15 W, and we established that we could reliably power the gateway using a 150 W (peak) solar panel together with a 100 Ah battery.

3.3   Sensing Devices

The sensing element of the solution attains low power and long range operation via the combination of the LoRa radio technology with the μPnP platform. μPnP provides zero-configuration customisation of wireless sensor nodes with diverse sensors at 10 million times lower power than USB and a cost overhead of just 1 cent per sensor. A technical description of the μPnP system is available in [15]. The devices themselves use Microchip's RN2483 LoRa radio module, which is connected to a μPnP board, allowing up to 3 sensors to be connected. A detailed technical description of the final solution can be found in [16].

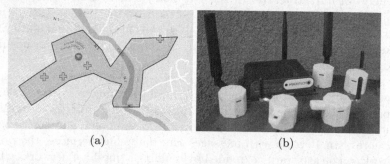

(a)   (b)

Fig. 1. LoRa deployment in Kikwit: (a) Range testing area; (b) LoRa gateway and fridge sensor devices

For this pilot, we have chosen this particular architecture based on pre-existing tools in order to enable rapid development and deployment, as well as flexibility for future expansion and experimentation (i.e. the ability to add new sensors and other custom devices).

3.4   Network Topology

Our pilot project initially concentrated on the implementation of a network based on a star topology (i.e. having centralised concentrators in the network), due to the small scale and relatively concentrated project sites involved in the initial pilot. However, one of the key benefits of the technology we have selected is the ability to flexibly expand the network as the project develops. Hence, this topology can be modified in the future to have either a star-of-stars or a mesh-based topology in order to expand the coverage as far as possible.

Mesh networking allows for the building of arbitrarily long-range networks by expanding the role of a low-power wireless device from a simple transmitter to a combined transmitter and router. All wireless devices then establish multi-hop routes to the gateway and therefore do not need to be within direct range (i.e. being in range of any of their peers is sufficient). This approach enables coverage over greater distances, without modification to the hardware. Our approach builds on classical approaches to low-power mesh networking such as Low Power Listening [17] and time synchronisation [18], though these must be adapted to the hardware platform developed.

3.5   Temperature Monitoring System

Our initial pilot concentrated on developing a robust automated temperature monitoring system for the fridges used by CPTS. We deployed two small dual 12V DC/220V AC-powered fridges, which enabled flexible operation either from solar panels or from the 12 V power outlet of a vehicle, and additionally by AC power when connected to a generator. One of the two fridges also featured the ability to freeze ice packs, extending the cooling capacity of the fridges during offsite blood collection drives at various locations in the community. We equipped these 'smart' fridges with our monitoring devices (sensors and a battery-powered LoRa end device) already integrated inside. We designed these 'LoRa MediFridges' to be completely independent units, with the flexibility to be used either onsite at the CPTS central office or on the road as mobile fridges for blood collection or distribution.

However, our objective was also to introduce a robust monitoring system to be used with the existing cooling infrastructure already in place. Hence, we additionally integrated our temperature-sensing devices into the existing solar-powered fridges already installed at the CPTS offices. Because the generator is used only sporadically to power computers or laboratory equipment for testing as needed, the blood, blood products, and testing reagents are regularly stored in the solar fridge. Unfortunately, the system is prone to temperature fluctuations and hence close monitoring of this fridge is essential. Our sensing device wás initially installed as a supportive monitoring system alongside the manual system, but the aim is that it can replace manual temperature measurements, reducing workload for CPTS staff and increasing the reliability of their monitoring system.

Based on consultation with the staff of the CPTS, we configured these devices to generate a sensor reading every 15 min. This interval was chosen to balance reactionary potential with battery life (i.e. sufficient frequency of measurement to enable timely intervention, but infrequent enough to ensure a battery life in the order of years [16]). These readings included information about the internal and external temperature (i.e. both inside the fridge and the ambient air temperature), and the humidity. Following initial deployment, we realised the need to monitor the solar system in order to predict the expected operational duration of the fridges. The flexible plug-and-play nature of μPnP [15] enabled us to quickly adapt the configuration to additionally include measurements of the voltage of the solar system, so as to be able to monitor the total energy input and consumption.

This sensor data is transmitted to the central gateway, where it is stored and a local web page is generated automatically. This web page is accessible via a WiFi network run by the gateway, and enables the CPTS staff to access and evaluate this data. If the temperature of one of the fridges rises above the optimal temperature range of 1 °C to 6 °C, the staff are able to intervene quickly to ensure the safe storage of the blood and blood products by either transferring them to another fridge operating at a safe temperature, using the generator or 12 V system to cool a mobile fridge as a temporary solution, or transferring the products to another fridge in Kikwit (such as at the general hospital) for safekeeping. For our own research purposes, we also transfer this data over a GSM modem to a central database in Belgium, where we also provide a web-based interface to access the data remotely (i.e. off-site locations and beyond the range of the local WiFi network). An example of the temperature trace from the solar-powered fridge is shown in Fig. 2. However, it is important to note that the local web interface does not depend on any external GSM network or internet connection to function, and the staff can access the information locally regardless of whether the data is transmitted to the remote database.

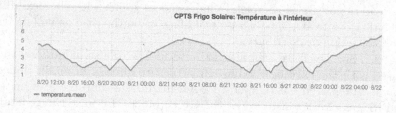

Fig. 2. Trace of daily temperature profile from solar-powered fridge

3.6 Limitations and Lessons Learned

Our experiences in implementing this pilot project revealed that there are several limitations to these technologies. With limited networking experience and informatics literacy, transferring sufficient knowledge and skills so that local actors can continue to use, apply, and extend the project outcomes after the completion of the pilot remains a challenge. This is particularly true given that we are collaborating with health professionals with no background in computer science, rather than specialists in this field. One potential solution is to incorporate a collaboration with local universities and incorporate training on networking and emerging IoT technologies and their local applications as part of informatics courses. This speaks to the need to foster local IoT innovation and experimentation [19] rather than merely transplanting solutions developed in Northern countries or other disparate contexts.

Moreover, our range test results in Kikwit indicate that the effective range of μPnP-WAN devices is not consistent with the coverage radius of the LoRa gateway [16]. This is attributed to interferences in the operational environment, and we expect that deploying the gateway in locations with higher altitude might alleviate this problem. However, it is not always practical to find such high-altitude locations, so other techniques to improve the range and reliability of the ad-hoc LoRa networks should be investigated. The redundancy offered by a mesh network, as described above, is also expected to improve reliability by providing multiple paths between the gateway and each LoRa device.

A final limitation relates to the scalability of network infrastructure installed in this environment. Although it has been shown that LoRa wide area networks scale well in urban areas to support thousands of devices per gateway [20, 21], the local political and economic context may hinder scalability. Even in rural areas, solutions like ours may readily integrate into particular projects or coordinated NGO programmes, but integration into weak and under-resourced state health infrastructures is more challenging. Hence, widespread deployments at national or regional levels may be slow or difficult without external (i.e. donor) support.

4 Conclusion and Future Work

This paper has described how emerging IoT technologies may be applied to facilitate the meaningful planning and responsible governance of development projects by providing accurate, complete, and timely information about the outcomes of project implementation. We have described the ways in which emerging technologies like LoRa are ideally suited to data collection and monitoring in decentralised and low-power environments, and our experiences applying this technology in the health sector in DR Congo.

In implementing our experimental pilot project in Kikwit, we have confirmed that IoT technologies like the LoRaWAN can indeed function in resource-limited contexts and areas with very little existing infrastructure. Although the project is in its infancy with preliminary results only, the technology shows sufficient potential to warrant further investigation and experimentation. Since there are few others using this technology in similar settings, the field of study would benefit greatly from further applied research projects on how to effectively integrate the IoT into development contexts.

While the scope of this research project to date has been limited to collaboration with the CPTS and monitoring the temperature of blood and blood products, the scope for expansion of this project is immense and the potential applications of similar technologies and systems are many. The most immediate and simplest opportunity for expansion is to extend our temperature monitoring system to other health-related institutions in the Kikwit area, such as the general hospital and the central office of the health zone. This would extend the scope of the cold chain monitoring beyond the domain of blood transfusion to include the surveillance of vaccines and life-saving medications that require refrigeration.

As described above, our research group is working on a mesh protocol for gaining ground and extending the reach of our LoRa network in Congo. As the size and range of the network expands, real-time monitoring of portable coolers (i.e. insulated boxes filled with cold packs and medical supplies) could for the first time extend the medical cold chain to rural health facilities. Scalability on this level would take time, resources, and coordination, but seems technically quite feasible.

Moreover, given the fact that GSM coverage in rural areas remains limited and unreliable, there is a second-order effect to be gained from rolling out a mesh network by creating new lines of communication between the smaller health centres and the central health offices. Once such a network is available, the possibilities of offering more than just temperature monitoring start to be realised. For example, one critical problem faced by the health sector is the logistics of provisioning all the local health centres with essential medicines. Given the poor state of the roads and long transport times, many deaths are caused by the inability to monitor and anticipate stock levels in the remote health centres and distribute medicines before they are needed (rather than merely responding to stock shortages).

The potential to automate the monitoring of stock and facilitate communication with a central distribution point is just one example of how the integration of novel distributed monitoring technologies and techniques could make a significant impact within developing countries. Given the vast selection of different sensors on the market, there are many possibilities to look beyond health and apply this type of IoT-based monitoring solution to other sectors and development projects (such as water quality or agricultural monitoring).

Acknowledgements. This research was partially supported by the Research Fund KU Leuven, the iMinds IoT research program, and the RINAiSense GRand FWO G.0453.15N. The second author was supported by Odysseus Grant FWO G.A005.14N. The authors wish to thank Dr Donald Mayuma and the staff of CPTS for their ongoing collaboration, Héritier Mbwabala for local assistance and logistical support, and VersaSense NV for the use of μPnP hardware.

References

1. LoRa Alliance: A technical overview of LoRa and LoRaWAN. Technical report (2015)
2. LinkLabs: How IoT medical devices are changing health care today (2016). https://www.link-labs.com/iot-healthcare/. Accessed 04 Jan 2017
3. Zennaro, M., Bagula, A.: IoT for development (IoT4D) (2015). http://iot.ieee.org/newsletter/july-2015/iot-for-development-iot4d.html. Accessed 04 Jan 2017
4. Saint, M., Garba, A.: Technology and policy for the internet of things in africa. In: TPRC 44: The 44th Research Conference on Communication, Information and Internet Policy 2016. SSRN (2016)
5. Partow, H.: Water issues in the DR Congo. challenges and opportunities. Technical report, United Nations Environment Programme (2011). http://postconflict.unep.ch/publications/UNEP_DRC_water.pdf. Accessed 12 Feb 2017
6. Fiordelli, M., Diviani, N., Schulz, J.P.: Mapping mHealth research: a decade of evolution. J. Med. Internet Res. **15**(5), e95 (2013)
7. Mechael, P., Batavia, H., Kaonga, N., Searle, S., Kwan, A., Goldberger, A., Fu, L., Ossman, J., et al.: Barriers and gaps affecting mHealth in low and middle income countries: policy white paper. Columbia university. Earth institute. Center for Global Health and Economic Development (CGHED): with mHealth alliance (2010)
8. Mechael, P.N.: The case for mHealth in developing countries. Innovations **4**(1), 103–118 (2009)
9. Phippard, T.M.: The (m)Health connection: an examination of the promise of mobile phones for HIV/AIDS intervention in sub-saharan africa. Master's thesis, The University of Western Ontario (2012)
10. Kuwekita, J.M., Bruyère, O., Guillaume, M., Gosset, C., Reginster, J.-Y.: Comment optimiser l'efficience de l'aide internationale, dans le domaine de la santé, en République Démocratique du Congo. Santé Publique **27**(1), 129–134 (2015)
11. Nsanga, K., Mulala, L.: Le Virus Ebola à Kikwit: mythe, mystère ou réalité. Et quinze ans après? Editions Baobab (1998)
12. SigFox: Sigfox technology. http://www.sigfox.com. Accessed 14 Mar 2016
13. Mutitech: Multiconnect conduit programmable gateway for the internet of things. http://www.multitech.com/documents/publications/data-sheets/86002170.pdf. Accessed 12 Feb 2017
14. Taoglas. Specification: 868mhz ism band dipole antenna. http://www.taoglas.com/wp-content/uploads/2015/06/OMB.868.B05F21.pdf. Accessed 12 Feb 2017
15. Yang, F., Matthys, N., Bachiller, R., Michiels, S., Joosen, W., Hughes, D.: μPnP: Plug and play peripherals for the internet of things. In: Proceedings of the Tenth European Conference on Computer Systems, EuroSys '15, pp. 25:1–25:14, New York, NY, USA. ACM (2015)
16. Ramachandran, G.S., Yang, F., Lawrence, P.W., Michiels, S., Joosen, W., Hughes, D.: μPnP-WAN: Experiences with LoRa and its Deployment in DR Congo. In: Proceedings of the 9th International Conference on Communication Systems and Networks (COMSNETS) (2017)
17. Polastre, J., Hill, J., Culler, D.: Versatile low power media access for wireless sensor networks. In: Proceedings of the 2nd international conference on Embedded networked sensor systems, pp. 95–107. ACM (2004)
18. Pister, K., Doherty, L.: Tsmp: Time synchronized mesh protocol. In: Proceedings of the IASTED Distributed Sensor Networks, pp. 391–398 (2008)

19. Masinde, M.: Iot applications that work for the african continent: Innovation or adoption? In: 2014 12th IEEE International Conference on Industrial Informatics (INDIN), pp. 633–638. IEEE (2014)
20. Mikhaylov, K., Petäjäjärvi, J., Haenninen, T.: Analysis of capacity and scalability of the lora low power wide area network technology. In: 22th European Wireless Conference on European Wireless 2016, pp. 1–6. VDE (2016)
21. Georgiou, O., Raza, U.: Low power wide area network analysis: Can lora scale? IEEE Wirel. Commun. Lett. (2017)

Designing a Framework for Smart IoT Adaptations

Asmaa Achtaich[1,3(✉)], Nissrine Souissi[1,2], Raul Mazo[3,4],
Camille Salinesi[3], and Ounsa Roudies[1]

[1] Univ. Mohammed V- Rabat, EMI, Siweb Team - Rabat, Morocco
asmaaachtaich@research.emi.ac.ma,
{souissi,roudies}@emi.ac.ma
[2] ENSMR, Département Informatique, Rabat, Morocco
[3] Université Paris, Panthéon-Sorbonne, CRI, Paris, France
{raul.mazo,camille.salinesi}@univ-paris1.fr
[4] Universidad EAFIT - Grupo GIDITIC, Medellin, Colombia

Abstract. The Internet of Things (IoT) is the science of connecting multiple devices that coordinate to provide the service in question. IoT environments are complex, dynamic, rapidly changing and resource constrained. Therefore, proactively adapting devices to align with context fluctuations becomes a concern. To propose suitable configurations, it should be possible to sense information from devices, analyze the data and reconfigure them accordingly. Applied in the service of the environment, a fleet of devices can monitor environment indicators and control it in order to propose best fit solutions or prevent risks like over consumption of resources (e.g., water and energy). This paper describes our methodology in designing a framework for the monitoring and multi-instantiation of fleets of connected objects. First by identifying the particularities of the fleet, then by specifying connected object as a Dynamic Software Product Line (DSPL), capable of readjusting while running.

Keywords: Multi-instantiation · IoT · Smart-environment · Dynamic software product lines · DSPL · Self-adaptation · Context · Environment · Fleet

1 Introduction

The Internet of things is a global infrastructure that enables advanced services by inter-connecting physical and virtual things like smartphones, sensors, computers, machines, vehicles, buildings, roads, cities or countries, and even people and animals [1]. These services vary from basic context information like location or weather, to much more complex setups. Smart environments are primary applications of the IoT, mainly concerned with issues related to pollution, limited resources, energy optimization, and fault tolerance.

Connected objects can monitor environment indicators like temperature, air and water quality, energy consumption, or radiation. This helps collect information about the surrounding, and prepare solutions to eradicate several phenomenon, or prevent some of the risks. In this context, our work consists of a platform that monitors a fleet of device to preform intelligent and dynamic change for an optimal configuration. When

© ICST Institute for Computer Sciences, Social Informatics and Telecommunications Engineering 2018
F. Belqasmi et al. (Eds.): AFRICATEK 2017, LNICST 206, pp. 57–66, 2018.
https://doi.org/10.1007/978-3-319-67837-5_6

a fleet is implemented, it bears a configuration (FConfig) that is characterized by the set of corresponding devices along with their respective configuration (DConfig). However, the IoT system is complex, rapidly changing, highly variable, heterogeneous, prone to risks and failure, and extremely dynamic. This implies that in the face of change, the system should have the ability to adapt itself in order to continue offering the needed performance. Dynamic proactive adaptation in particular is required to provide adjustments at runtime [2]. Furthermore, and thanks to IoT devices which are growing exponentially in number and performance, it is much more conceivable to collect real time context data, and react accordingly. Additionally, a Device Management (DM) platform monitors every device in the fleet. It can inspect specific information about the services provided by the device (coffee readiness, light status, expired merchandize, speed of car, motor condition, ...), it can collect information about the context of the fleet (temperature, light, location, ...) and it can report on the characteristics of the devices themselves (battery life, memory, software version, etc.). In addition to that, and poster to processing the collected data, it is responsible for controlling the fleet in order to adjust its behavior.

In this sense, the paper describes our process in designing a framework for the smart monitoring and reconfiguration of a fleet of connected devices. The paper starts by presenting a motivational example–a smart irrigation fleet, which will be depicted all along the development of our framework. Our process will then be elaborated. The first step identifies the requirements for the management of fleets of connected objects. The second step discusses the particularities of IoT devices and their surroundings. Three representative dimensions are conceived; the system, the context, and the environment. The third step studies the self-adaptation approaches, and selects the Dynamic Software Product Lines (DSPL) paradigm as the mechanism that fits best our set of requirements. The fourth and final step introduces an architecture skeleton; it considers the outcome of the previous stages; the three dimensions on the one hand, and the engineering processes involved in DSPL on the other hand.

The paper is structured as follows: Sect. 2 presents a motivational example. Section 3 describes our methodology by presenting the requirements needed from the DM platform, describing the characteristics of IoT environments and overviewing the mechanisms for self-adaptation. Section 4 presents the DSPL based framework. And finally, Sect. 5 presents the related works before concluding.

2   Motivational Examples

In this section, we intend to illustrate the need for proactive self-adaptation of fleets of connected objects. We consider the following irrigation system example: Dust and air humidity sensors, temperature sensors, water sprinklers, water taps, and a smartphone compose a fleet of devices, installed in an agriculture field. Sensors collect data about the dust and air humidity, and about the temperature. When humidity is low, the tap or sprinkler provides dust with the needed water. When the temperature is too high or too low, alerts are sent to the smartphone. The fleet does not take into consideration the specific knowledge related to the domain of agriculture. For instance, instead of watering the plants a days before a rainy day, the fleet could consider the weather forecast to readjust its configuration, and wait for the rain instead of unnecessarily using the water supplies. In this scenario, the proactive adaptation would be possible by implementing a Device Management (DM) Platform that monitors devices and their surroundings, processes the data, and reconfigures the fleet by reconfiguring associated devices.

3   Methodology

As we intend to design a framework that manages run-time variability in a fleet of connected objects, the following section outlines our methodology.

3.1   Main Requirements Elicitation

In order to insure the proper management of the fleet, the DM is required to provide the necessary mechanisms to monitor IoT devices, to propose best-fit adaptions, to manage different levels of variability and to support a large number of connected devices. Our system's requirements can be identified as follow.

Smart proactive self-adaptation: the platform should provide the necessary mechanisms to analyses collected data and adapt the system in problematic situations. In a resources constrained environment like ours, every planned adaptation should be subject to validation to insure its necessity.

Uncertainty management: It is not always possible to predict the events that will trigger a reconfiguration. Thus, the platform is required to evaluate the qualities the system offers in comparison with the ones requested by users.

Variability management: in a fleet of connected devices, variability can be captured at different levels. The platform should be able to manage this separately throughout the system's lifecycle.

Physical abstraction: the platform should support communication with heterogeneous devices and various technologies in order to monitor and actuate. This requirement will not be discussed in this paper. Only preliminary concepts will be introduced.

3.2   Identifying Dimensions for IoT Systems

In IoT applications, it is important to take into consideration the mutual dependency between objects and their surroundings -context and environment; change in the surrounding has repercussions on the proper functioning of devices. Similarly, the reconfiguration of the fleet changes the state and behavior of the surrounding. We observed that relevant information comes from three main elements, that we call dimensions. The **system** is the fleet. It is represented by the embedded devices and their configurations. It is managed in a way that its outcome allows the achievement of goals specified by the domain expert. The **context** is everything that surrounds the systems, and has an impact on it. Context is represented by measurements captured by devices that surround the system. Context data can also originate from the user, and it can be time or space bound. Finally, the **environment** illustrates knowledge related to a domain. It holds universal information that might not have a direct impact on the system at a time being. However, it could be significant in other dispositions.

It is important to note that these dimensions are dynamic. Devices that form the system at a particular configuration might not be the same involved in another instance of the same fleet. They could become part of the context. Similarly, information that had an impact on the system in a configuration, might become irrelevant in another, and be part of the environment instead. This confirms the need for variability management. One configuration could correspond to fleet is installed in a covered field during the summer. This installation protects the plants from the burning sun and harmful UV, and helps control the temperature inside the covers. For this installation, the **system** is the water sprinkler, the water tap, and the smartphone. The **context** is the inside temperature, and the dust humidity. And finally, the **environment** is the outside temperature, the weather forecast, the national irrigation laws and the agriculture best practices. During the spring, the field is uncovered. The configuration then switches, the fleet is now installed in an open space. The **system** is still the water sprinkler, the water tap, and the smartphone. The **context** on the other hand now includes the brightness, the air temperature, the dust and air humidity, and the weather forecast. The **environment** contains national irrigation laws and the agriculture best practices. In accordance with these dimensions and with the requirements presented above, a DM platform is required to adjust the fleet to answer the user's needs. The next session discusses self-adaptation mechanisms and selects the best fit for our application.

3.3   Selecting a Self-Adaptation Mechanism

A Self-Adaptive Software (SAS) is a system that can automatically modify itself in the face of a changing context, to best answer a set of requirements. The Self-adaption capacity can be provided by programming languages in the form of exceptions, parameters or conditions. However, adaptation through these mechanisms is application specific, error prone and poorly scalable. In contrast to these mechanisms, numerous external approaches contribute to the development of runtime adaptation of software. The following will present an overview of the most notable -but not all- approaches for designing self-adaptive systems.

Overview of self-adaptive approaches. Different approaches for SASs can be found in the literature. Reviews and surveys in the matter are available in [3,4]. This section enumerates the most notorious ones, and the design technics they fall into. *Architecture-based* self-adaptive techniques formulate and process changes in an architectural model [5] that describes the properties of software through a set of bound components and interconnections. The two concepts are strictly separated, which allows their rearrangement and replacement. The Rainbow Framework [6] and the three Layer Architecture [7] are the most acclaimed architecture-based approaches for SASs. *Agent-based* approaches model systems as a collection of autonomous agents which can interact within an environment to realize common goals; they create a Multi-Agent System (MAS). In MASs, agents are systems that sense the environment they are part of, and act on it in order to realize a purpose [8]. *Reflection* is the capability of a system to observe and modify its composition at runtime [9]. This technic is used to inspect the internal behavior of a system by implementing additional components for monitoring purposes. It is also used to adapt behavior or structure of a system by changing or replacing or adding features. Reflective middleware like ReIOS [10] are a prominent way to reason about self-adaptation. *Model-driven engineering* (MDE) shifts the focus to the creation and use of domain models, to automate code generation. Models abstract the application and its context, as well as the relationships between them. With regards to self-adaptive systems, MDE provides means for designing manageable systems along with reconfiguration mechanisms to generate executable applications, supported by runtime models during execution [11]. The MUSIC Framework [12] and the Dynamic Software Product Line (DSPL) [13] are model driven approaches. The latter uses models at runtime to address variability and context changes during system execution.

The DSPL mechanism. DSPL uses software product lines principles to build systems that can adapt to context fluctuation, new user requirements and variant QoS states. These principles include software reuse, variability modeling and management, and automatic product derivation.

We consider the DSPL paradigm the most fitting approach to provide autonomic scalable support for a fleet of connected devices, from design to execution [14]. First, DSPLs provide a systematic and non-restrictive way to deal with SASs [15], also they successfully realize the MAPE-K loop [16] as tested by Bencomo et al. in [17]. Besides, on the one hand, monitoring and controlling are the main activities for the fleet management. On the other hand, these same two activities are central tasks in DSPLs, which makes the paradigm a good fit for the self-adaptation of the fleet. Also, with regards to uncertainty, the quality of a product can be measured against user requirements by the mean of Goal-based approaches. Goal models can represent the system requirements at the domain level of (D)SPLs, in the form of variable reusable components. Furthermore, variability is a key challenge in the management of a fleet of connected things; it takes place at different levels. Static variability is concerned with similarities and variations between devices, dynamic variability is dealing with the runtime reconfiguration, and temporal variability, describes the alterations of the three dimensions. Dealing with variability is by far the greatest asset of DSPL, since it adopts essential concepts from SPL [18].

The fleets–an irrigation system installed in different fields—can be considered as a DSPL. Each fleet is a product that shares common characteristics with other fleets, but still answers the specific needs of the customer it serves. For instance, some of the devices installed in Sarah's field are like the ones at Omar's. Still, unlike him, Sarah is also interested in measuring the fertility of the soil, and applying fertilizers when needed. A fleet has the capacity to re-adjust itself when requirements are no longer fulfilled. A New FConfig implies a different set of devices with a different DConfig.

4   Designing a Fleet as a DSPL

The first level in the process is the creation of assets. As described in Fig. 1, a meticulous study of the domain in question helps define the qualities the system should satisfy, while specifying the variability and the variation points. The result of a domain study is a fleet line (a). The second level is the creation of the final product. The requirements of each customer are described in formal language. The selection of features is carried out accordingly, and then adjusted to fit the exact needs of the customer. Features are finally derived, linked, tested and deployed in order to instantiate the Product—the fleet (d).

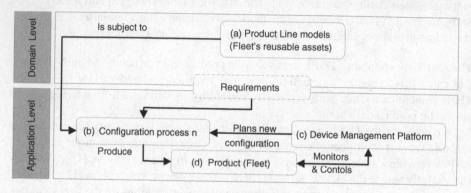

Fig. 1. The DSPL Process

DSPLE takes the SPL process one phase further. Each product is thoroughly monitored (c) to determine the structural or behavioral state that dissatisfies requirements. When these are no longer fulfilled, a new configuration is planned (b). This one achieves the optimal satisfaction of primary goals. Features are then re-selected, re-adjusted, re-derived and re-linked (re-tested and re-deployed) to create a new product—a new configuration for the fleet. This process is repeated whenever the system fails to fulfill requirements, in light of contextual change.

From one engineering process to the other, the fleet's three dimensions defined in (3.2) have different designations, as described and illustrated in Fig. 2. At the domain level, each one of the concepts contributes to the creation of assets. With regards to the system (1), a domain expert thoroughly studies the domain in order to determine the functionalities the system should provide and qualities to comply with. In this sense, the system is where domains requirements are extracted, which are then translated to goals, features, components or assets. Context (2) is where the initial requirements are updated to answer the needs that weren't captured by domain experts, but arose after the deployment of the fleet. Environment (3) holds more generic information about domains and devices. It can contribute to the evolution and extensibility of the system by supporting an open Marketplace. This one could supply the system with new components, device specifications, documentation, and other related information.

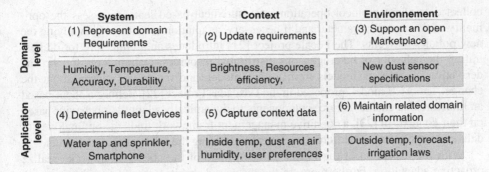

	System	Context	Environnement
Domain level	(1) Represent domain Requirements	(2) Update requirements	(3) Support an open Marketplace
	Humidity, Temperature, Accuracy, Durability	Brightness, Resources efficiency,	New dust sensor specifications
Application level	(4) Determine fleet Devices	(5) Capture context data	(6) Maintain related domain information
	Water tap and sprinkler, Smartphone	Inside temp, dust and air humidity, user preferences	Outside temp, forecast, irrigation laws

Fig. 2. A DSPL three-dimensional Framework

At the **domain level**, each one of the concepts contributes to the creation of assets. With regards to the system (1), a domain expert thoroughly studies the domain in order to determine the functionalities the system should provide and qualities to comply with. In this sense, the system is where domains requirements are extracted, which are then translated to goals, features, components or assets. Context (2) is where the initial requirements are updated to answer the needs that weren't captured by domain experts, but arose after the deployment of the fleet. Environment (3) holds more generic information about domains and devices. It can contribute to the evolution and extensibility of the system by supporting an open Marketplace. This one could supply the system with new components, device specifications, documentation, and other related information. At the **application level**, the monitoring and controlling aspects take place. In relation to the system (4), for each product, devices are monitored in order to determine situations when reconfiguration is required. Sensed or calculated information, feedbacks, battery level, computational performance, network and data accessibility, and other characteristics are relevant. Context (5) on the other hand deals with stakeholders that surround the system, and have an impact on it. Devices that are not part of the system, but contribute to its activity are part of the context, user activity and logs also matter, the time and space of the fleet is also responsible of how it is configured. The environment (6), finally, is place to generic information about the surroundings of the system, that might, but still do not have an impact on the fulfillment of requirements. Devices around the fleet can be in this category, laws, rules or conditions constrained by a time or place are too, part of the environment. Monitoring the environment gives the platform proactive qualities, this helps avoid waste of resources in unnecessary adaptations.

5   Related Works

To face the growing complexity of IoT environments, several researchers have identified the need for Frameworks and architectures that support the management of fleets of cooperative devices, considering self-adaptation a core requirement. Inox [19] combines IoT and service architectures to provide enhanced application and service deployment capabilities. The architecture enables the service and network infrastructure with self-management capabilities. In [20], the authors propose an architecture, where agents collect data about protocol operations, measurement-based learning assess the optimality of the control parameter and if necessary, adaptation is realized by applying the new policies to agents. The Focale project [21] introduces an architecture for orchestrating the behavior of heterogeneous distributed resources. Data models support the derivation of different models from a core model, and ontologies reason about the change. The ACE model, proposed in the Cascadas Project [22], defines a agent-based architecture that enables service components to dynamically adapt their behavior based on their context. In [23], a cognitive management framework finds the optimal way to deliver an application in different contexts by enabling the reuse of virtual objects.

With the exception of the Focale Project, none of the above frameworks realize proactive adaptation. Furthermore, in the discussed architectures, no mechanism was proposed to validate the need for intelligent adaptation. Finally, variability is not considered a fundamental concern, thus not managed.

Several SPL based architectures can also be found in the literature. In [24], a DSPL based architecture, combined with preference based reasoning, provides the necessary mechanisms for reasoning about change; this allows the realization of decentralized self-managed system. Gaia-PL [25] is an extension of the Gaia platform for the analysis and design of multi-agent systems in active spaces. A requirement specification pattern captures the behavior of a system in dynamic conditions, and reuses the software assets for future similar systems. In [26], the author proposes a multi-view blueprint architecture, a basis for future smart city projects, based on the SoaSPLE [27] framework for run-time variability management of service-oriented software product lines. Finally, authors in [28] propose a SPL based process for the development of connected devices, defined by the means of CVL, to provide reuse mechanisms for the development of a family of agents.

In contrast with the aforementioned (D)SPL based approaches, our framework introduces variability management at different stages of the process, as explained previously, including static (devices), dynamic (configurations) and time-bound (dimensions alterations) variability. None of the proposed SPL based approaches introduce the environment dimension, necessary for a smart proactive adaptation.

6   Conclusion and Perspectives

As a result of a successful COP22 [29], held in 2016 in Marrakech, several Paris agreements were put into practice, including new funds to support climate technologies in developing countries. The IoT paradigm supports this claim by enabling services that manage limited resources, insure service durability, maintain the quality of service, etc. This is possible by supplying connected devices with the necessary mechanisms to readjust their behavior in the face of resource shortage, internet interruptions or service unavailability.

Connected objects can monitor environment indicators, and then a DM Platform processes the information about the surrounding, and prepares solutions to best answer the needs of users. Our work consists of designing a framework for the monitoring and control of a fleet of connected devices, which allows preforming intelligent and dynamic changes for optimal configurations. The first step in our process defines the main requirements needed from the DM platform. The second step defines the characteristics of the fleets, its context and its environment, along with their mutual dependencies. The third step selects DSPL among the various self-adaptation mechanisms as a basis for the framework composition. Considering it is capable of managing uncertainty by capturing inconsistency and readjusting the system's configuration. Eventually, the various modules of the framework are depicted.

This paper has investigated the problem regarding IoT fleets adaptation and proposed a framework for developers to build adaptable applications. Future work includes the validation and implementation of the framework using the VariaMos [30] Tool [31], and an agriculture field case study.

Acknowledgment. This work was supported by the Moroccan « Ministère de l'Enseignement Supérieur, de la Recherche Scientifique et de la Formation des Cadres » , by the « French Embassy in Morocco » , and by the « Institut Français du Maroc » .

References

1. I. T. Union: Overview of the Internet of Things (2012)
2. Alférez, G.H., Pelechano, V., Mazo, R., Salinesi, C., Diaz, D.: Dynamic adaptation of service compositions with variability models. J. Syst. Softw. **91**(1), 24–47 (2014)
3. Salehie, M., Tahvildari, L.: Self-adaptive software: landscape and research challenges. ACM Trans. Auton. Adapt. Syst. **4**(2), 1–42 (2009)
4. Krupitzer, C., Roth, F.M., VanSyckel, S., Schiele, G., Becker, C.: A survey on engineering approaches for self-adaptive systems. Pervasive Mob. Comput. **17**, 184–206 (2015)
5. Denko, M.K., Yang, L.T., Zhang, Y.: Software architecture-based self-adaptation. Auton. Comput. Netw., 1–458 (2009)
6. Cheng, S.W., Garlan, D., Schmerl, B.: Evaluating the effectiveness of the rainbow self-adaptive system. In: Proceedings of 2009 ICSE Workshop on Software Engineering for Adaptive and Self-Managing Systems, SEAMS 2009, pp. 132–141 (2009)
7. Kramer, J., Magee, J.: Self-managed systems: an architectural challenge. Fut. Softw. Eng. (2005)
8. Filipe, J., Fred, A., Sharp, B.: Toward a self-adaptive multi-agent system to control dynamic processes. Commun. Comput. Inf. Sci. **129** (2011)
9. Baumer, E.P.S., Khovanskaya, V., Matthews, M., Reynolds, L., Schwanda Sosik, V., Gay, G.: Reviewing reflection: on the use of reflection in interactive system design. In: Proceedings of the 2014 Conference on Designing Interactive Systems—DIS '14, pp. 93–102 (2014)
10. Mongiello, M., Boggia, G., Di Sciascio, E.: ReIOS: reflective architecting in the internet of objects. In: Proceedings of the 4th International Conference on Modelling of Engineering Software Development, pp. 384–389, 2016
11. Szvetits, M., Zdun, U.: Systematic literature review of the objectives, techniques, kinds, and architectures of models at runtime. Softw. Syst. Model. **15**(1), 31–69 (2016)
12. Rouvoy, R., Barone, P., Ding, Y., Eliassen, F., Hallsteinsen, S., Lorenzo, J., Mamelli, A., Scholz, U.: MUSIC: middleware support for self-adaptation in ubiquitous and service-oriented environments. Lecture Notes on Computer Science (including Subseries Lecture Notes on Artificial Intelligence and Lecture Notes on Bioinformatics), vol. 5525, pp. 164–182 (2009)

13. Capilla, R., Bosch, J., Trinidad, P., Ruiz-Cortés, A., Hinchey, M.: An overview of dynamic software product line architectures and techniques: observations from research and industry. J. Syst. Softw. **91**(1), 3–23 (2014)

14. Mazo, R., Dumitrescu, C., Salinesi, C., Diaz, D.: Recommendation heuristics for improving product line configuration processes. Recomm. Syst. Softw. Eng., 511–537 (2014)

15. Hinchey, M., Park, S., Schmid, K.: Building dynamic software product lines. Computer (Long. Beach. Calif.) **45**(10), 22–26 (2012)

16. IBM: Autonomic computing white paper: an architectural blueprint for autonomic computing. IBM White Paper, p. 34 (2005)

17. Bencomo, N. Lee, J., Hallsteinsen, S.: How dynamic is your dynamic software product line? Work. Dyn. Softw. Prod. Lines (2010)

18. Dumitrescu, C., Mazo, R., Salinesi, C., Dauron, A.: Bridging the gap between product lines and systems engineering: an experience in variability management for automotive model based. In: Proceedings of the 17th International Software Product Line Conference (SPLC), Aug 2013

19. Clayman. S., Galis, A.: INOX: a managed service platform for inter-connected smart objects stuart. In: Proceedings of the Workshop on Internet Things Services Platforms—IoTSP '11, pp. 1–8 (2011)

20. Athreya, A., DeBruhl, B., Tague, P.: Designing for self-configuration and self-adaptation in the Internet of Things. In: Proceedings of the 9th IEEE International Conference on Collaborative Computing: Networking, Applications and Worksharing, pp. 585–592 (2013)

21. Strassner, J., Agoulmine, N., Lehtihet, E.: FOCALE: a novel autonomic networking architecture. Int. Trans. Syst. Sci. Appl. J., 64–79 (2007)

22. Baresi, L., Di Ferdinando, A., Manzalini, A., Zambonelli, F.: The CASCADAS framework for autonomic communications. Auton. Commun., 1–374 (2009)

23. Vlacheas, P., Giaffreda, R., Stavroulaki, V., Kelaidonis, D., Foteinos, V., Poulios, G., Demestichas, P., Somov, A., Biswas, A., Moessner, K.: Enabling smart cities through a cognitive management framework for the internet of things. IEEE Commun. Mag. **51**(6), 102–111 (2013)

24. Ayala, I., Horcas, J.M., Amor, M., Fuentes, L.: Using models at runtime to adapt self-managed agents for the IoT. Sensors, 155–173 (2015)

25. Dehlinger, J., Lutz, R.R.: Gaia-PL: a product line engineering approach for efficiently designing multiagent systems. ACM Trans. Softw. Eng. Methodol. **20**(4), 17:1–17:27 (2011)

26. Abu-Matar, M.: Towards a software defined reference architecture for smart city ecosystems. In: Proceedings of 2016 IEEE International Smart Cities Conference, pp. 1–6 (2016)

27. Abu-Matar, M., Gomaa, H.: An automated framework for variability management of service-oriented software product lines. In: Proceedings of 2013 IEEE 7th International Symposium on Service-Oriented Systems Engineering SOSE 2013, pp. 260–267 (2013)

28. Ayala, I., Amor, M., Fuentes, L., Troya, J.: A software product line process to develop agents for the IoT. Sensors **15**(7), 15640–15660 (2015)

29. COP22: [Online] http://cop22.ma/en/

30. Mazo, R., Salinesi, C., Diaz, D., Muñoz-Fernández, J.C., Rincón, L., Salinesi, C., Tamura, G.: VariaMos: an extensible tool for engineering (dynamic) product lines. In: Proceedings of the 24th International Conference on Advanced Information Systems Engineering (CAiSE Forum'12), pp. 374–379 (2015)

31. Muñoz-Fernández, J.C., Tamura, G., Raúl, M., Salinesi, C.: Towards a requirements specification multi-view framework for self-adaptive systems. In: Proceedings of XL Latin American Computing Conference (CLEI), vol. 18(2), pp. 1–12 (2014)

ABAC Based Online Collaborations in the Cloud

Mohamed Amine Madani[1]([✉]), Mohammed Erradi[1], and Yahya Benkaouz[2]

[1] Networking and Distributed Systems Research Group, SIME Lab, ENSIAS,
Mohammed V University in Rabat, Rabat, Morocco
`amine.madani@um5s.net.ma` , `mohamed.erradi@gmail.com`
[2] LCS, Department of Computer Science, FSR, Mohammed V University in Rabat,
Rabat, Morocco
`y.benkaouz@um5s.net.ma`

Abstract. Nowadays sharing data among organizations plays an important role for their collaboration. During collaborations, the organizations need to access shared information while respecting the access control constraints. In addition, most organizations rely on cloud based solutions to store their data (e.g. openstack). In such platform, data access is regulated by Access Control Lists (ACLs). ACL defines static access rules. It assumes the knowledge of the whole set of users and possible access requests. This make ACL unusable in collaborative context due to the dynamic nature of collaborative sessions. In this paper, we consider ABAC, a flexible and fine-grained model, as an access control model for cloud-based collaborations to overcome the ACL limitations. We provide an architecture that integrate ABAC in the storage level of a cloud platform.

Keywords: ABAC model · Swift · Collaborative session · Access control

1 Introduction

Nowadays, sharing information among multiple organizations plays an important role to ensure an optimal utilization of distributed resources to improve productivity and profits. In order to reach this objective, a tight collaboration among organizations should be established. Collaborative applications allow a group of users to collaborate, communicate and cooperate through distributed platforms in order to perform common tasks, such as document sharing.

As most organizations rely on cloud-based solutions to store their data, cloud platforms [1] provide a considerable convenience to support the collaboration as well as the information sharing [8]. In this direction, OpenStack cloud platform represents a very interesting solution. OpenStack [6] is an open source IaaS (Infrastructure as a Service) software adopted by many cloud service and technology providers such as Rackspace, IBM, Dell and RedHat.

During collaborations, the organizations need to access and use the information shared by other collaborating organizations. This information often contains sensitive data. It is meant to be shared only during specific collaborative sessions

© ICST Institute for Computer Sciences, Social Informatics and Telecommunications Engineering 2018
F. Belqasmi et al. (Eds.): AFRICATEK 2017, LNICST 206, pp. 67–76, 2018.
https://doi.org/10.1007/978-3-319-67837-5_7

[5]. This arises the access control issue [4]: The organizations need strong access control model to permit or deny a specific request of other organizations.

Using OpenStack cloud platform, the collaborating organizations store their data and information as objects in the Swift storage [7] (an object storage service in OpenStack). Swift uses the access control lists (ACL) to manage the access permissions. However, ACL model is too simple, static, and a coarse-grained model that does not provide the rich semantics for the collaboration. During a collaborative session, users may intervene dynamically without a prior knowledge of which user will access which objects. Specifying access rules during a collaboration is a difficult even an impossible task to accomplish using ACL. A fine-grained access control model is mandatory to support the requirements of the collaborative systems [5].

In this direction, Attribute Based Access Control model (ABAC) is of a great interest. ABAC model [9, 10] overcomes the limitations of the classical access control models (i.e., ACL, MAC and RBAC). This model is adaptive and flexible. ABAC is more suitable to describe complex, fine-grained access control semantics, which is especially needed for collaborative environments. In ABAC, access requests are evaluated based on the user attributes, the object attributes and the environment attributes. Therefore, in this paper, our main contributions are twofold: (1) Ensuring the access control dynamicity in collaborative session on the cloud based on the ABAC model. (2) Providing an architecture to integrate ABAC in the storage level of the cloud and providing an enforcement model.

The paper is organized as follows: Sect. 2 presents the background of this work. In Sect. 3, we present the related work. Section 4 describes the suggested architecture and the enforcement model. Section 5 discusses the implementation performance. Finally, we conclude in Sect. 6.

2   Background

This section aims to present the necessary background of this work. This section mainly focus on the presentation of the concept of Cloud based collaborative application. Then, it gives an overview of the OpenStack cloud platform. Finally, it presents the attribute based access control model.

Cloud based collaborative applications. Collaborative applications are among the services that can be provided by the cloud computing. They enable collaboration among users from the same or different tenants of a given cloud provider [2, 3]. During collaborations, the participants need to access and use resources held by other collaborating users. These resources often contain sensitive data. They are meant to be shared only during specific collaborative session [5]. The collaborative session is an abstract entity, comprising a set of users, called members of the session, playing the same or different roles. These users may have concurrent access to shared objects in this session depending on the access control policies. As most organizations rely on cloud-based solutions to store their data, cloud platforms provide a considerable convenience to support the collaboration. In this direction, OpenStack cloud platform represents a very interesting solution.

Openstack. OpenStack is a robust open-source IaaS software for building public, private, community or hybrid clouds. OpenSteck is adopted by many cloud providers such as Rackspace, IBM and RedHat. OpenStack contains the following components: Nova, Swift, Glance, Cinder, Keystone, and Horizon. Each component acts as a service which communicates with other sevices via message queues. Keystone provides authentication and authorization for all OpenStack services. In our work, we focus on the Swift object storage. Swift is a multitenant, highly scalable and durable software defined storage system designed to store files, videos, virtual machine snapshots and other unstructured data [7]. It allows building, operating, monitoring, and managing distributed object storage systems that can scale up to millions of users.

The Account Server is responsible for listings of containers, while Container Server is responsible for listings of objects. A container is a mechanism that stores data objects. An account might have many containers, whereas a container name is unique. A user represents the entity that can perform actions on the object in the account. Each user has its own account and is associated to a single tenant. Swift uses the access control lists (ACL) to manage the access permissions. In fact, the ACL model defines static access rules. It is not suitable for collaborative environment. In this direction, Attribute Based Access Control model (ABAC) is of a great interest.

ABAC Model. ABAC is an adaptive and a flexible access control model for the collaboration in the cloud. The core components of ABAC model [9] are:

- U, O and E represent finite sets of existing users and objects and environments respectively. A is a finite set of actions might be noted $A = \{create, read, update, delete\}$.
- $UATT$, $OATT$ and $EATT$ represent finite sets of user, object and environment attribute functions respectively.
- For each att in $UATT \cup OATT \cup EATT$, $range(att)$ represents the attribute's range, which is a finite set of atomic values.
- $attType : UATT \cup OATT \cup EATT \rightarrow \{set, atomic\}$, specifies attributes as set or atomic values.
- Each attribute function maps elements in U to an atomic value or a set
  - $\forall ua \subseteq UATT. \ ua : U \rightarrow Range(ua) \ if \ attType(ua) = atomic$
  - $\forall ua \subseteq UATT. \ ua : U \rightarrow 2^{Range(ua)} \ if \ attType(ua) = set$
- Each attribute function maps elements in O to an atomic value or a set
  - $\forall oa \subseteq OATT.oa : O \rightarrow Range(oa) \ if \ attType(oa) = atomic$
  - $\forall oa \subseteq OATT.oa : O \rightarrow 2^{Range(oa)} \ if \ attType(oa) = set$
- Each attribute function maps elements in E to an atomic value or a set
  - $\forall ea \subseteq EATT.ea : E \rightarrow Range(ea) \ if \ attType(ea) = atomic$
  - $\forall ea \subseteq EATT.ea : E \rightarrow 2^{Range(ea)} \ if \ attType(ea) = set$
- An authorization that decides on whether a user u can access an object o in a particular environment e for the action a, is a boolean function of u, o, and e attributes: Rule: $authorization_a(u, o, e) \rightarrow f(ATTR(u), ATTR(o), ATTR(e))$.

3   Related Work

In the Task based access control [13] (TBAC), the permissions are granted in steps that are related to the tasks progress. The TRBAC [14] model is constructed by adding task to the RBAC model. In TRBAC, the user has a relationship with permissions through roles and tasks. On the other hand, in the Team Access Control Model (TMAC) [12], the permissions are granted to each user through its role and the current activities of the team. These models enable fine-grained access control but they do not incorporate contextual parameters into security considerations and do not support dynamic collaboration during collaborative sessions.

Current access control models for cloud are built on role-based access control (RBAC). There have been very few works for implementing ABAC in cloud. Attributes based access control (ABAC) [10] model brings out many advantages over traditional identity or role based models. Jin et al. [15] present an ABAC framework for access control in cloud IaaS. This paper provides formal models for the operational and administrative aspects of this framework for cloud IaaS. Authors present the implementation of the models based on the open source cloud platform OpenStack. However, this ABAC framework is not dedicated for the swift environment.

Biswas et al. [16] proposes an extension of Swift Object Server where policies might be specified on a Swift object at the content level and let different users access different parts of it. Biswas et al. [17] presents an attribute based protection model for JSON documents. Security-label attribute values are assigned to JSON elements and authorization policies are specified based on these attribute values. This approach is specific to JSON documents, whereas our suggested architecture might be applied to any objects.

4   Architecture and Enforcement Model

In this section, we present the implementation of the ABAC model on the swift storage component. First, we describe the architecture of the extended ABAC module. Then, we present the enforcement model. Finally, we evaluate the implemented approach to demonstrate its feasibility.

4.1   System Architecture

We implemented the ABAC model on the swift storage component. This component acts as a service that communicates with other components (Nova volume, nova compute, nova network, glance and keystone) via message queues. These components are loosely coupled. Keystone is the identity service used by OpenStack for authentication and authorization. It provides a token signed by each users private key.

Let us consider a telemedicine scenario where the School Hospital (SH), the Emergency Medical Services (EMS), and the Home Hospital (HH) are three collaborating organizations. These organizations share a common private cloud openstack. We consider that these organizations use the swift component for the storage service. In this use case, each organization is assigned to a swift account. (e.g. the accounts ACC_SH, ACC_EMS and ACC_HH represent the organizations SH, EMS and HH respectively).

This cloud provides a service of collaborative sessions for these organisations. This service allows a group of users, from different tenants, to collaborate in order to observe and treat a patient admitted in the Home Hospital (HH) emergency. In this example, we have a collaborative session CS1 of a telemedicine type. During a collaborative session, users may intervene dynamically without a prior knowledge of which user will access which object.

In order to support ABAC Model in the OpenStack Swift environment and overcome the limitations of Swift ACL, we propose to extend the Swift component by implementing a new ABAC Module (Fig. 1). The ABAC module is

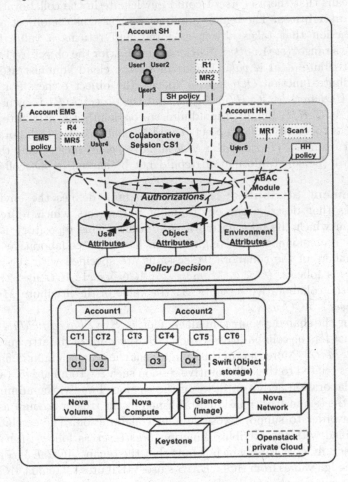

Fig. 1. The system architecture

composed of five components: User attributes, object attributes, environment attributes, authorizations and the policy decision component. In the following, we describe each of these components:

- **User attributes:** The security administrator defines the user attributes as a function that takes user as input and returns a value from the attribute's range. ($user1 : attr1 : val1$) means that for the user $user1$ the value of the attribute $attr1$ is $val1$. For example, a user attribute function such as $Role \in UATT$ maps $user1 \in U$ to a value $neurologist$. Furthermore, the cloud administrator defines the attribute function $UOwner$ to specify the user owner. For instance ($user1 : UOwner : ACC\_SH$) means that the user $user1$ is owned by the account ACC_SH. Finally, the administrator defines the attribute function $JoinCS$ to specify which users could join the collaborative sessions. The value of this attribute is either true or false. ($user1 : JoinCS : true$) means that the user $user1$ could participate in the collaboration.
- **Object attributes:** The tenant administrator assigns the object attributes as a function that takes object as input and returns a value from the attribute's range. ($obj1 : attr1 : val1$) means that for the object $obj1$ the value of the attribute $attr1$ is $val1$. Furthermore, the cloud administrator defines the attribute function $OOwner$ to specify the object owner. For instance ($MR1 : UOwner : ACC\_HH$) means that the object $MR1$ is owned by the account ACC_HH. Finally, the administrator defines the attribute function $SharedCS$ to specify which objects could be shared in the collaborative session. For example, ($Per\_info1 : SharedCS : false$) means that the object Per_info1 (personal information) could not be shared in the collaborative session.
- **Environment attributes:** The security admin defines the environment attributes that describe the environment parameters which represent the context in which the information access occurs. This repository is responsible for users management (e.g. to join/leave the collaborative session). The members of the collaborative sessions are specified with the attribute $Member$ as follows: ($CS1 : Member : \{ACC\_user1, ACC\_user2\}$) means that for the collaborative session $CS1$ the value of the attribute $Member$ is $\{ACC\_user1, ACC\_user2\}$.

  Regarding the shared resources management: ($CS1 : Shared : \{MR1, MR2\}$) means that for the collaborative session $CS1$ the value of the attribute $shared$ is $\{MR1, MR2\}$. Moreover, in this component the tenant admin defines other attributes related to the collaborative session such as: Template [5] (a pattern for a collaboration activity), State of the session. Finally, the administrator specifies the tenant trust relation established by the truster account as defined in [11] in order to support cross-domain collaboration. These relationships are specified with the attribute function $trustUser$ as follows: ($ACC\_SH : trustUser : ACC\_EMS$), which means that the tenant ACC_EMS is authorized to assign values from ACC_EMS's user attributes to Tenant ACC_SH's users that will join the collaborative sessions. In order to support the resources sharing in a collaborative session owned by another tenant, the tenant administrator defines a new trust relationship by using the attribute function *trustObject* as follows: ($ACC\_SH : trustObject : ACC\_EMS$), which means that the tenant ACC_EMS is authorized to assign values from ACC_EMS's object attributes to tenant ACC_SH's objects that will be shared in the collaborative sessions.

- **Authorizations:** The administrator specifies the authorizations policy. In our scenario, we consider that each tenant defines its policy rules. Note that at this level, we suppose that the security policy rules are valid and conflict-free. The policy rules are specified here as follows: $read - u : role : tenant\_admin \wedge cs : template : neuroEmergency \wedge cs : member : u \wedge cs : shared : o \wedge o : objecttype : MR \wedge u : UOwner : UH \wedge o : OOwner : UH$, which means that for the action 'read', this authorization is valid if only if : (1) The user u plays the role tenant_admin in the session cs; (2) There is a collaborative session cs that is an instance of the template $neuroEmergency$; (3) The user u is member of the collaborative session cs; (4) The object o is shared in the session cs; (5) The object type of o is the MR (medical_record); (6) The user u is owned by the tenant UH; (7) The object o is owned by the tenant UH.
- **Policy decision:** This component is responsible for evaluating the access request to the resources in the collaborative session based on the collected attributes values and authorizations. When a user sends a request to access a resource stored in the cloud swift, the policy decision component evaluates this request according to the policy rules in order to decide whether the user is authorized to access this resource or not.

4.2 Enforcement Model

The ACL model defines static access rules. During a collaborative session, a set of users from the same or different tenants join this session and share multiple resources. In our use case, $user1$, $user2$, $user3$, $user4$ and $user5$ are the members of the collaborative session $CS1$ and the objects $MR1$ and $Scan1$ are shared in this session.

A general authorization process for Swift component with ABAC module is illustrated in Fig. 2. When the user $user1$ attemps to access the resource $MR1$ stored in the swift. First, (1) The user requests keysone to get his/her token. (2) Keystone generates a token and sends it to the user. (3) The user sends a request to ABAC module by using his/her token to access the resource $MR1$. The Policy decision component receives this request to evaluate it. (4) During the evaluation process, the policy decision component requests the components: user attributes, object attributes and environment attributes. (5) to receive user1's attributes, $MR1$'s attributes and the attributes related to the collaborative session wherein this user is member. (6) The policy decision component requests the authorizations component and (7) receives all the policy rules stored in this component. These attributes and policy rules will be used by the policy decision to evaluate access request in order to decide whether the user is authorized to access this resource or not. (8) the policy decision will execute an ACL command to assign the authorization decision (permit or deny) to the user in the swift environment.

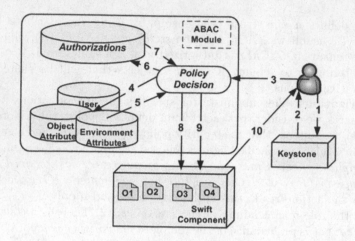

Fig. 2. The enforcement model

(9) The policy decision component executes a swift API command in the swift component using *user*1's token in order to send the *user*1's access request to swift. (10) *user*1 access to the resource *MR*1 if the authorization decision is permitted.

5   Implementation and Evaluation

In this paper, we implement the ABAC model on the swift storage component of openstack. Our experiments were run on a virtual machine with the following characteristics (Memory 1024 MB, 2 cores CPU, Hard Disk 30 GB). We consider the download time of a Swift object with and without ABAC module. We observe that the performance of enforcing our approach depends on many factors, such as numbers of rules, number of attributes and number of concurrent collaborative sessions. In our analysis, we have used a synthetic dataset that contains up to 500 rules, 200 user attributes and 25 concurrent collaborative sessions.

Figure 3(a) shows that the average time to authorize the access to a Swift object increases with 25% and 30.5% for policies of 100 and 500 rules respectively using the ABAC Module. The waiting time for getting a policy decision becomes larger when there are too many authorizations to be collected. We acknowledge that our implementation works well for a medium number of authorizations.

Furthermore, we compute the running time for access/deny decisions to a Swift object with and without ABAC module for 200 rules and user attributes with 40 to 200 UA assignments. Figure 3(b) shows that the average time for download of a Swift resource increases with 26% and 33% for 40 and 200 user attributes assignments respectively using ABAC Module. We acknowledge that our implementation works well for a medium number of authorizations.

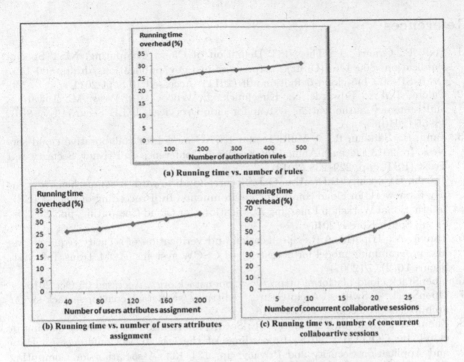

(a) Running time vs. number of rules

(b) Running time vs. number of users attributes assignment

(c) Running time vs. number of concurrent collaboartive sessions

Fig. 3. Running time overhead for access/deny decisions

Finally, we compute the running time for access/deny decisions to a Swift object with and without ABAC module for 500 rules, 80 UA assignments and number of concurrent collaborative sessions with 5 to 25 active ones.

Figure 3(c) shows that the average time for access/deny decisions to Swift resources increases with 30.5% and 61% for 5 and 25 concurrent collaborative sessions respectively using the ABAC Module. We observe that our implementation works well for a medium number of active concurrent collaborative sessions. The overhead reaches 61% in an unusual situations where there are 25 concurrent parallel collaborative sessions.

6   Conclusion

In this paper, we provide an architecture that integrates ABAC in the storage level of the cloud platform. This arcitecture is implemented on the cloud platform Openstack to allow the use of the access control policies based on the ABAC model. It interacts with the Swift component of Openstack for policy enforcement. Therefore, this arcitecture provides a fine-grained access control to support collaborations between multiple organizations allowing a secure data sharing during a collaborative session. The evaluation results have shown that the suggested approach has a very limited overhead when the ABAC module is used.

References

1. Mell, P., Grance, T.: The NIST Definition of Cloud Computing. NIST Special Publication 800–145 (Draft). http://csrc.nist.gov/publications/drafts/800-145/Draft-SP-800-145-cloud-definition.pdf (2011). Accessed 10 Sept 2011
2. Calero, J.M.A., Edwards, N., Kirschnick, J., Wilcock, L., Wray, M.: Toward a multi-tenancy authorization system for cloud services. IEEE Secur. Priv. 8(6), 48–55 (2010)
3. Tang, B., Sandhu, R.: A Multi-Tenant RBAC model for collaborative cloud services. In: 2013 Eleventh Annual International Conference on Privacy, Security and Trust (PST), pp. 229–238 (2013)
4. Takabi, H., Joshi, J.B.D., Ahn, G.J.: SecureCloud: towards a comprehensive security framework for cloud computing environments. In: Proceeding of the 1st IEEE International Workshop Emerging Applications for Cloud Computing, pp. 393–398. Seoul, South Korea (2010)
5. Tanvir, A., Tripathi, A.R.: Specification and verification of security requirements in a programming model for decentralized CSCW systems. ACM Trans. Inf. Syst. Secur. 10(2), 7 (2007)
6. OpenStack cloud platform. http://www.openstack.org/. Accessed 05 Oct 2016
7. OpenStack Swift Architecture. https://swiftstack.com/openstack-swift/architecture/. Accessed 05 Oct 2016
8. Zhang, Y., Krishnan, R., Sandhu, R.: Secure information and resource sharing in cloud. In: CODASPY 2015—Proceedings of the 5th ACM Conference on Data and Application Security and Privacy, pp. 131–133. Association for Computing Machinery, Inc. (2015)
9. Jin, X., Krishnan, R., Sandhu, R.: A unified attribute-based access control model covering DAC, MAC and RBAC. In: Cuppens-Boulahia, N., Cuppens, F., Garcia-Alfaro, J. (eds.) DBSec 2012. LNCS, vol. 7371, pp. 41–55. Springer, Heidelberg (2012). doi:10.1007/978-3-642-31540-4_4
10. Yuan, E., Tong, J.: Attributed Based Access Control (ABAC) for web services. In: ICWS, pp. 561–569. IEEE Computer Society (2005)
11. Aydoğan, R., Festen, D., Hindriks, K.V., Jonker, C.M.: Alternating offers protocols for multilateral negotiation. In: Fujita, K., Bai, Q., Ito, T., Zhang, M., Ren, F., Aydoğan, R., Hadfi, R. (eds.) Modern Approaches to Agent-based Complex Automated Negotiation. SCI, vol. 674, pp. 153–167. Springer, Cham (2017). doi:10.1007/978-3-319-51563-2_10
12. Thomas, R.: TMAC: a primitive for applying RBAC in collaborative environment. In: 2nd ACM, Workshop on RBAC, Fairfax, Virginia, USA, pp. 13–19 (1997)
13. Thomas, R., Sandhu, R.: Task-based Authorization Controls (TBAC): a family of models for active and enterprise-oriented authorization management. In: 11th IFIP Working Conference on Database Security, Lake Tahoe, California, USA (1997)
14. Sejong, O.H., Park, S.: Task-role-based access control model. Inf. Syst. 28(6), 533–562 (2003)
15. Jin, X., Krishnan, R., Sandhu, R.: Role and attribute based collaborative administration of intra-tenant cloud iaas. In: 2014 International Conference on Collaborative Computing: Networking, Applications and Worksharing (CollaborateCom), pp. 261–274 (2014)
16. Biswas, P., Patwa, F., Sandhu, R.: Content level access control for OpenStack swift storage. In: CODASPY, pp. 123–126 (2015)
17. Biswas, P., Sandhu, R., Krishnan, R.: An attribute based protection model for JSON documents. In: NSS, pp. 303–317 (2016)

Smart Energy and Disaster Management

Evaluating Query Energy Consumption in Document Stores

Duarte Duarte and Orlando Belo[✉]

ALGORITMI R&D Centre, University of Minho, 4710-057 Braga, Portugal
obelo@di.uminho.pt

Abstract. Today's system users demand fast answers when querying their own databases. Their impatience still high when waiting for the results of a query when they take more than one or two seconds to appear on the screen. However, having fast querying answers it is not the only aspect that determines the quality of a database system we are using, but also the energy consumption involved with. The development of database systems increasingly economic in terms of energy consumption has led to great technological advances in this area. Today, many of the entities that manage large data base systems pay particular attention to this issue, not only for environmental reasons but also for economic reasons, obviously. In this paper we address the issue of queries energy consumption evaluation in database systems, with particular emphasis to those that are executed in a environment of a document store. Based on the information provided by the execution of a query in MongoDB, we designed and developed a process that determines the energy consumption of queries launched in a document store, approaching different alternatives in query designing, implementation and execution.

Keywords: Document stores · NoSQL · Query processing · Energy consumption plans · Green computing · Green queries · And MongoDB

1 Introduction

For a long time, relational database management systems have dominated database systems market. Although still constitute the most common data model used in database systems, from the time intensive data processing applications (big data applications) began to be common. Thus, other data models began to gain their place in this market, having very sophisticated solution for large databases, with performance, storage and scale characteristics quite interesting when compared to the traditional relational data model—e.g., key-value, wide-column, graphs and document stores [10]. In general terms, we can say that these data models are the ones that support today the large emergence of the overall NoSQL approaches. They sustain a large number of real world big data applications, providing support for large scalable, reliable and fast databases. However, as it happens in relational database systems, NoSQL systems consume also a lot of energy in querying processing. In order to evaluate their energy consumption, we selected one of the NoSQL systems that is quite popular and highly adopted in many database systems applications: the document stores, also known as document-oriented

© ICST Institute for Computer Sciences, Social Informatics and Telecommunications Engineering 2018

F. Belqasmi et al. (Eds.): AFRICATEK 2017, LNICST 206, pp. 79–88, 2018.
https://doi.org/10.1007/978-3-319-67837-5_8

databases [12]. The use of this type of NoSQL database is growing significantly as well is the energy concern in the IT domain. This induced us to study and develop a process to allow for evaluating the energy consumption carried out by queries executed in a document store, providing as well as some specific information for design and implement less energy consuming queries. Our idea is quite simple. The power consumption of a query alone is something that we could classify as ridiculous. However, in an environment of a document store in which thousands of queries are executed every day, at the month-end the sum of the energy consumption of all queries is no longer a ridiculous thing, on the contrary.

In this paper we present the work we have done for evaluating querying energy consumption in a document store management system. The main goal of this work was to establish an effective way to determine energy consumption of different querying approaches that produce the same results, pointing out the less energy-consumption one without degrading its execution time, if possible. We intend to contribute for reducing as much as possible the energy consumption of querying processes in document stores without affecting its performance on providing results. Next, we present a brief related work about energy consumption in database systems (Sect. 2), exposing the way how a document store system process a query (Sect. 3), and how we evaluated the energy consumption of a query in a document store maintained in MongoDB [11] (Sect. 4), with particular emphasis on its implementation and validation. Finally, we present the usual section of conclusions and future work (Sect. 5).

2   Related Work

In 2008, Khargharia et al. [5] warned of the need to manage well the consumption of energy and to create environmental standards for reducing power consumption in computer platforms, with a framework and a methodology for autonomous energy management in data centers. But it was only the following year, with the appearance of Claremont report [1] that concerns about power consumption in database systems were well evidenced for all stages of their development process. In that same year, also Harizopoulos et al. [4] alerted architects and database system builders about the great energy consumption the systems they built do, pointing out several relevant aspects that could improve substantially the reduce of energy consumption. Meanwhile, other initiatives were done. Note, for example, the works done by Lang and Patel [7] and Lang et al. [8], in which were designed and developed, respectively, some energy efficient data processing techniques changing performance by energy reduction, and a framework for energy-aware database query processing, augmenting query plan optimization and adding some complementary information for energy consumption prediction, and producing an energy response time profile. In the same year, Rasmussen [13] presented another approach for energy consumption estimation of database operations, and Kunjir et al. [6] demonstrated some valid alternatives to reduce the peak of energy consumption on database management systems in tasks involving complex SQL queries processing. Later, in 2014, Gonçalves et al. [3] presented another method for estimating at compile time the energy consumption of database operators integrated in a query execution plan, building up its corresponding energy consumption plan for executing the query. Later, the same authors extended their work to the data warehousing systems domain, evaluating the energy consumption of a conventional star-query launched in a data warehouse [2]. All the works referred here are only a small part of a large set of initiatives especially oriented to reduce the energy consumption in many functionalities and services of database systems. The majority of these works approached querying processing in relational databases systems. To the best of our knowledge, and based on the search we made in the literature and in the Web, there is not for now any kind of initiative covering the issue of energy consumption in NoSQL database systems or document stores in particular.

3   Querying Processing in Document Stores

Studying the basic structure of a query in a document store and the execution plan built by the system to execute it, we get detailed information about the most elementary element used and the resources involved with, processing time and memory usage. To support this work over document stores we selected one of the most successful products in this field, which has been the preference of many NoSQL users for the last few years: MongoDB [10]. Basically, processing a query is an act of converting a search instruction for a given database written in some querying language and translating it into a set of primitive commands understandable by a system database. Additionally, processing a query also includes choosing the most efficient method to get the results corresponding to the querying instruction. In a relational database system, the queries are usually defined in SQL. However, this is not the case in non-relational databases, including document stores systems. In MongoDB queries are made in JavaScript. They have a different processing when compared to conventional relational database systems. A query in MongoDB is processed into two main steps: planning and execution. In the first step, the system aims to discover the best way to execute the query, assessing what it needs to be executed, the order for executing the various elements of the query, and how it will perform them defining a querying plan. Then, in the second step, the system performs the querying plan defined in the previous phase, using when possible the indexes defined on the collection in which the query will be executed so that its results may be obtained faster.

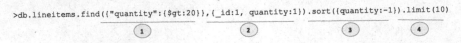

Fig. 1. An example of a query in MongoDB.

To understand a little better what we done to evaluate the energy consumption of a query, it is useful to see how queries are in fact implemented in MongoDB. Queries in MongoDB return a set of documents that are contained in a given collection. For this, MongoDB provides a specific method: *db.collection.find()*. Let's see how this happens, analyzing the execution of a very simple query that is presented in Fig. 1—a query that provides us the first 10 orders recorded in a document store that have a quantity greater than 20. The query is organized in four distinct blocks, which are marked, respectively, with 1, 2, 3 and 4. The block 1 includes a predicate defining what you want to search, which is, in this case, all documents in the collection that has orders with a quantity greater than '20 '- *{ "quantity": {$gt: 20}}*. Next, in block 2, a projection is set, indicating which fields should be included the results—*{_id: 1 quantity: 1}*, and in block 3 is indicated which is the field that will define the presentation order of the results and the sort criterion—*{quantity: −1}*, which is in this case a descending sort ('−1'). Finally, the block 4 includes the results cursor modification (*limit (10)*), which limits the number of documents in the result set. After defining the query we want to process, we submit it to the MongoDB's engine to be executed. The choice of an execution plan is made using a specific caching system, which maintains all the execution plans used previously that were considered viable for correspondent queries. Then the plan that was choose for the query will always be used in all future executions of the same query. However, if there is no implementation plan already established for the query, MongoDB will generate a new execution plan for it. The execution plan capable of responding to a particular query can be obtained adding the *explain()* command to the query. The explain command allows for consulting the execution plan for a given query and for obtaining statistics about its execution. The results produced by the command explain are presented in the form of a state tree. Figure 2 shows a small excerpt of an execution plan that was generated by MongoDB for the query presented previously in Fig. 1.

```
{
    "queryPlanner" : {
        "plannerVersion" : 1,
        "namespace" : "tpch.lineitems",
        "indexFilterSet" : false,
        "parsedQuery" : {
            "quantity" : {
                "$gt" : 20
            }
        },
        "winningPlan" : {
            "stage" : "PROJECTION",
            "transformBy" : {
                "_id" : 1,
                "quantity" : 1
            },
            "inputStage" : {
                "stage" : "SORT",
                "sortPattern" : {
                    "quantity" : -1
                },
                "limitAmount" : 10,
                "inputStage" : {
                    "stage" : "SORT_KEY_GENERATOR",
                    "inputStage" : {
                        "stage" : "COLLSCAN",
                        "filter" : {
                            "quantity" : {
                                "$gt" : 20
                            }
                        },
                        "direction" : "forward"
                    }
                }
            }
        }
    },
    (...)
```

Fig. 2. An excerpt of a query's execution plan.

MongoDB leaves "footprints" during the execution of a query. They can be analyzed later, in order to understand the various states passed by MongoDB's engine during the execution of the query. For example, in Fig. 3 we can see the tree of corresponding states to implement the query of Fig. 1. The execution of the query was divided into five states, namely: (a), (b) the CollScan, (c) the Filter, (d) Sort, (e) Limit and, finally, (f) Projection. The CollScan is able to do research on a collection and return the documents in this collection. These documents are passed to the Filter condition and are filtered according to the query that has been set. In this case the query restricted all documents had to exceed 20 units. The remaining documents carried over to the Sort state where they will be sorted according to defined key.

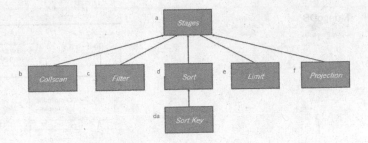

Fig. 3. The state tree of the execution of a query.

4 Defining an Energetic Comsumption Plan

The model we propose allows for a document store system administrator to compare the energy level consumption made by different queries. With this it is intended that, in addition to the definition of an execution plan for the query, something quite usual in most DBMS, you can now also possible to calculate the total energy consumption made in implementation. With this information we can improve the query or choose another to produce the same result. Let's see now, how we defined the energy measurement process of a query in MongoDB (Fig. 4a). In general terms, a query (A) is sent for execution (a) and analysis to the environment for energy consumption assessment (c). Then, using a specific meter (c), the measurement of the energy consumption is made (c1) from the time the query starts to run (b). Finishing the execution of the query also finishes the measurement of its energy consumption (c2). Then, the measurement process ends, returning a set of documents as the result of the query along with some energy consumption data gathered during the execution of the query. However, we can see a more low level view presenting the main tasks of the querying and energy measurement processes (Fig. 4b). As we can see, the process starts sending the query (A) for the energy consumption evaluation environment and preparing its execution (a). Then, the system gets the most efficient execution plan (b) for the query in the caching system and initiates the execution of the query (c) and, simultaneously, the energy meter starts measuring the energy consumption of the query (d). When the execution of the query ends, the energy measurement process is terminated, and the querying results are joined (e), integrating the documents that satisfy the query and the correspondent energy consumption data. Finally, the system returns the results (f) in a JSON file (B).

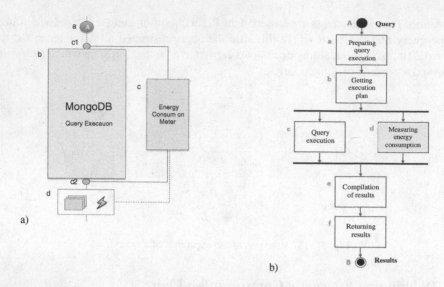

Fig. 4. A schematic view of the energy consumption process.

To support the execution and energy consumption tests we used an operational system integrating four processors Intel(R) Core(TM) i3-2100 CPU @ 3.10 GHz, each one with 8 GB of RAM, using as operating system the Ubuntu 14.04.4 LTS, and as document store management system MongoDB, version 3.2.6. The energy consumption meter was implemented in RAPL Power Meter using the driver RAPL (Running Average Power Limit) from Intel. For programming the services of the energy consumption meter we used jRAPL, a variant of the JAVA programming language for the RAPL Power Meter. Using the jRAPL, the results of the evaluation of the energy consumption of the query are a combination of three distinct values, which are related namely with the energy consumption of the: RAM, processing unit, and evaluation process programs [9].

In order to implement the energy measurement process of a query in MongoDB it was necessary to create a specific mechanism to start the measurement process, execute the query, obtain the results (related to the execution of the query and its energy consumption) and finally, finish the process. All this was done in jRAPL. Thus, to determine the energy consumed by a query with a nice accuracy level, we executed 25 times all the queries we designed for our tests, always measuring each time the energy consumption. The final energy consumption of the query was calculated using the average of all energy consumption values recorded each time the query was executed. Despite the meter provide the total value of the energy consumption of all the queries, we need to have into account that this value can be influenced by other sources that usually affect the operation of the system, and of course its energy consumption. In order to withdraw the amount of energy absorbed by these sources, we had to analyze the energy consumption of the system in an idle state, having no query or application running. Thus, the system was monitored 100 times, during 10 s each monitoring time, and then the average energy consumption value was calculate taking into account all the measurements made each time the system was monitored in idle status.

To demonstrate the utility of the consumption model we developed, and evaluate the energy consumption of a given query in a document store, we prepared ten distinct queries. Then, we grouped them two by two. Each group of two queries returns the same results, which means that the queries are equivalent, but are executed in different ways. For this, one query group was implemented using Map/Reduce (M/R), and the other was implemented using the MongoDB's aggregation functionality (Aggregation). All the queries were used over the same document store in a MongoDB system, containing a collection of 150 000 documents produced by the TPC-H [14] and converted for a format compatible with MongoDB, mapping the relational data to a document store with embedded documents containing replicated data along different documents. This is necessary due to the fact that it is not possible to join documents in MongoDB. To validate the consumption model we developed, both in terms of execution time and energy consumption, we selected a specific set of queries that were used over a document store containing a single collection ("LineItems") of 150 000 documents—Fig. 6 presents an example of one of the queries we selected, which returns a price summary report.

```
Query1 M/R

1     var red = function(doc, out) {
2       out.count_order++;
3       out.sum_qty += doc.quantity;
4       out.sum_base_price += doc.extendedprice;
5       out.sum_disc_price += doc.extendedprice * (1 - doc.discount);
6       out.sum_charge += doc.extendedprice * (1 - doc.discount) * (1 +
        doc.tax);
7       out.avg_disc += doc.discount;};
8     var avg = function(out) {
9       out.avg_qty = out.sum_qty / out.count_order;
10      out.avg_price = out.sum_base_price / out.count_order;
11      out.avg_disc = out.avg_disc / out.count_order;
12    };
13    db.lineitems.group( {
14    key : { returnflag : true, linestatus : true},
15    cond : { "shipdate" : {$lte: 19980801}},
16    initial: { count_order : 0, sum_qty : 0, sum_base_price : 0,
17    sum_disc_price : 0, sum_charge : 0, avg_disc : 0},
18    reduce : red,
19    finalize : avg
20    });
```

Fig. 5. An example of a query in MongoDB M/R – Query1.

All queries follow the model presented in Fig. 5, M/R and another in Aggregation and then were tested and analyzed their execution plans and energy consumption. As mentioned above, in MongoDB resort to explain command. However, explain returns a JSON document and to be more easily interpretable JSON was converted to a visual level. However, the explain command is only valid in the aggregation model as M/R does not. In terms of consumption, for each query is returned a list that discriminate three types of consumption, namely memory consumption, CPU consumption and package execution consumption. In Fig. 6a and b, respectively, we can see the results for the three types of consumption of Query 1 for the case of use of aggregate framework and Map/Reduce respectively. With results equal to these and for all queries used for testing was possible to reach a representative chart of all queries executions (Fig. 7).

a)
```
Power consumption of dram: 0.00538629999937256 power consumption of cpu:
0.510784899999998 power consumption of package: 0.661329599999953 time:402
```

b)
```
Power consumption of dram: 0.0290893000004871 power consumption of cpu:
3.13843540000016 power consumption of package: 3.94761509999989 time:2186
```

Fig. 6. Consumption results for Query 1 using aggregation (a) and using M/R (b).

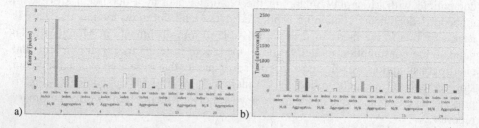

Fig. 7. Energy consumption (a) and execution time (b) of all queries.

Figure 7 presents the energy consumption of all the queries used in this work. In this figure, we can see that all the queries that have a lower energy consumption, except query 1—the case of Map/Reduce—which had a great energy consumption. Furthermore, the use of indexes in the queries also allowed for saving energy, except in the case of query 1, just as before. As expected the use of indexes has clear advantages in having better query execution time (except again for test 1), but would be expected to their use would a disadvantage. It is something that occurs with the use of indices inserts become slower and more costly the energy level. To verify this property we used two tests, one of 50 000 insertions and another 100 000. These two tests were carried out for two cases as and without indexes in the collection, before insertion already in the collection 100 000 documents—all the tests were performed 25 times each.

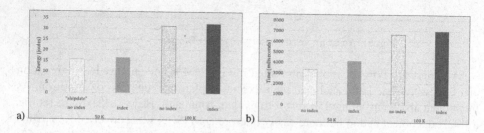

Fig. 8. Energy consumption (a) and execution time (b) of insert operations.

Regarding the execution time, it seems that the use of indexes has some impact, as expected. More specifically, the impact we measured was about 25.6% and 4.5%, respectively, for the execution of 50 000 and 100 000 insert operations in the document store. This is due to the work that is required to add these new documents to the data structure (a tree) that contains the correspondent indexes. In Fig. 8, we can see that the use of indexes has an impact on the energy level for insert operations as it happened for the execution time. This impact is about 5.6% and 3.4%, respectively, for the same insert operations cases done before −50 000 and 100 000 inserts. With this, we verified the advantage acquired when we done the inserts using a document store—an associated negative weight. With regard to the energy consumption, despite the higher consumption this is not very significant. Regarding the execution time for a large number of insert operations, it has a reduced impact. In fact this impact is more relevant in the document store if compared to the one of common search queries, as it happens usually in any database. However, in a regular day of operation, in a database system insert operations are much lower than the number of search operations.

5   Conclusions

Today, in all branches of activity, companies are discussing and promoting energy consumption measures and actions in order to have more efficient energy consumers. In information technology such concern is rising each passing day, with particular emphasis in databases. See, for instance, the case of Google. The Google's search engine makes a day about 3.5 billion searches, and an abysmal number of 1.2 thousand of billions searches per year, worldwide. Thus, if there is a way to save a tiny amount of energy, even small, for each of these searches, it will be possible to transform that saving in a huge amount of energy at the end of a year of activity. With this, companies with a similar magnitude to Google can reduce significantly their energy costs and contribute to the reduction of their ecological footprint—in the case of Google this is already a concern.

In this work we presented and described a tool we implemented for helping document stores administrators to assess the energy consumption of the different queries that are usually launched in these systems. The way two different queries producing equal results interact with the engine of a document store may cause a significant difference in the energy consumed by each one of them. Modifying a query to optimize its energy consumption could not be always possible, since such improvement can worse its own execution time. Thus, sometimes the differences in the implementation of a query do not allow for any kind of improvement in terms of energy consumption, due to some kind of application or operational requisites. However, this was something that was not observed in this work. We verified that the fastest queries were also the most energy efficient, which is a very encouraging result. Despite this, more extensive tests must be done to reinforce these results. Finally, we need also to do all the tests performed in this study using a different document store management system, as well as a different application context with other operational conditions, in order to verify the findings we got here—shorter execution time, lower energy consumption. However, this cannot be generalized at the moment to all document stores management systems, since they all have different kinds of implementations.

Acknowledgments. This work has been supported by COMPETE: POCI-01-0145-FEDER-007 043 and FCT—Fundação para a Ciência e Tecnologia within the Project Scope: UID/CEC/ 00319/2013.

References

1. Agrawal, R., Ailamaki, A., Bernstein, P., Brewer, E., Carey, M., Chaudhuri, S., Doan, A., Florescu, D., Franklin, M., Garcia-Molina, H., Gehrke, J., Gruenwald, L., Hass, L., Halevy, A., Hellerstein, J., Ioannidis, Y., Korth, H., Kossman, D., Madden, S., Magoulas, R., Ooi, B., O'Reilly, T., Ramakrishnan, R., Sarawagi, S., Stonebraker, M., Szalay, A., Weikum, G.: The claremont report on database research. Commun. ACM **52**(6), 56–65 (2009)
2. Belo, O., Gonçalves, R., Saraiva, J.: Establishing energy consumption plans for green star-queries in data warehousing systems. In: Proceedings of the 2015 IEEE International Conference on Green Computing and Communications (GreenCom 2015), Sydney, Australia, pp. 11–13 (2015)
3. Gonçalves, R., Saraiva, J., Belo, O.: Defining energy consumption plans for data querying processes. In: Proceedings of the 4th IEEE International Conference on Sustainable Computing and Communications (SustainCom 2014), Sydney, Australia, 3–5 Dec 2014
4. Harizopoulos, S., Shah, M., Meza, J., Ranganathan, P.: Energy efficiency: the new holy grail of data management systems research. In: CIDR (2009)
5. Khargharia, B., Hariri, S., Yousif, M.: Autonomic power and performance management for computing systems. In: Proceedings of 2006 IEEE International Conference on Autonomic Computing, pp. 145–154 (2006)
6. Kunjir, M., Birwa, P., Haritsa, J.: Peak power plays in database engines. In: Proceedings of the 15th International Conference on Extending Database Technology, pp. 444–455 (2012)
7. Lang, W., Patel, J.M.: Towards eco-friendly database management systems. In: CIDR (2009)
8. Lang, W., Kandhan, R., Patel, J.M.: Rethinking query processing for energy efficiency: slowing down to win the race. IEEE Data Eng. Bull. **34**, 12–23 (2011)
9. Liu, K., Pinto, G., Liu, Y.: Data-oriented characterization of application-level energy optimization. In: Lecture Notes in Computer Science (including subseries Lecture Notes in Artificial Intelligence and Lecture Notes in Bioinformatics), pp. 316–331 (2015)
10. Moniruzzaman, A., Hossain, S.: Nosql database: new era of databases for big data analytics-classification, characteristics and comparison. Int. J. Database Theory Appl. **6**(4), 1–14 (2013)
11. MongoDB: MongoDB. https://www.mongodb.com (2016). Accessed 19 Aug 2016
12. Person. L.: World NoSQL Market—opportunities and forecasts, 2013–2020 (2015)
13. Rasmussen, N.: A.p.c. determining total cost of ownership for data centers and network room infrastructure. www.apcmedia.com/salestools/CMRP-5T9PQG/CMRP-5T9PQG_R4_EN.pdf(2011). Accessed from 3 Sept 2016
14. TPC-H: TPC-H, An ad-hoc decision support benchmark. http://www.tpc.org/tpch/(2016). Accessed from 19 Aug 2016

Joint Energy Demand Prediction and Control

Mehdi Merai[✉] and Jia Yuan Yu

Concordia Institute of Information System Engineering, Concordia University,
Montreal, QC H3G 1M8, Canada
m_erai@encs.concordia.ca

Abstract. Joint electricity predictor and controller (JEPAC) is a system that allows energy suppliers to better predict their electricity grid activity and then, optimize their energy production, management and distribution. In fact, the more accurate the prediction is, the lesser its negative impact on the economy and environment. Once the JEPAC system is installed in the energy consumer place, it will collect indoor ambient parameters and energy usage and thus predict the individual future consumption. This prediction will be frequently transmitted to the energy supplier as a formatted commitment then later, the same device will try to respect this commitment by adjusting wisely the user's appliances and HVAC. As a result, the energy supplier will then crowdsource the global energy demand by aggregating highly detailed individual consumption commitments. This will allow a better prediction and control of the future energy demand.

Keywords: Machine learning · Smart grid · Energy prediction and control · HVAC · Micro grid

1 Introduction

Forecasting accurate electricity consumption is a challenge. To perform this task, electricity suppliers use aggregate prediction due to the lack of information about individual electricity usage and behavior. If the utility suppliers predict energy consumption at the scale of the individual service subscriber, they can better manage their electricity grid; consequently, optimizing their energy production (for example; utilizing more renewable energy for example) and improve their distribution [2]. In this article, we propose a system that jointly predicts individual energy consumption and at the same time, wisely adjusts the HVAC in order to maximize the fit with the performed prediction. Then, the predicted individual usage details will be transmitted to the energy supplier as a commitment in a structured format that can be automatically processed. The energy consumption commitment will include a highly detailed prediction performed based on the frequency defined by the energy supplier. This process will be performed without impairing the privacy of the user. The individual energy usage will be locally performed and the commitment will only include timely aggregated energy consumption prediction. The energy supplier will therefore crowdsource all predicted data to build an accurate and detailed energy demand prediction. Ultimately the system will contribute to the emergence of a new electricity consumption

© ICST Institute for Computer Sciences, Social Informatics and Telecommunications Engineering 2018
F. Belqasmi et al. (Eds.): AFRICATEK 2017, LNICST 206, pp. 89–96, 2018.
https://doi.org/10.1007/978-3-319-67837-5_9

paradigm. In fact, by helping energy supplier to better predict the energy demand, the latter will directly benefit of an important positive economic and environmental impacts that could be shared with the consumer as part of a reward system.

In Sect. 1, we introduce the JEPAC hardware architecture and the ambient parameters it collects. The Sect. 2 describes the machine learning technics executed by the device in order to predict the future energy consumption for an individual residence. In Sect. 3, we describe how the performed predictions are collected by the energy supplier and how JEPAC maximizes the respect of those predictions. In Sect. 4, we share the results of JEPAC device execution experience. Finally, in Sect. 5, we describe our future work perspectives.

2   Ambient Parameters Collection

In order to collect and determine indoor ambient parameters, the JEPAC device will use several sensors like temperature, humidity, Lux, etc., (a) [6]. The collected information is directly consumed for the needs of the device (to adjust HVAC or to perform an accurate prediction) or used to infer other information like user behaviour (example: sleeping mode, travel mode, etc.), [4]. The JEPAC device will certainly insure its primary role; adjusting appliances in order to reach a specific configuration of ambient parameters (like temperature, humidity, etc.) like shown in (d). As part of the system, the ambient parameters configuration could be specified by the end user or automatically determined [9]. Indeed, the JEPAC device will be connected to the internet via a regular internet router (c_1). It requires an internet connection to get access to some web services that provide external useful data that can't be collected by its own sensors like

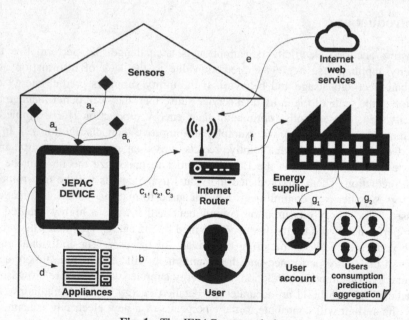

Fig. 1. The JEPAC system design

outdoor weather. The internet access represented by f will also allow the JEPAC device to send energy consumption commitments to a specific software hosted by the energy provider (c_2) to update the JEPAC embedded software when it is necessary (c_2).

3 Regression Based Prediction

By collecting indoor, outdoor and behaviour usage data [8], the JEPAC device will learn appliances configuration related to each ambient parameter combination (indoor measurements, outdoor measurements and other useful data like energy consumer behaviour). Then, the JEPAC device will use the predicted appliance configuration to deduct the user future energy consumption that will be communicated as a commitment.

In order to perform the energy consumption prediction, JEPAC uses an embedded machine learning algorithm [7] and produce a commitment. It includes the energy consumption prediction details during the entire following day. The prediction granularity is by default fixed to one prediction each hour. It means that each commitment will include 24 predictions that cover the energy consumption of the proceeding day. The number of predictions per day could differ depending on the accuracy level requested by the energy supplier. As represented in Table 1, the training set will be organized in separate slots, each represents a unique daily hour. Those slots will be used as a training base for a set of regressions that output a set of predictions related to each slot. Given that our regression model includes multiple regressor variables, we opted for multiple linear regression [1], i.e., for all $s = 1, 2, ...$:

$$\widehat{Y}_S = \widehat{\theta}_S \cdot X_S$$

$$\widehat{\theta}_S = \arg \min_{\omega \varepsilon \mathbb{R}^d} \sum_{j=1}^{s-1} (Y_j - X_j \cdot \omega)^2$$

The entire slots predictions will represent the daily prediction that will be commuted as a commitment between the user and the energy supplier. It means that during a day, the machine learning will predict a set of $\hat{Y}$ where $\hat{Y}_s = \{\hat{Y}0, ..., \hat{Y}s\}$ and s is the time slot identification. The training set consists of a consistent dataset composed of n records where each one is formed by a vector X which is paired with a value Y. Considering X_s as inputs vector in the slot S having I features and N samples. We can note it as follow: $X_s = \{x_s, 0,0 \dots x_s, i, n\}$ where x_s, i, n is the ith input feature of the

Table 1. Training set for energy consumption prediction

Slot 0		Slot S	
X_0	Y_0	Xs	Ys
$X0, 0, 0 \cdots X0, i, 0$	$Y0, 0$	$Xs, 0, 0 \quad \cdots \quad Xs, i, 0$	$Ys, 0$
$\vdots$	$\vdots$	$\vdots \qquad\qquad \vdots$	$\vdots$
$X0, 0, n \cdots X0, i, n$	$Y0, n$	$Xs, 0, n \quad \cdots \quad Xs, i, n$	Ys, n

nth JEPAC collected sample in a time slot *s*. *Y* is collected by the energy supplier using the smart meter installed at the user location.

3.1 Prediction Driven Control

The JEPAC device will act as a controller by adjusting the user appliances in order to respect the predicted electricity usage committed with the energy supplier. The appliance control can also be managed based on the user preferences and behaviour (sleeping mode, travel mode, outside mode, etc.). In fact, JEPAC gives the priority to the manual configurations in order to allow the user to have the final control of his appliances. JEPAC extends the reactive systems like the proportional controllers. Those ones are mainly based on a feedback loop that control their behavior dynamically. A simple reactive system acts as a proportional controller [10]. Like the non-smart thermostats, the proportional controller collects a current state $y(t)$ through its sensors and compares it with a desired one $z(t)$. Then, it calculates the difference between these values in order to determine the error $e(t)$ that will proportionally adjust the system to reach the desired output.

In general, the proportional controller algorithm follows a mathematical model that Eq. 1 describes. We consider that $u_{out}(t)$ refers to the proportional controller algorithm output. In our case, JEPAC is coupled with an HVAC system. So $u_{out}(t)$ refers to the control action taken by JEPAC and decides how much electricity the appliance system should supply to reach the setpoint. Kc refers to the proportional gain that adapts the magnitude of input signal collected by the JEPAC system to the magnitude used for by the JEPAC controller. However, in our system the reference setpoint is automatically defined and results from the combination between the commitment $c(t)$ and the user manual configuration $z(t)$. $y(t)$ refers to the current ambient state collected by the JEPAC system through its sensors. Finally, u_0 refers to the control action taken by JEPAC which is necessary to maintain ambient parameters at the steady state when there is no error.

$$. u_{out}(t) = K_c(z(t) - y(t)) + u_0 \tag{1}$$

The JEPAC augments the proportional controller by taking the committed energy consumption into consideration. As in Fig. 2, rather than trying to reach only a user defined setpoint $z(t)$, the current system reference will consider a combination of the energy consumption commitment $c(t)$ (resulting from the learning model) and the user desired setting $z(t)$. The JEPAC system is composed by coupling the prediction system (represented by the orange boundary) and the controller (represented by the blue boundary). The prediction system forecasts the future energy consumption, and sends it to the energy supplier as a commitment $c(t)$. This commitment will be used the following day in conjunction with the manual settings $z(t)$ in order to control the HVAC. More specifically, the system will update the reference initially defined by the user with a temporary setpoint respecting the commitment made between the energy consumer and the energy supplier. The difference between the commitment setpoints and the user defined ones should be smaller than a certain ratio in order to ensure that the system meets at a certain level the user comfort desires. Also, the end user has the possibility to explicitly ignore the commitment setpoint.

In general, by adding the commitment data to the initial control system reference, different strategies with different advantages and costs can be considered. As represented in the Eq. 2, the function $f(c(t), z_s(t))$ that represents the new control system entry can be updated by the user as needed. More strategies will be part of our future work.

$$u_{out}(t) = K_c(f(c(t), z(t)) - y(t)) + u_0 \tag{2}$$

Algorithm 1. Future consumption prediction and commitment

Result: Energy supplier aggregates individual predictions to evaluate the global energy demand

1. Use an existing training set to train the machine learning algorithm;

for *each day d (example: Sep 1st)* **do**

    for *each time slot s (example: 13h00)* **do**

        1 Provide an energy consumption prediction $\hat{Y}_s$;

        2 Add $\hat{Y}_s$ to the commitment $c(t)$ (that includes the next day electricity consumption);

    end

    3.1 As soon as the commitment $c(t)$ is fully completed, display its content in a user-friendly way (Optional step);

    3.2 Wait for the users' commitment confirmation $c(t)$ (Optional step); 4 Send the commitment $c(t)$ to the energy supplier;

    5 At d, energy supplier will $c(t)$ energy consumption commitment; 6 At $d+1$, Adjust the users' appliances in order the respect the energy consumption communicated in $c(t)$;

    7 At $d+1$, the energy supplier compares real energy consumption et to the predicted one $e'(t)$ previously communicated in $c(t)$ to produce δ. δ measure how much the energy consumption prediction (already received) fits with the real consumption;

    8 In addition to $e(t)$, the energy supplier will use δ rate to determinate the right charging formula;

end

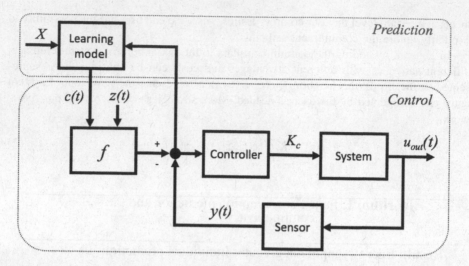

Fig. 2. Joint energy demand prediction and control

3.2   The Energy Demand Prediction

As in g_1 (Fig. 1), the energy supplier will receives energy consumption commitments from users. It aggregates those commitments $c(t)$ in order to build a larger prediction concerning specific clusters of energy consumers like an energy consumer in some specific area. This aggregation will be performed by a software hosted by the energy supplier. In fact, thanks to the formatted structure of data provided through the users commitments, the electricity demand can be predicted through a simple aggregation of the commitments records. Furthermore, energy supplier can perform a horizontal aggregation; Aggregating all the energy consumption prediction records provided by different commitments in a specific for a specific time [5]. As a result, the energy supplier can predict easier the future activity of its electricity grid. For example; it can determine how many turbines it has to activate, estimates better the electricity demand in a specific geographic zone and improves renewable energy use thanks to more predictable energy demand [5]. As represented in g_2, by using δ rate, the energy supplier will reward the user based on the fitting level between the real and the predicted energy consumption. The more the commitment $c(t)$ (predicted energy consumption) is respected, the more the reward will be. To encourage energy consumers adhesion, the commitment respecting rate will be used exclusively to reward the user. In case of non respect, the user will pay the energy supplier with the regular pricing formula. He will only lose the reward.

4 Simulation

For experimentation, we use a public dataset provided by OpenEI that includes 8760 data records collected hourly at the same residential place.[1] Each data record includes energy consumption details such as heating, electrical devices, etc. This dataset was used to train a machine learning algorithm in order to perform the energy consumption prediction. The data is ordered by time stamps and splitted into 24 slots where each one represents a unique daily hour (Example: 13h00). The JEPAC machine learning algorithm runs a set of multiple linear regressions applied on each time slot. In terms of technology, we use Statsmodels Python module to implement multiple linear regression using an ordinary least squares method to perform the multiple linear regressions [3].

4.1 Tests and Results

Once trained, JEPAC system was able to predict the next day energy consumption details with an accuracy equal to 91,83% for all of the 24 time slots. In Fig. 3, we used an error bar representation to visualize the predicted energy consumption during one day. It also includes the prediction errors in comparison with real energy consumption for the same day. We noticed that the prediction accuracy was lower in a small number of time slots due to the lack of data used for the simulation (in our case, it concerns the time slots 18:00, 19:00 and 20:00. This gap will be naturally filled once the training set grows up. Once a consistent training set will be constituted, the JEPAC machine learning algorithm will be able to extend its prediction over one day. Finally, once the prediction will be performed, it can be sent to the energy supplier as well as to support the JEPAC controller to better adjust the user devices' respecting the energy consumption commitment [5].

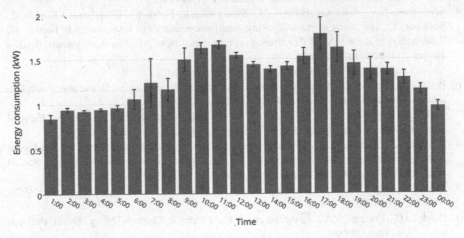

Fig. 3. Energy consumption prediction for an entire day (kW)

---

[1] Link: OpenEI.org - EPLUS TMY2 RESIDENTIAL BASE.

5   Future Work

Our future work will focus on two main research paths: Firstly improving and expending our prediction driven control system and secondly building an incentive plan for reward distribution by taking into regards the engagement user.

5.1   Expension of the Current JEPAC System

Our future work will extend the combination strategy between the manual and the commitment based setting. Represented by the function $f(c(t), z(t))$, we intend to build a more complex combination function that combines user's convenience and commitment respect.

5.2   Reward Distribution Incentive Plan

In order to encourage users to respect the commitment, the energy supplier should have an efficient incentive plan. In our future work, we intend to build an incentive and fair rewards distribution model that could improve users' envolvement in such energy consumption program.

References

1. Peck, E., Montgomery, D., Vining, G.: Introduction to Linear Regression Analysis, 4th edn. Wiley (2015)
2. Rogers, A., Jennings, N.R., Ramchurn, D., Vytelingum, P.: Putting the smarts into the smart grid: a grand challenge for artificial intelligence. Commun. ACM **55**(4), 86–97 (2012)
3. Hayashi, F.: Econometrics. Princeton University Press (2000)
4. Srinivasan, S.V., Gao, G., Holben, B., Stankovic, J., Field, E., Whitehouse, K., Lu, J., Sookoor, T.: The smart thermostat: using occupancy sensors to save energy in homes. In: Proceedings of the 8th ACM Conference on Embedded Networked Sensor Systems, SenSys 10, pp. 211–224. ACM (2010)
5. Yu, J.Y.: Distributed Forecasting and Pricing System (2014)
6. Peffer, T., Aragon, C., Perry, D., Pritoni, M., Meier, A.: How people use thermostats in homes: a review. Build. Environ. **46**(12), 2529–2541 (2011)
7. Parker, L.E., Edwards, R.E., New, J.: Predicting future hourly residential electrical consumption: a machine learning case study. Energy Build., 591–603 (2012)
8. Newman, M.W., Yang, R.: Learning from a learning thermostat: lessons for intelligent systems for the home. In: Proceedings of the 2013 ACM International Joint Conference on Pervasive and Ubiquitous Computing, UbiComp 13, pp. 93–102. ACM (2013)
9. Iskin, I., Daim, T.U.: Smart thermostats: are we ready? Int. J. Energy Sect. Manage. **4**(2), 146–151 (2010)
10. Doyle, J.C., Francis, B.A., Tannenbaum, A.R.: Feedback Control Theory. Dover Publications, New York (2009)

Big Data, Data Analytics, and Knowledge Management

Trust Assessment-Based Multiple Linear Regression for Processing Big Data Over Diverse Clouds

Hadeel El-Kassabi[1,2]([✉]), Mohamed Adel Serhani[2],
Chafik Bouhaddioui[2], and Rachida Dssouli[1]

[1] Concordia Institute for Information Systems Engineering,
Concordia University, Montreal, Canada
h_elkass@encs.concordia.ca,
rachida.dssouli@concordia.ca
[2] College of Information Technology, UAE University,
Al Ain, United Arab Emirates
{serhanim, chafikb, htalaat}@uaeu.ac.ae

Abstract. Assessing trust of cloud providers is considered to be a key factor to discriminate between them, especially once dealing with Big Data. In this paper, we apply Multiple Linear Regression (MLR) to develop a trust model for processing Big Data over diverse Clouds. The model relies on MLR to predict trust score of different cloud service providers. Therefore, support selection of the trustworthiness provider. Trust is evaluated not only on evidenced information collected about cloud resources availability, but also on past experiences with the cloud provider, and the reputation collected from other users experienced with the same cloud services. We use cross validation to test the consistency of the estimated regression equation, and we found that the model can perfectly be used to predict the response variable trust. We also, use bootstrap scheme to evaluate the confidence intervals for each pair of variables used in building our trust model.

Keywords: Trust · Multiple Linear Regression · Cloud · Big Data · Community management

1 Introduction

With the abundance of cloud services sharing the market space, it becomes challenging to select the appropriate, and trustworthy cloud providers that guarantee user's quality preferences and ensure continuity of service provisioning especially when dealing with Big Data. Big Data processing requires trustworthy cloud provider who ensures service delivery with high QoS guarantee. The dynamic nature of cloud makes it hard to evaluate the trust of cloud providers to process Big Data as it is dynamic in nature and can be subject of continuous resource availability, high dependability, and fault tolerance. Previous trust models are non-dynamic and lack of real-time adaptability, which makes them unsuitable in the context of Cloud and Big Data. Building trust only based reputation can be irrelevant if the users are untrustworthy or subjective. Also,

© ICST Institute for Computer Sciences, Social Informatics and Telecommunications Engineering 2018
F. Belqasmi et al. (Eds.): AFRICATEK 2017, LNICST 206, pp. 99–109, 2018.
https://doi.org/10.1007/978-3-319-67837-5_10

trust models have used local trust and recommendation trust using weights that are not necessarily dynamic and suitable to the user's preferences. Therefore, we need trust to be dynamic and relies on evidenced information collected about cloud resources availability, past experiences with the cloud provider, and the reputation calculated from other users experienced with the same cloud services. The trust model we aim to develop in this paper will fulfill the following requirements: (1) Supports dynamic trust score calculation and update, (2) Provides credibility validation through community management system, and (3) Collects reputation information dynamically using reputation request messages broadcasted to community members.

In this paper, we first describe trust approaches in Cloud. We then, formalize trust evaluation of cloud providers using Multiple Linear regression. Afterwards, we describe our trust prediction scheme, and we evaluate it using data generated from a simulator we have developed for this purpose.

2 Background and Related Work

2.1 Properties of Trust

Few research initiatives described various properties of trust some of which are Subjectivity, Dynamicity, and Context Dependency [1]. Trust by nature is subjective because it depends on user's opinion and it is based on personal perspective and preference. However, assessing trust objectively depends on real evidenced measurements, which make it challenging to achieve due mainly to two factors: incompleteness and uncertainty. Subjective assessment is usually studied using probability set and fuzzy set techniques [2]. Another property of trust is dynamicity, where the trust is subject to time elapse, amount of interaction, external factors like authority control and contract rules, and even physical resource capabilities decay over time. This necessitates the periodic refreshment of trust evaluation. Trust also is context depended because an entity can be trusted in a service domain but not in another. This property is modeled in various works in the literature as in [2–4].

2.2 Trust Model Approaches

Many classifications of Trust model for clouds were proposed in the literature. Authors in [5] described four main categories: self-managed case-based, SLA-based, broker-based, and reputation-based approaches. Other classification schemes relied either on the user or provider perspectives, or both, in building trust model such as in [6]. While in [7] trust models were classified into policy, reputation, recommendation, and prediction, the necessity of prediction models arise when there is no previous communication with the cloud service provider. Additionally, a reputation-based trust model is based on the opinions of other users towards service providers. We further classify reputation-based models into service quality-based and resource quality-based models. The service quality-based model performs trust assessment based on the Quality of Service of the cloud. However, the resource quality-based model relies on the cloud resources quality and availability to evaluate the trust.

Many trust model approaches relied on previous experience with the service provider. Authors in [8] built trust score evaluation based on historical records were the Last-K algorithm is adopted. Nevertheless, this method could decrease accuracy because of the limited number of used quality attributes. Other approaches adopted game theory to evaluate trust like in [9–11].

Trust model based on service quality reputation has been proposed in [12], where kept information about service providers are kept in a registry using a discovery system. The credibility of a service provider was evaluated using the ratio of the period of time over which a service is provided to the number of times the service is offered to evaluate. In [13], the trust score of a cloud resource is evaluated based on multiple QoCs attributes. The weights were manually and evenly distributed, so it was inflexible to user quality preferences for services. In the context of Big Data and cloud computing, authors in [3] suggested a category-based context-aware and recommendation incentive-based reputation mechanism to enhance the accuracy and protect data against attacks. Authors in [14] suggested a trust framework for cloud service selection that uses QoCs monitoring and feedback ratings in trust assessment.

Prediction-based trust models typically use statistical techniques for trustworthiness evaluation and prediction. In [7], they study the capabilities and the historical reputation of the service provider and predict its future behavior. These approaches use Fuzzy logic, Bayesian inference, or regression models to estimate the trust of service providers calculated as the probability of providing satisfactory QoCS to users [15]. These models are usually used when there is no previous historical interaction with the cloud service provider. They are also resilient to false reputation attacks especially the logistic regression models that are known to detect outlier values [16]. Bayesian inference is widely used as it considers trust as a probability distribution and is simple with strong statistical basis. However, the belief discounting technique is resilient to false attacks [15]. The fuzzy logic uses approximation to evaluation trust based on ranges between 0 and 1 rather than binary sets. It is widely used despite it incur some implementation complexity and low malicious behavior detection [2].

2.3 Trust Score Computation Approaches

A simple way to evaluate reputation scores is to calculate the difference between the number of positive ratings and the number of negative ratings, which was used in eBay's reputation forum [17]. Yet, this approach might give weak results. A refined method was proposed by some commercial websites such as Epinions and Amazon, where they compute the average of all the ratings. Other approach suggested using a weighted average of all the ratings based on the rater's age, credibility, and difference of the rate value to existing ratings. Similar approach was also used in [18]. Other computational reputation models include Bayesian Systems, Regression Analysis, Belief Models, Fuzzy Models, and Flow Models. However, not all of the aforementioned approaches are used for cloud provider trust evaluation because of unsuitability or simply untried.

The different computation methods are also associated with how the trust scores are scaled. The different scales for trust that are represented in literature include binary, discrete, nominal scale, and continuous values [1]. One problem with several trust score evaluation methods is that they are based on sophisticated and time-consuming mathematical models. This is unsuitable for a Big Data environment with its own special characteristics (multi-Vs). Most of the aforementioned trust models are non-dynamic in nature and unsuitable for Big Data and the cloud environment. Some base their trust only on reputation, which can be misleading especially if the users are untrustworthy or subjective. Other trust models have used local trust and recommendation trust using weights that are not necessarily dynamic.

3 Trust Evaluation Model

3.1 Problem Definition

In this section, we describe the trust evaluation problem in competing cloud environment as follows: a user wants to select a Cloud Service Provider (CP) to execute some Big Data processing task. Given a history of previous service interactions received from members of community, the user will predict whether CP_i is trustworthy or not. We define a trustworthy CP as being able to satisfy a set of QoCSs. The goal is to reach a high prediction accuracy.

For each service interaction with CP_i at time t, a record containing the observed quality level of this service y_k^t by user k with respect to a set of quality attributes a_{ki}^t that is a real value $[0,1]$; where:

$$CP = \{cp_i | i = 1, 2, 3, \ldots n\} \tag{1}$$

$$A = \{a_j | j = 1, 2, 3, \ldots m\} \tag{2}$$

$$P^t = \{p_1, p_2, p_3 \ldots p_m\} \tag{3}$$

where t is the time stamp of the observed service transaction, cp_1, cp_2 ... cp_n are the possible n alternative cloud service providers CPs available to the user k, a_1, $a_2, \ldots, a_m$ represent QoCS attributes (criteria) such as reliability, availability, and throughput. p_1, $p_2, \ldots, p_m$ represent the performance level of a_1, $a_2, \ldots, a_m$ respectively.

Then, *trust* is the score that CP_i will achieve according to set of QoCS at time t described by p^t vector. Let $y_i^t = y_{ki}^t \cup \{y_{ui}^t, k \neq u\}$ where y_{ui}^t is an observation of neighbor u about a prior service experience with CP_i provided to user k. The observation record is in the form of $\{P^t, y^t\}$ specifying the performance of each quality attribute at time t. Let $y_i = \{y_i^t, t = 1, \ldots, N\}$ represent the set of observations gathered by a user k which includes both self-experience and collected observations from neighbors in $[0, N]$. And, let $p = \{P^t, t = 1, \ldots, N\}$ be the corresponding performance level of the quality attributes in $[0, N]$.

We suggest to use Multiple Linear Regression (MLR) to solve this problem and model the relationship between the trust score which we consider the dependent variable y and some explanatory (also named independent) variables p using a linear function of the independent variables [19].

$$E\left[y_i^t|p_i\right] = \beta_0 + \sum_{i=1}^{m} \beta_i P_i + \varepsilon \qquad (4)$$

where $\beta i = [\beta_i, \ i = 1, 2, 3, \ldots m]$ is a column vector of coefficients that are estimated values from the available data, and ε is the 'noise' which is a random variable having an independent normal distribution with mean equals to zero and unknown constant standard deviation σ.

We estimate the values for β_i coefficients by minimizing the sum of squares of differences between the predicted values and the observed values in the data given by:

$$\sum_{i=1}^{N} \left(y_i - \beta_0 - \beta_1 x_{i1} - \cdots - \beta_m x_{im}\right)^2 \qquad (5)$$

Let the ordinary least squares (OLS) $\hat{\beta}_0, \hat{\beta}_1, \ldots, \hat{\beta}_m$ be the optimized coefficients that minimize Eq. 5. Then we substitute the computed values in the linear regression model in Eq. 4 to predict the trust score for one CP according to the following:

$$\hat{y} = \hat{\beta}_0 + \sum_{i=1}^{m} \hat{\beta}_i P_i \qquad (6)$$

To summarize, history experience $\{p, y_i\}$ is a collection of self-experience QoS performance of CP_i and reputation provided by neighbors upon their experience dealing with CP_i. We perform the multiple linear regression processing for each CP calculating the expected $\hat{y}$. The selected CP would be the one with the highest $\hat{y}_i$ value, i.e. the one with highest predicted trust score, which means the highest probability of providing satisfactory QoS performance. The algorithm shown in Fig. 1 describes the CP selection process according to trust score prediction using MLR algorithm. A trust score is predicted for each CP_i. The algorithm then recommends a CP_i having the highest score.

Algorithm 1 Multiple Linear Regression for CSPs Trust Score Prediction

Input: *CSPList* //List of CSPs
CSPServiceLog //Service Log of all CSPs
ReqAttrVals //list of Required QoS attributes

Output: CSP with Highest Predicted Trust Score

```
 1: procedure PREDICTCPTRUST(CSPList, CSPServiceLog, ReqAttrVals)
 2:     for all csp ∈ CSPList do
 3:         attScore ← 0
 4:         Evaluate Bs coefficients according to Eq.5 and Eq.6
 5:         for attLabel ← 1, nAttributes do //in ReqAttrVals
 6:             attScore ← attScore + ReqAttrVals[attLabel] * B[attLabel]
 7:         end for
 8:         CSPListScore[csp] ← attScore
 9:     end for
10:     return max(CSPListScore)
11: end procedure=0
```

Fig. 1. MLR algorithm for cloud service provider (CP) selection

3.2 Community Management

Our trust evaluation scheme depends on the CP's reputation within the community neighborhood. Initially it requires establishing a degree of trust towards information providers, and then the neighbors need to be motivated and willing to offer reputation information. Hence, we propose a community management system to facilitate the aforementioned requirements. Community is defined in the Oxford dictionary as "the condition of sharing or having certain attitudes and interests in common". With this viewpoint, the community members dealt with the possibility of acquiring CP reputation information from other community members. Many Community management initiatives were presented in the literature as in [20, 21]. An important issue in community management would be the adaptability to the cloud environment dynamic changes and being robust against false information or malicious attacks. We propose a third party entity to maintain a database of community members' information. A user will send request to join the community, and when accepted, the new member is provided with an identification number.

4 Trust Prediction Scheme

Figure 2 describes the set of entities involved in our trust prediction system.

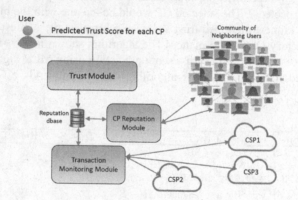

Fig. 2. Trust prediction scheme

Trust Module: It is responsible for analyzing the reputation database to predict the trust score for each cloud provider, and producing a selection decision to the user using the algorithm explained in Sect. 3.1. It generates a predicted trust score for each cloud service provider (CSP) from the logs containing QoS performance and trust score generated by neighbors. The user will choose the CSP having the highest probability of giving a satisfactory QoS.

Transaction Monitoring Module: It monitors all communications with other cloud providers and logs the performance information. A record for each communication transaction exchanged between the user and the cloud provider is logged to the database called reputation database. This record contains QoS evidence that can help to evaluate a cloud provider's trust score. This information might contain for example, the invocation time, data size, response time, cost and distance between the user and cloud and success status (success or fail).

CP Reputation Module: This module is responsible for sending requests to other neighboring users asking for their own previous experience with other CSPs. In addition, it handles replies received. The request message contains the list of the CSPs to be evaluated. Each reply message contains a list of cloud providers; their QoS performance and their trust scores calculated by the neighboring users. It also analyzes all the reply messages and stores this information in the *Reputation* database and is eventually communicated to the ***Trust module*** for the final trust evaluation. The request messages are sent periodically and the reply messages are collected during this time period. The reputation database is updated whenever a reply message is received.

Reputation Database: It is a local database containing the self-experience and the collected logs from neighbors who were asked to provide their own historical experience with each CSP. Each log contains QoS performance values and the trust score. For scalability reasons, we keep the most recent transaction logs.

5 Implementation and Experimentations

In this section, we describe the experimentations we have conducted to evaluate our proposed trust model. We explain experimental setup, and then we describe the simulator system including all modules.

5.1 Trust Prediction Implementations

The following is the implementation details of the main components involved in our trust prediction model which we have developed in Java to test our proposed trust model. Our simulator implemented all modules described in Sect. 4 including user modules, which are the trust module, CP reputation manager, transaction monitoring module, cloud provider's components, as well as neighbor components (e.g., other users). The simulation generates database logs that are analyzed using Weka MLR to predict the trust scores for each CP.

We considered the following default simulation parameters: Number of cloud providers: 1 to 50, number of nodes within each cloud: 1 to 100, cloud provider's properties: proximity, average node performance and unit storage price, node properties: available resources, memory, disk space, processing power, round trip delay (RT) and bandwidth, QoCS attributes: data size, distance, cost, response time, availability and confidence, and number of community members: 3 to 100 neighbors.

All statistical results were obtained using R language and the packages MASS, DAAG and RELIMPO.

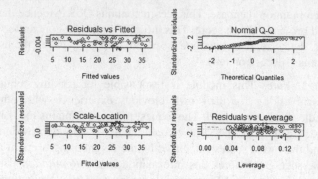

Fig. 3. The regression residuals plot

5.2 Experiments

In this experiment, we generate 50 observations from one provider of the dependent variable Trust denoted by Y and *six* explanatory variables data size (X_1), distance (X_2), availability (X_3), response time (X_4), confidence (X_5) and cost (X_6). First, the variable cost can't be included in the model generated by one provider. It can only be used to compare between different providers. We tested the correlation between the explanatory variables and the response variable, and we can clearly conclude that the correlations are significant with all independent variables except the confidence variable (X_5). Also, we note that the data size and the response time are highly correlated ($r = 1$). Therefore, the estimated regression equation is expressed by

$$\hat{y} = 0.00631 + 0.0243X_1 + 0.0165X_2 + 0.0194X_3.$$

The three variables have a significant positive effect (all p-values are close to zero). This means that the trust will increase with the increase of each of these explanatory variables. As depicted in Fig. 3, the residuals satisfy the assumptions of normality (p-value for Shapiro-Wilk normality test is 0.1689), constant variance and independence. Using the cross-validation procedure to evaluate the consistency of the estimated regression equation, using three folds, we found that the model can perfectly be used to predict the response variable *trust* as depicted in Fig. 4.

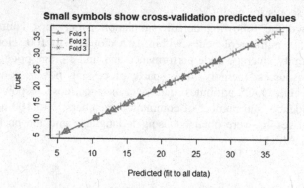

Fig. 4. Cross-validation for predicted values.

By calculating the relative importance for each explanatory variable, we found that the *data size* has the most relative importance for explaining the *trust* variable, roughly more than 62% followed by the distance variable, which has 25% of importance. The three variables explained 100% of the variability of the *trust* variable. To evaluate if the difference between the relative importance for trust is significant, we used the bootstrap procedure to calculate the confidence intervals of the difference between the relative importance of each pair of variables, see Fig. 5.

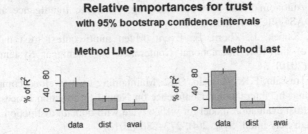

Fig. 5. 95% bootstrap confidence interval of relative importance for the *trust*.

Using the LMG metric, the 95% bootstrap confidence interval (BCI) of the relative importance of data size variable is (51.43%, 71.56%) while using the LAST metric; we note that the coefficient of determination is explained only by the data size and distance variables. In this case, the 95% BCI of the relative importance of data size variable is (78.29%, 89.32%).

6 Conclusion

In this paper, we proposed a Trust model for processing Big Data over different clouds. The model applies the MLR to predict trust scores for different cloud providers. Trust is evaluated based on evidenced information collected about cloud resources availability, past experiences with the cloud provider, and the reputation collected from other users experienced with the same cloud services. The trust model we have developed supports dynamic trust score calculation and update, provides credibility validation through community management system, and retrieves dynamically reputation scores. The model has been evaluated with few experiments and the results we have achieved prove that our Trust model exhibits high prediction accuracy. To evaluate the prediction accuracy, the consistency of the estimated regression equation, and the trust significance, we used the cross-validation method. As a result, we found that the model can perfectly be used to predict the response variable trust. Finally, we estimated and compared the relative importance of each explanatory variable in the model using the bootstrap confidence intervals for the difference between the relative importance of each pair of variables. We found that the data size variable explains the largest relative importance in the proposed trust model followed by the distance variable.

References

1. Cho, J.-H., Chan, K., Adali, S.: A survey on trust modeling. ACM Comput. Surv. (CSUR) **48**(2), 28 (2015)
2. Kanwal, A., Masood, R., Shibl, M.A.: Taxonomy for trust models in cloud computing. Comput. J. **58**, 601–626 (2014)
3. Lin, H., Hu, J., Liu, J., Xu, L., Wu, Y.: A context aware reputation mechanism for enhancing Big Data veracity in mobile cloud computing. In: IEEE International Conference on Computer and Information Technology, Ubiquitous Computing and Communications; Dependable, Autonomic and Secure Computing, Pervasive Intelligence and Computing (CIT/IUCC/DASC/PICOM) (2015)
4. Malacka, O., Samek, J., Zboril, F.: Event driven multi-context trust model. In: 2010 Proceedings of the 10th International Conference on Intelligent Systems Design and Applications (2010)
5. Hussain, W., Hussain, F.K., Hussain, O.K.: Maintaining trust in cloud computing through SLA monitoring. In: International Conference on Neural Information Processing (2014)
6. Wu, J.-B.: A trust evaluation model for web service with domain distinction. Int. J. Granul. Comput. Rough Sets Intell. Syst. **2**(4), 273–280 (2012)
7. Noor, T.H., Sheng, Q.Z., Zeadally, S., Yu, J.: Trust management of services in cloud environments: obstacles and solutions. ACM Comput. Surv. (CSUR) **46**(1), 12 (2013)
8. Qi, L., Dou, W., Zhou, Y., Yu, J., Hu, C.: A context-aware service evaluation approach over Big Data for cloud applications. IEEE Trans. Cloud Comput. **PP**(99), 1
9. Gokulnath, K., Uthariaraj, R.: Game theory based trust model for cloud environment. Sci. World J. (2015)
10. Yahyaoui, H.: A trust-based game theoretical model for web services collaboration. Knowl. Based Syst. **27**, 162–169 (2012)
11. Hassan, M.M., Abdullah-Al-Wadu, M., Almogren, A., Rahman, S.K., Alelaiwi, A., Alamri, A., Hamid, M.: QoS and trust-aware coalition formation game in data-intensive cloud federations. Concurr. Comput. Pract. Exp. **28**, 2889–2905 (2015)
12. Muchahari, M.K., Sinha, S.K.: A new trust management architecture for cloud computing environment. In: IEEE International Symposium on Cloud and Services Computing (ISCOS) (2012)
13. Kim, H., Lee, H., Kim, W., Kim, Y.: A trust evaluation model for QoS guarantee in cloud systems. Int. J. Grid Distrib. Comput. **3**(1), 1–10 (2010)
14. Tang, M., Dai, X., Liu, J., Chen, J.: Towards a trust evaluation middleware for cloud service selection. Future Gener. Comput. Syst. **74**, 302–312 (2016)
15. Guo, J., Chen, R.: A classification of trust computation models for service-oriented internet of things systems. In: 2015 IEEE International Conference on Services Computing (SCC) (2015)
16. Wang, Y., Lu, Y.-C., Chen, I.-R., Cho, J.-H., Swami, A., Lu, C.-T.: LogitTrust: a logit regression-based trust model for mobile ad hoc networks (2015)
17. Resnick, P., Zeckhauser, R.: Trust among strangers in internet transactions: empirical analysis of eBay's reputation system. Econ. Internet E-commer. **11**(2), 23–25 (2002)
18. Nitti, M., Girau, R., Atzori, L.: Trustworthiness management in the social internet of things. IEEE Trans. Knowl. Data Eng. **26**(5), 1253–1266 (2014)

19. Freedman, D.A.: Statistical Models: Theory and Practice. Cambridge University Press, Cambridge (2009)
20. He, D., Peng, Z., Hong, L., Zhang, Y.: A social reputation management for web communities. In: International Conference on Web-Age Information Management (2011)
21. Gutowska, A., Sloane, A.: Evaluation of reputation metric for the B2C e-Commerce reputation system. In: WEBIST (2009)

Opinions Sandbox: Turning Emotions on Topics into Actionable Analytics

Feras Al-Obeidat[1], Eleanna Kafeza[1], and Bruce Spencer[2(✉)]

[1] Zayed University, Abu Dhabi, UAE
[2] University of New Brunswick, Fredericton, NB, Canada
bspencer@unb.ca

Abstract. The Opinions Sandbox is a running prototype that accesses comments collected from customers of a particular product or service, and calculates the overall sentiment toward that product or service. It performs topic extraction, displays the comments partitioned into topics, and presents a sentiment for each topic. This helps to quickly digest customers' opinions, particularly negative ones, and sort them by the concerns expressed by the customers. These topics are now considered issues to be addressed. The Opinions Sandbox does two things with this list of issues. First, it simulates the social network of the future, after rectifying each issue. Comments with positive sentiment regarding this rectified issues are synthesized, they are injected into the comment corpus, and the effect on overall sentiment is produced. Second, it helps the user create a plan for addressing the issues identified in the comments. It uses the quantitative improvement of sentiment, calculated by the simulation in the first part, and it uses user-supplied cost estimates of the effort required to rectify each issue. Sets of possible actions are enumerated and analysed showing both the costs and the benefits. By balancing these benefits against these costs, it recommends actions that optimize the cost/benefit tradeoff.

Keywords: Social commerce · Opinion extraction · Topic extraction · Actionable analytics

1 Introduction

Sentiment analysis and topic extraction have been very active research fields in recent years. The emergence of social media and the availability of a vast amount of user-produced information, make it possible to automatically identify users' emotions about the topics they discuss. Although data from a variety of social media have been analyzed for different purposes, the processing of data related to users' opinions as expressed in reviews has been of major interest.

Existing work has focused on providing useful information to users who want to check the sentiment expressed by others with respect to a business, service or product before buying it or marketers who want to know the general sentiment for their brands [5]. While the problem of topic extraction and discovering of sentiments polarity has been recently addressed in the literature [2–4]. there is

© ICST Institute for Computer Sciences, Social Informatics and Telecommunications Engineering 2018
F. Belqasmi et al. (Eds.): AFRICATEK 2017, LNICST 206, pp. 110–119, 2018.
https://doi.org/10.1007/978-3-319-67837-5_11

no existing work to examine how topics and related sentiments can be used for providing actionable analytics for businesses. By actionable analytics, we mean data analysis and metrics that can enable businesses to better understand and improve their clients' opinions about their products and services.

In this work, we propose the *Opinions Sandbox*, a framework integrating topic extraction, sentiment analysis for extracting topics and their associated sentiments from an opinion database, and analytics for recommending actions. We propose a set of metrics that can contribute to developing exact strategies for influencing customers' opinions. Our methodology is based on existing popular techniques, including Latent Dirichlet Allocation (LDA) [6] for topic extraction, and the "bag-of-words" sentiment analysis algorithm where polarity is determined based on the frequency of occurrence of positive/negative words in a document. As a next post-processing step, we apply a procedure to incrementally inject into the corpus, comments that express opinions with the polarity of our choice. Thus we have a clear perceptive on how to influence the corpus. Although, business cannot inject opinions in social media, our Opinions Sandbox tool, gives insights on the number and style of opinions that could be generated for the specific topic and the specific customer base. Injected comments simulate the future situation after the business owner has taken steps to rectify the conditions that led customers to express negative opinions. This allows the business owner to determine the effect of various rectifying steps, and to decide which to do. We describe our running prototype that implements the these ideas.

We experiment on our ideas using the Opinosis 1.0 dataset [16] that contains reviews for many businesses. Our approach can be easily extended to any type of social media content. We use LDA and a frequency-based algorithm for opinion mining but our approach can work with any selection and combination of topic analysis and sentiment analysis algorithms. Our contribution is to provide actionable analytics for creating efficient strategies that can influence the opinions and the discussions of the customers.

The rest of this paper is organized as follows: we discuss related work, present the Opinions Sandbox idea, and describe an example implementation that provides recommendations that balance minimizing costs with maximizing social opinion. We discuss the main points and point to future work.

2   Related Work

While the problem of topic extraction has been addressed in the past, in recent years research is relating topic extraction with sentiment analysis. In their work [8] the authors are interested to mine users' opinions on Weblogs, analyzing the sentiments for subtopics. In their approach the authors propose a probabilistic mixture model called Topic Sentiment Mixture (TSM) where words are sampled by a mixture model of background language, topic language and two sentiment language models. They present a mechanism for extracting subtopics, associating with every subtopic a positive or a negative sentiment and how the opinions over a topic change over time. Their approach does not use LDA and the sentiment model is applied as a post-processing step to the topic discovery.

In their work [2] the authors present JST, a method that is using a weakly-supervised approach to draw words taking into consideration both topics and sentiment labels from a corpus of documents thus extending LDA. As a result, JST performs document level sentiment classification where topics and sentiments are detected simultaneously while it can extract sentiment oriented topics effectively evaluating the sentiment of each topic. In [1] the authors extend JST proposing the Sentiment LDA, where sentiment labels are associated to topics instead of documents and introduce sentiment dependency in their calculations. In more recent work, [11], the authors argue that the sentiment should not be used to influence the topic as done in JST but sentiment polarities as well as topics of text should be analyzed at the same time. They propose Double Latent Dirichlet Allocation (DLDA) for sentiment analysis in short texts. A review of on LDA-based topic extraction in sentiment analysis is presented in [7].

As already presented, there is a diversity of approaches in the literature regarding the extraction of topics and their associated sentiments. In our work, we are not attempting to provide yet another approach in addressing this problem, but we are making a next step and we are considering the following problem: given any approach on topic-sentiment analysis how can we improve the sentiment and how much will it cost to do so.

3   The Opinions Sandbox

Given a set of reviews about a specific product, service or business, such as a specific hotel in a city, we execute Latent Dirichlet Analysis [6], which partitions the reviews into disjoint sets. Each set pertains to a specific aspect mentioned in the reviews, such as the check-in experience, or the cleanliness of the rooms. LDA also generates a set of words associated with each set, from which it is possible to get some idea of the unifying themes and concerns discussed in a given set of comments.

Some of the reviews for a given topic express a positive sentiment, such as "The check-in procedure was a good experience." or "The cleanliness of the room was very satisfactory", while others express a negative sentiment. Some reviews express a combination of views. There are a variety of techniques to assess the overall sentiment or mixture of sentiments attached to a review, and also to any set of reviews, including the entire set. The proposal in this paper is a framework that depends on the existence of some method of extracting the sentiment, but is not dependent on any particular method.

The Opinions Sandbox uses the subsets of reviews as generated by LDA partitioning, and the sentiment assessed for each partition subset, to generate actionable recommendations aimed at addressing the issues mentioned in the reviews and improving future sentiment analysis results. The Opinions Sandbox is a recommendation system to be used by business owners to address their clients' concerns and thereby improve their online profile.

The business owner works cooperatively with the Opinions Sandbox to identify the issues that are both addressable and damaging to the overall sentiment.

After the reviews are partitioned by LDA, the sentiment of each partition is assessed. The business owner can see which partition is least positively assessed and can see the unfavourable reviews in that partition, starting with the least positive. He or she assesses the issues mentioned in the partition assesses whether and to what extent each can be addressed. The Opinions Sandbox generates positive reviews in sufficient number and strength to counter the negative reviews that the business owner is considering to address. Given the generated positive comments, the sentiment within the Opinions Sandbox will rise for the topic. The business owner continues until sufficient positive reviews are generated so that sentiment assessment achieves a level that is satisfactory to the business owner. This gives the business owner a clear understanding of the degree of work that needs to be done in order to redress issues mentioned by customers in the reviews.

Thus the Opinions Sandbox provides an aid by which the business owners can efficiently traverse the set of online reviews and quickly identify any deficiencies in their business offering. First, it use partitioning to cluster the issues on similar topics. Second it assessing the sentiment on each topics. Third it takes advice from the business owner who estimates the degree of work needed to address those issues. Fourth it predicts the overall change in the online opinion after that work is done, by creating simulated positive comments that might arise when the work is done, and re-assesing the sentiment that would result. Finally, it presents a set of options ordered by degree of work, which the business owner can consider as a set of recommendations that maximize his or her return on investment while addressing issues that aggravate customers and negatively affecting the online reviews.

4   An Opinions Sandbox Example Implementation

The Opinions Sandbox is a framework and we also provide a specific implementation in R/Shiny [12]. The framework depends on an LDA-based partitioning of comments and on some technology for assessing sentiment. The implementation uses a concrete method for partitioning documents in the tm package [13] and the topicmodels package [14]. Topic selection is done both by Gibbs [10] and CTM [9] techniques. The user is shown both results. While there are a variety of techniques for assessing comments, the implementation currently uses a straightforward opinion assessment based on assigning sentiment to certain words, either positive and negative. The sentiment of any collection of words, whether a single comment, a cluster of comments, or the entire set of reviews, is based on the number of occurrences of positive and of negative words. The Opinions Sandbox implementation is illustrated using comments collected online and made available publicly from the Opinosis 1.0 Dataset [16]. This dataset consists of 51 files, each containing about 100 comments, selected from various sources.

More specifically, our opinion assessment strategy applies to a single review or to a set of reviews. It considers each review or set of reviews to be a bag of words, which is a multiset, *i.e.* a set of word instances. We use a given set P of words associated with positive sentiment such as "good" and "satisfactory", and a set N of negative words. These categories are provided by the General Inquirer dataset [15]. Given a bag B of word instances, comprising either a single review or a set of reviews, we assess each word instance as either having no sentiment or of having positive or negative sentiment according to whether it belongs to the positive set P or to the negative set N. We associate a sentiment metric S based on each word occurrence: S is the fraction of sentiment words in B that are positive.

$$S(B) = |\{B \cap P\}|/|\{B \cap (P \cup N)\}|$$

Similarly we compute the $N(B)$ to measure the negativeness of the corpus B.

$$N(B) = |\{B \cap N\}|/|\{B \cap (P \cup N)\}|$$

In the Opinions Sandbox framework, it is suggested to simulate the effect of addressing client's issues by creating and injecting positive comments into the reviews. However, in our initial implementation we circumvent this step, because of the simplicity of the sentiment assessment. When the business owner identifies a set of comments to have been addressed, we simulate the result of that work having been done by increasing the positive word count by a number equal to the negative word count. In effect, this simulates having each negative opinion countered by a new positive opinion. For instance, suppose there are 100 sentiment words in a set of reviews, of which 40 are positive and 60 are negative. Given our assessment method, this would generate an assessment of $40/(40 + 60) = 0.4$. Once the business owner deems them as addressable, the future assessment is predicted to be $(40 + 60)/(40 + 60 + 60) = 0.625$, as if 60 new opinions, each expressing a positive sentiment, were added. This strategy will always increase the sentiment of a given set of comments, and will always convert an assessment below 0.5 to one above 0.5.

We also consider a more powerful injection mechanism, where the positive comment completely counters the effect the negative comment. In our previous example with 40 postive and 60 negative comments, the effect of adding 60 new postive comments to counter the negative comments brought the sentiment to 0.625. However, if the positive comments nullify the negative comments, the new sentiment is $(40 + 60)/(40 + 60)$. Currently our system uses this mechanism. The goal, then, is to create a sentiment of 1.0 for the whole corpus.

5   System Description

The flow of the Opinions Sandbox system is described in Fig. 1. The user is free at any time to restart at any section, for instance, to consider a new business, or analyse a new partition. Screen shots of the running system are shown in Figs. 2, 3, 4, 5 and Table 1, which shows the user accessing various parts of the flow mentioned in Fig. 1.

We consider a specific example of a hotel in the San Francisco area. During the review, the business owner is deemed to want to address the comments in

1. Select the business, service or product, Figure 2.
2. Load the comments.
3. Select the number of topics of interest, or use the suggested topics
4. Partition the comments into topics, Figure 3.
5. For each partition:
   a) Review the comments, Figures 5.
   b) Estimate and provide the cost of addressing all comments in each topic.
6. Review the report telling the effect of addressing comments, the cost of doing so and the effect on sentiment, Table 1.

Fig. 1. User's steps: flowchart for opinions sandbox

Opinions Sandbox

Select an entity

bestwestern_hotel_sfo ▾

| Random Topics | Suggested Topics |

Number of topics to view

7

Create Topics

Fig. 2. The start screen allows the user to select reviews for a business, product or service and to choose a number of topics. Thus user can also select from a precomputed selection of topics from this dataset, which is available within the Opinosis 1.0 dataset.

each of the seven topics. The cost of doing so is estimated to be 500, 400, 800, 800, 1200, 1400, and 800, respectively, in some unspecified monetary units. We do so by placing different weight on each of the two criteria, and by ordering the various combinations either by sentiment or by cost. Table 1 show the partial enumeration of the 2^n possible choices of addressing or not addressing each of the $n = 7$ topics. If nothing is done, the cost is zero and the sentiment is predicted to remain at 0.73. If all of the comments are addressed, the cost is 5900, but the online sentiment will have a positive comment for every negative comment, and thus under the stronger form of injection, achieves a high score of 1.

We also provide in this paper the cost and expected resulting sentiment for each of the 2^7 combinations of the the seven sets of comments, in Table 1. As that

Topics

Gibbs	CTM

Show [5 ⬍] entries   Search: [   ]

Topic 1 ⬍	Topic 2 ⬍	Topic 3 ⬍	Topic 4 ⬍	Topic 5 ⬍	Topic 6 ⬍	Topic 7 ⬍
hotel	rooms	location	free	room	service	staff
best	clean	wharf	wine	bathroom	parking	friendly
although	nice	fisherman's	coffee	tuscan	location,	helpful
food	small	perfect	morning	excellent	valet	desk
restaurant	comfortable	cable	really	inn	friendly	front

Fig. 3. Once the number of topics is selected, the user can review the topics that were selected. The user can choose either Gibbs or CTM sampling for partitioning into topics.

Topic 6 (0.52) 136p 125n
Topic 5 (0.64) 147p 84n
Topic 1 (0.73) 308p 116n
Topic 3 (0.75) 357p 116n
Topic 2 (0.77) 446p 134n
Topic 7 (0.78) 366p 104n
Topic 4 (0.79) 384p 103n

Fig. 4. Within a drop down selection list, the user can see the current sentiment for each topic, as well as the number of positive and negative comments. The topics with lowest sentiment are at the top of the list.

table shows, the result of addressing all of the comments is an absolutely positive online sentiment, assuming the stronger form of comment injection where the new positive comment is assumed to override the existing negative comment.

The system then blends two criteria in Table 1, cost and benefit, to make a recommendation of which jobs to do. The blend can be oriented toward lower cost by slightly weighting the cost criterion. In this case the system recommends addressing the comments for topics 1, 2 and 3 at a cost of 1700 to raise the sentiment to 0.86. The system can also be tuned to consider higher sentiment as more important. In this case, the system recommends addressing comments in topics 1, 2, 3, 4 and 7 at a cost of 3,300 and raise the sentiment to 0.93.

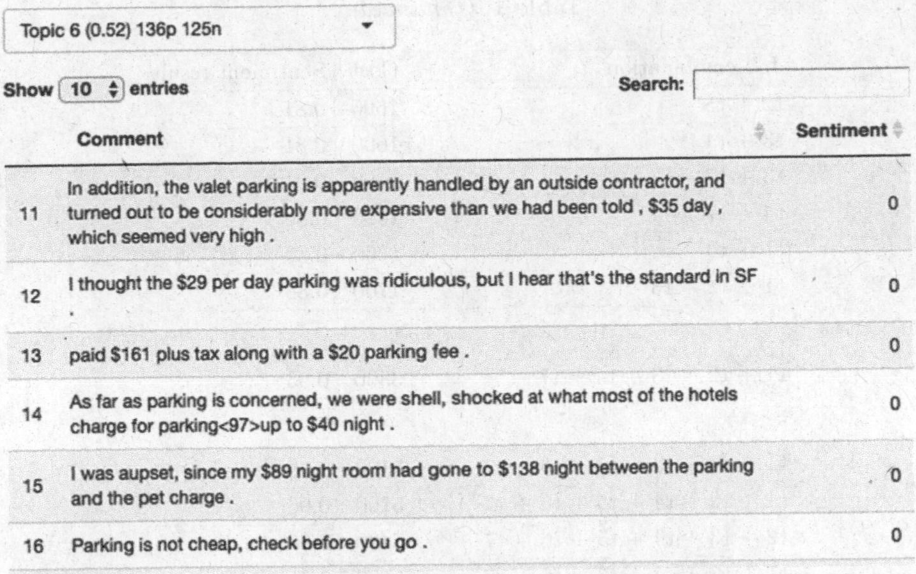

Topic 6 (0.52) 136p 125n ▾

Show [10 ⬍] entries   Search: [   ]

Comment	Sentiment
11 In addition, the valet parking is apparently handled by an outside contractor, and turned out to be considerably more expensive than we had been told , $35 day , which seemed very high .	0
12 I thought the $29 per day parking was ridiculous, but I hear that's the standard in SF .	0
13 paid $161 plus tax along with a $20 parking fee .	0
14 As far as parking is concerned, we were shell, shocked at what most of the hotels charge for parking<97>up to $40 night .	0
15 I was aupset, since my $89 night room had gone to $138 night between the parking and the pet charge .	0
16 Parking is not cheap, check before you go .	0

Fig. 5. Comments are presented along with their sentiment. Parking issues elicit negative sentiment in Topic 6.

Table 1. Description and cost for each job, and the resulting sentiment

Job combination	Cost	Sentiment result
do nothing	0	0.73
t2	400	0.78
t1	500	0.77
t3	800	0.77
t4	800	0.77
t7	800	0.77
t1 + t2	900	0.82
t5	1200	0.76
t2 + t3	1200	0.82
t2 + t4	1200	0.81
t2 + t7	1200	0.81
t1 + t3	1300	0.81
t1 + t4	1300	0.81
t1 + t7	1300	0.81
t6	1400	0.78

(*continued*)

Table 1. (*continued*)

Job combination	Cost	Sentiment result
t2 + t5	1600	0.81
t3 + t4	1600	0.81
t3 + t7	1600	0.81
t4 + t7	1600	0.80
t1 + t5	1700	0.80
t1 + t2 + t3	1700	0.86
⋮	⋮	⋮
t1 + t2 + t3 + t4 + t7	3300	0.93
⋮	⋮	⋮
t1 + t2 + t3 + t5 + t6 + t7	5100	0.96
t1 + t2 + t4 + t5 + t6 + t7	5100	0.96
t2 + t3 + t4 + t5 + t6 + t7	5400	0.96
t1 + t3 + t4 + t5 + t6 + t7	5500	0.95
t1 + t2 + t3 + t4 + t5 + t6 + t7	5900	1.00

6   Conclusions and Future Work

The Opinions Sandbox is a tool that helps business owners to assess the severity of online criticisms. It first partitions the set of online reviews according to topic. Each partition pertains to one or a small set of issues to which the business owner can respond. After working with the business owner to identify the issues, how to resolve them and the degree of effort required, the Opinions Sandbox then injects positive comments that counter the effect on the existing negative comments, thus simulating future situation where the issues are addressed. It allows the business owner to contrast the current online sentiment with a forecast of the future sentiment. The Opinion Sandbox helps the business owner to quantify the amount of work to address issues mentioned, and the result that doing so is likely to have on the online opinion. It enumerates the combinations of actions that can be taken, and the effect of each on the online opinion, so that the most cost-effective method can be found for addressing some or all of the issues. In summary, the Opinions Sandbox helps the business owner to quickly understand the online issues, to consider the possible redress actions, and to find a selection of actions that provides the most expedient way to improve online sentiment.

This product is particularly relevant for developing economies, and in regions including the Middle East and North Africa, where online tourism attracts potential customers making their first visit. These customers rely heavily on online recommendations, sometimes only on these recommendations, before making significant purchases. In future we will experiment with different topic classification techniques, and with different techniques for measuring sentiment. Comment synthesis is a relatively new area and we plan to contribute. We are also planning trials with clients in the tourism industry, where opinions have direct economic impact.

References

1. Li, F., Huang, M., Zhu, X.: Sentiment analysis with global topics and local dependency. In: Proceedings of AAAI, pp. 1371–1376 (2010)
2. Lin, C., He, Y., Everson, R., Ruger, S.: Weakly supervised joint sentiment-topic detection from text. IEEE Trans. Knowl. Data Eng. **24**(6), 1134–1145 (2012)
3. Chen, X., Tang, W., Xu, H., Hu, X.: Double Lda: a sentiment analysis model based on topic model. Paper presented at the 2014 10th International Conference on Semantics, Knowledge and Grids, 27–29 Aug 2014
4. Yin, S., Han, J., Huang, Y., Kumar, K.: Dependency-topic-affects-sentiment-Lda model for sentiment analysis. Paper presented at the 2014 IEEE 26th International Conference on Tools with Artificial Intelligence, 10–12 Nov 2014
5. Go, A., Bhayani, R., Huang, L.: Twitter Sentiment Classification Using Distant Supervision. Technical Report, Stanford University (2009)
6. Blei, D.M., Andrew, Y.N., Michael, I.J., Lafferty, J.: Latent Dirichlet allocation. J. Mach. Learn. Res. **3**(4/5), 993–1022 (2003)
7. Rana, T.A., Cheah, Y.-N., Letchmunan, S.: Topic modeling in sentiment analysis: a systematic review. J. ICT Res. Appl. **10**(1), 76–93 (2016)
8. Mei, Q., Ling, X., Wondra, M., Su, H., Zhai, C.: Topic-Sentiment Mixture: Modelling Facets and Opinions in Weblogs, pp. 171–180 (2007)
9. Blei, D.M., Lafferty, J.D.: A correlated topic model of science. Ann. Appl. Stat. **1**(1), 17–35 (2007)
10. Phan, X.H., Nguyen, L.M., Horiguchi, S.: Learning to classify short and sparse text & web with hidden topics from large-scale data collections. In: Proceedings of the 17th International World Wide Web Conference (WWW 2008), Beijing, China, pp. 91–100 (2008)
11. Xue, C., Tang, W., Xu, H., Hu, X.: Double Lda: a sentiment analysis model based on topic model. In: Proceedings of the 2014 10th International Conference on Semantics, Knowledge and Grids, pp. 49–56. IEEE Computer Society (2014)
12. http://shiny.rstudio.com/
13. Feinerer, I., Hornik, K.: https://cran.r-project.org/web/packages/tm/tm.pdf
14. Grün, B., Hornik, K.: https://cran.rproject.org/web/packages/topicmodels/topicmodels.pdf
15. http://www.wjh.harvard.edu/inquirer/
16. Ganesan, K.A., Zhai, C.X., Han, J.: Opinosis: a graph based approach to abstractive summarization of highly redundant opinions. In: Proceedings of the 23rd International Conference on Computational Linguistics (COLING '10) (2010)

E-Healthcare Knowledge Creation Platform Using Action Research

May Al Taei[(✉)], Eleanna Kafeza, and Omar Alfandi

College of Technological Innovation, Zayed University, Dubai, United Arab Emirates
{May.AlTaei,Eleana.Kafeza,Omar.AlFandi}@zu.ac.ae

Abstract. There has been a long discussion on knowledge creation in the health care environment. Recently, the action research approach is attracting considerable attention. Action research supports a learning process where collaboratively the healthcare stakeholders are cooperating to produce knowledge that will influence their practice. Usually physicians are involved in case study research where information is produced but it is not used to offer insights back to the community. In this paper we propose a healthcare learning platform (HLP) that enables members of the health multidisciplinary communities to collaborate, share up-to-date information and harvest useful evidence. In this e-health platform knowledge is created based on patient feedback, the dynamic creation of communities that involve the participation of several stakeholders and the creation of an action learning environment where problem identification, investigation and planning, action and reflection is a cycle that enables knowledge and experience to contribute to healthcare knowledge creation.

Keywords: E-health · Knowledge creation · Action research

1 Introduction

E-health systems have been evolving the last years towards the direction of generating increased knowledge, value and innovation [3]. Tacit knowledge that resides on the peoples' mind and innovation that can be derived by human interactions are new aspects that need to be considered when we evaluate healthcare systems. Healthcare professionals are exploring new ways if interactions and knowledge sharing and in that process they have incorporated social media in their practice. In [2] the authors show that the benefits of staying connected with colleagues, sharing knowledge and benchmarking have contributed towards the use of social media. On the other hand, time, trust and information anarchy when using social media create reservation. In a similar study [5] a strong network with several related participants, with trust and shared language can be a motivating factor for participating in knowledge creation and knowledge sharing activities. Hence there is a need for an e-health platform that will cater to an adequate set of professionals creating dense network, that will use a variety tools of digital communications tools, that will foster a cross-disciplinary approach and will do in a structured and trusted environment.

© ICST Institute for Computer Sciences, Social Informatics and Telecommunications Engineering 2018
F. Belqasmi et al. (Eds.): AFRICATEK 2017, LNICST 206, pp. 120–125, 2018.
https://doi.org/10.1007/978-3-319-67837-5_12

On the other hand, in the discussion of knowledge creation, the action research approach is attracting considerable attention. Action research supports a learning process where collaboratively the stakeholders are cooperating to produce knowledge that will influence their practice. Action research is cyclic process where the participants are sharing information, planning and design action in order to address a problem, then they reflect and they re-execute the cycle [10]. Although usually physicians are involved in case study research where information is produced, it is not used to offer insights back to the community.

In this work we propose an innovative platform in the context of e-health that will enable the sharing of information and contribute towards knowledge creation. Our proposal is motivated by the recent observation in the bibliography that sharing best practices, mistakes and feedback exchanges, contributes to better and innovative health care services.

2   Related Work

In recent research on healthcare systems, the need for the development of user-centered systems which span across different domains of health and incorporate ethical and social care aspects has been identified [1]. The need of digital collaborative environments has been identified in the literature, where the authors in [4] present a survey of knowledge exchange portals and conclude that they are beneficial because they provide a one-stop point for information sharing while identifying the need to further examine their contribution to evidence-informed decision making. Out platform is making a next step and provides a digital place where not only content is retrieved but people are communicating, different levels and type of data are provided and this is done across disciplines in a dynamic environment.

An interesting approach on patient value co-creation is presented in [6] where the authors identify its need and importance and examine the factors that motivate the patients to active participation. In the same context in a previous work [7] the authors identify as cooperation, co-learning, connecting with family, friends, doctors and other health professionals, co-production and positive thinking as activities that can contribute to measure for patient value co-creation. Our approach considers all these aspects and provides a digital environment that supports and strengths all the above activities.

Although several digital solutions have been proposed in the literature for healthcare collaboration most of them caster only to a subset of collaboration. For example, in [7] the authors propose a platform for safe and easy communication between patients and healthcare providers. In [8], the authors propose a cloud based solution for sharing of clinical images between clinicians and researchers. While the authors in [9] identify the problem of poor collaboration of clinicians and statisticians and provide a platform to enhance this collaboration.

From the above discussion it is evident that there is lack of a platform that will be able to be dynamically create and provide a forum consisting form a diverse set of healthcare stakeholders, enabling knowledge exchange and creation. This gap is addressed by our research and by our proposed platform.

3   The Healthcare Learning Platform (HLP)

In this paper we propose the Healthcare Learning Platform (HLP), as a new and innovative approach towards knowledge creation. HLP platform creates a collaborative environment where users can exchange information and create knowledge. The platform supports the action research knowledge creation cycle with a variety of tools. The main parts of the platform are the stakeholder involvement, the community action research module and the stakeholder profiling. Figure 1 presents the HLP system architecture.

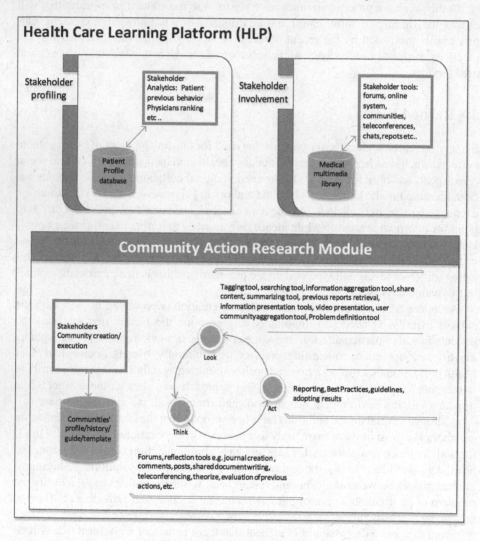

Fig. 1. HLP system architecture

3.1 Stakeholder Involvement

Stakeholders like patient will participate in the platform contributing with their lived experiences being able to convey the experience through a diverse set of tools and formats i.e. uploading images, videos, chatting in forums etc. Our learning platform values the idea that patient experience and feedback is central to the healthcare learning process and should be recorded and taken into consideration. Such participation challenges the traditional way of knowledge creation where a set of experts choose the information based on which knowledge is created. It suggests an expectation of a partnership with the patients and other stakeholders where through a collaborative relationship she/he can contribute to learning.

This module will enable the upload of learning material and information, in various formats and from various tools and it will provide a set of tools that the stakeholders can use for uploading the data, for labeling thus adding semantics information to the data module. Stakeholders can communicate and interact in this process as well, outside and within the communities.

HLP adopts a critical reflective approach that enables dialogue to happen. It incorporates evidence based practice but at the same time it considers the knowledge contributed by the patients and other relevant stakeholders. These lived experiences are creating multiple stories and present multiple possibilities. In this way, physicians can critically reflect on their own practices and result in the transformation of their practical knowledge.

3.2 Stakeholder Profiling

Each user/stakeholder will participate in the platform with a profile. The profile will register a physician with relevant information. The profile of a user will constitute with information provided by the user himself and statistics that are derived based on the user behavior within the platform.

The information derived by user participation will be extracted by the evidence of user behavior within the platform. This information shall consist of metrics like the number of communities that the user participated, the number of posts he contributed to the communities, the number of cases he shared, the number of times the patients commended on the user (positively/neutral/negative), the number of times the fellow doctors commented on the cases/data the user uploaded to the platform and the nature of comments (positive/neutral/negative). The stakeholder profiling will have a part that will be public so that other members can view information about the user and a private one. It will be mainly used by the community creation submodule of the Community Action Research Module. Communities will be created by marching the community requirements to users' profiles. As a result, HLP will support a dynamic community creation and deletion environment that will be able to address the changing needs and unexpected requests for knowledge creation.

3.3 Community Action Research Module

HLP is supporting community based action research for healthcare. Communities are statically and dynamically created within the platform based on their common interest on a problem. The purpose of each community is to contribute to extending and augmenting the understanding of the problem and its surrounding environment and thus resolve the problem while creating new knowledge.

The main principle of community creation is to support a multidisciplinary group where several stakeholders will participate. Possible participants could be physicians of different level of expertise, physicians from different disciplines, researchers, clinical staff, patients etc. Several search tools and guidelines will be offered for the static and dynamic creation of the communities.

HLP will support the basic action research routine: look, think and act by providing a road map where participatory action research can take place. In the look phase information will be gathered from different resources. This information will be structured and the participants will contribute to define and describe the problem. In the second phase the exploration and analyze process will occur. Physicians will comment on the information, analyze it, interpret and explain it (how and why things are as they are and try to theorize). In the last stage action will occur. A report will be build that will describe plans for future action. This process will be re-cycled as the same or similar problems will re-occur and the communities will discuss them. In each cycle the report from previous cycles and previous communities will be considered as part of the collected information and will be evaluated and added to the cycle. The community will reflect on the previous results, and decide upon modification on their actions.

This knowledge creation is a collective process where the links and the relationships within the community are empowered. Since these steps cannot occur in a strict sequential manner, HLP for each community will provide tools (i.e. libraries for information uploading, sorting and collection, tags to characterize a contribution to the community as look, think or act, grouping of the posts based on the tags etc.) so that each community member will be able to express his/her opinion but at the same time the platform will contribute to maintain an action research approach towards producing a result.

HLP provides the platform for the interested parties to make meaning of their experiences as a result of their own experience and their relationships to others in the context of their environment. It enables the implementation of participatory action research approach enhanced with the use of communication technologies thus improving the engagement and community interactions compared to traditional approaches. For example, physicians can create online journals where they can record their experience on a subject and reflect on the changes as influenced by other physicians, their data, the patients' info and the clinical and other relevant participants.

In this process the participants will have the chance to reflect on the situation and they can address misconceptions, misinterpretations, share a broader set of information and be involved in a constructive analysis. This sharing of a diverse knowledge, cases, opinions and expertise by physicians and patients will improve the community life by improving healthcare practice. The idea behind the HLP platform is not only to produce knowledge that will potentially be published in journals or magazines or that will provide a set of best practices. It goes beyond these objectives and aims to make a difference and improve the everyday life of the participants. Hence physicians that participate in HLP platform should improve their everyday practice and their reputation, patients should have a better treatment, academics should be able to produce quality research etc.

4 Conclusions and Future Work

In this paper we presented a system architecture for an innovative system for e- health-care knowledge creation. Our proposed solutions take into consideration that there is a need for a multidisciplinary involvement and interaction when creating knowledge in the healthcare field. Moreover, it addressed the problem that knowledge creation can be better served not by specific platforms that enable communication among specific stake-holders but by a generic platform that will allow the dynamic creation and termination of communities based on the information needs and the stakeholders' skills, treating each problem separately. As a future work, we intent to implement a pilot project and run a pilot study.

References

1. May, C.R.: Making sense of technology adoption in healthcare: meso-level considerations. BMC Med. **13**, 921 (2015)
2. Panahi, S., Watson, J., Partridge, H.: Social media and physicians: exploring the benefits and challenges. Health J. **22**(2), 99–112 (2016)
3. Miller, L.M.: E-health: knowledge generation, value intangibles, and intellectual capital. Int. J. Healthc. Manag. **8**(2), 100–111 (2015)
4. Quinn, E., Huckel-Schneider, C., Campbell, D., Seale, H., Milat, A.: How can knowledge exchange portals assist in knowledge management for evidence-informed decision making in public health? BMC Public Health **12**(14), 443 (2014)
5. Zhao, J., Sejin, H., Wi, R.: The influence of social capital on knowledge creation in online health communities. Inf. Technol. Manag. **17**(4), 311–321 (2016)
6. Zhao, J., Wang, T., Fanm, X.: Patient value co-creation in online health communities: Social identity effects on customer knowledge contributions and membership continuance intentions in online health communities. J. Serv. Manag. **26**(1), 72–96 (2015)
7. Font, J., Magdalena, D., Soldevila, M., Pascual, J.: Canal Paciente. Platform for collaboration and communication between patients and healthcare providers. Int. J. Integr. Care (IJIC) **16**(6), 1–2 (2016)
8. Doel, T., Shakir, D., Pratt, R., Aertsen, M., Moggridge, J., Bellon, E., David, A., et al.: Gift-cloud: a data sharing and collaboration platform for medical imaging research. Comput. Methods Programs Biomed. **139**, 181–190 (2017)
9. Raptis, D., Mettler, T., Tzanas, K., Graf, R.: A novel open-source web-based platform promoting collaboration of healthcare professionals and biostatisticians: A design science approach. Inf. Health Soci. Care **37**(1), 22–36 (2012)
10. Sankara, S., Dick, B., Passfield, R. (eds.): Effective Change Management Through Action Research and Action Learning: Concepts, Perspectives, Processes and Applications, pp. 1–20. Southern Cross University Press, Lismore, Australia (2001)

Web Services and Software Engineering

Framework for Dynamic Web Services Composition Guided by Live Testing

Mounia Elqortobi[✉], Jamal Bentahar, and Rachida Dssouli

CIISE, Concordia University, 1455 Boulevard de Maisonneuve O,
Montreal, QC H3G 1M8, Canada
m_elqort@live.concordia.ca,
{jamal.bentahar,rachida.dssouli}@concordia.ca

Abstract. Web services allow businesses to offer their services and consumers to retrieve and use them. Businesses own some services and can reuse services that belong to other businesses to perform new transactional activities. By doing this, they achieve outsourcing, cost, and resources optimization. The advances in design principles, architectures, protocols and languages have helped to solve some of the problems related to the composition of business applications. Web service composition technology emerged as a new approach for efficient automation and integration of business processes based on Service-Oriented Architecture (SOA). SOA provides a set of principles to create distributed computing systems that support the creation of loosely coupled applications in heterogeneous and distributed environment. Service computing or engineering covers the entire lifecycle of services that include: modeling, creation, realization, deployment, publication, discovery, composition, delivery, collaboration, monitoring, adaptation, optimization, and management. In this paper we propose an architecture for dynamic composition of web services that is guided by live testing technique. The main focus is on the framework and composition requirements.

Keywords: Web services · Dynamic composition · Live testing · Runtime monitoring · Runtime trace analysis · Architecture framework

1 Introduction

Service-Oriented Architecture (SOA) consists of a wide range of standards, specifications and tools. Standards from W3C and OASIS have been established to manage web service lifecycles and service-client communication. These standardized protocols and proposed languages played key roles in the development of web services. The challenges in service composition are mainly related to live real-time dynamic service composition: (1) efficient web service discovery; (2) efficient selection of basic services at run time; (3) on the fly verification and validation of composite web service; (4) user preferences driven discovery of basic web services; (5) context aware composition of services; (6) end to end quality proprieties of composed services: determination and guaranty; (7) dynamic assessment of quality of service; (8) verification of web service selection for transactional composition; (9) billing and pricing management; (10) service

© ICST Institute for Computer Sciences, Social Informatics and Telecommunications Engineering 2018
F. Belqasmi et al. (Eds.): AFRICATEK 2017, LNICST 206, pp. 129–139, 2018.
https://doi.org/10.1007/978-3-319-67837-5_13

management, monitoring and adaptation; (11) intellectual and ownership rights. In this paper we only address a subset of the listed challenges.

The paper has the following sections: background information, related work, requirements for dynamic composition of web services, architecture framework for dynamic composite of web services, and then the conclusion.

2   Background Information

Service composition is used for application integration. A service is a means to transfer information from one component to the other. It can transfer information such as a message. A service is operable from any type of platform or operating system. It is in itself flexible. It is well known that a service has the following set of principles to be followed: (1) standardized contract; (2) loose coupling; (3) abstraction; (4) service reusability; (5) service autonomy; (6) service statelessness; (7) service discoverability; (8) composability. It is also known that Service Oriented Architecture (SOA) has 6 core values: business, strategic goals, intrinsic inter-operability, shared services, flexibility, and evolutionary refinement. The remaining parts of this section present the life cycle of web service composition, and related of service composition, dynamic composition, live testing and testability, runtime monitoring, runtime verification and runtime trace analysis.

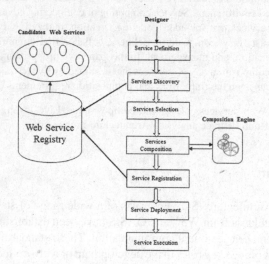

Fig. 1. The life cycle of services composition [30].

To better understand what is involved in composition of services, we introduce its lifecycle. The life cycle of web services composition is now well described in the literature [30]. It is composed of several phases (Fig. 1 shows the life cycle) that starts with a user's request for an added value service that doesn't exist as a standalone service. The request is forwarded to a service designer that will define the new service as a composition of existing services. Composition templates or design pattern can help.

This will trigger several activities that compose this life cycle such as services discovery, services selection, and composition of a service. An obtained composite service will be registered, and it will be deployed and executed as per the user's request.

To our knowledge there is no work addressing dynamic composition of services that is guided by live testing. In the following, we will address related work of all activities that are required by runtime composition of web services that is guided by live testing.

2.1 Dynamic Composition of Services

There are two types of service composition: (1) static that is done at design time [3]; and (2) dynamic that adapt to dynamic environment changes [1, 3, 42]. The authors of [4] offer a survey reviewing web composition. Paper [25] offers a framework for dynamic web service composition to different components. They use a graph-based approach to the web service composition. They take into consideration both functional and non-functional properties. The authors in [5, 6] identify a lifecycle for a web service composition. In each, a business aspect to identify the need for the composite web service is identified. In [2], there is a proposal for an approach that will render the composition of web services by rendering them self-aware of the context in which they are being composed. They intend to augment the semantics defining a web service in order to allow it to grow and adapt their behavior to a changing context. The authors have generated a UML activity diagram portraying a scenario to which an OWL-Ctx ontology representing their context, hence supporting their approach. In [17], context awareness is also in study for parallel multi-core components. This entails the possibility of executing multiple tasks in parallel which improves speed.

Nonfunctional requirements are important to service users. In [8], requirements are accessibility, availability, reliability, and performance. Additional requirements in [8] are mentioned such as execution price, execution duration and reputation. The requirements are non-functional characteristics that aim to ensure that both the client and service provider's experience with web services is up to scale. The authors in [7] have adapted a model they named *publish-find-bind* by integrating certification and verification transitions in relation to the quality of service. In [9] a concern related to security is raised in terms of authentication, authorization, confidentiality, cryptography, accountability, security administration, and non-repudiation.

Dynamic composition of web services palliates a known issue with static composition of web services: the inability to adapt to a changing context. This type of composition opens the path for live-testing as it pushes research towards self-awareness and context-awareness [10, 11, 27, 31]. Self-awareness of the web service would facilitate and optimize the dynamic composition due to the ability to satisfy fluctuating business requirements, in being aware of the new context, and integrating it. The challenge is the performance and the means for data storage. The amount of data needed for a service can be voluminous, and its performance could be affected. Making a context self-aware has been discussed and analyzed in many articles such as in [2, 10, 11, 17]. In [12], the authors discuss the design of an architecture to support and maintain self-awareness and enable live-testing through dynamic composition of web services.

2.2   Live Testing and Testability Related Work

Testing is the most used validation technique. It is expensive and technically challenging. A lot has been done on software testing. In this paper, the focus is on testing web services for their composition [43]. Live testing/runtime testing is an emerging research topic that is necessary to update at runtime composition of services with high availability requirements. Runtime testing is performed during the normal operation of services within its execution environment [38]. Most of the runtime testing approaches are platform dependent. For general work on runtime testing, concepts can be found in Brenner et al. publication [35]. All the proposed runtime testing techniques assume a predefined set of test cases. The research question is how to select a subset of test cases to be applied in relation with an observed event, a property violation, or an identified context. Runtime testing is applied in areas of embedded systems as a built-in-test [37], finance and e-commerce, as well as telecommunication systems. Gonzalez et al. [36] defined prerequisites to runtime testing, such as test sensitivity and test isolation notions, which are also important for runtime composition. A most recent work on safe and efficient runtime testing of distributed systems has been proposed by Lahami et al. [38] where the distribution of monitors and tester is the main focus. This work uses a set of predefined test cases. This limits their ability to generate additional test cases to adapt to unforeseen bugs and to diagnose their causes. The originality of our proposed framework is the architecture that allows the generation of test cases on the fly. The generation algorithm is guided by runtime trace analysis and objectives.

2.3   Runtime Monitoring, Verification and Trace Analysis

Early work on software monitoring focused on off-line monitoring, where data is collected at runtime and analyzed off-line. Runtime verification is an approach that allows insertion of services properties into the systems' code and verify them at execution time. The objective is to verify that services' properties are not violated, and the traces satisfy the composite service specification. The research challenges of runtime monitoring and runtime verification include constructing efficient monitors under the assumption of resources sharing with the observed service. The main concepts and foundations of runtime monitoring can be found in Viswanathan's PhD thesis and a survey [32, 33]. Survey and future challenges of distributed monitoring are addressed in [34]. Model based runtime verification/monitoring has been addressed in several papers listed in Zhao's early work [41].

Runtime trace analysis faces the same challenges as runtime monitoring and verification activities. They both require a valid specification of expected behavior, computation and memory resources. In addition, they should not interfere with the service and degrade its performance. Trace analysis is more specific to service behavior with the intention to detect nonconformance to the specification. Very often, they differ in the level of granularity in data collection, a trace analyzer is high level granularity in comparison to a monitor. To the best of our knowledge, a runtime composition of distributed services supported by guided live testing has not been studied yet.

3   An Architecture Framework for Dynamic Composite Web Services

We propose an architecture framework for live testing guided dynamic composition based on a broker (see Fig. 2). These types of architecture were used for QoS based selection of services for composition [37, 39]. We propose that the composition broker not only guides the client in offering web services composition, but also handles the guided dynamic composition itself and the verification aspect of the composition. In this architecture, modules for dynamic web service composition and live testing are located on the same system for efficiency and performance reasons. Depending on a type of service and the resources available at service provider, as well as the flexibility in instrumenting the service, the monitor can be either an insertion of monitoring code or a mobile agent attached to the monitored service. If the provided platform does not allow such insertion, then observation, monitoring and data collection are performed at the broker side. Runtime monitoring also helps in acquiring self-awareness during dynamic composition which allow adaptation of services.

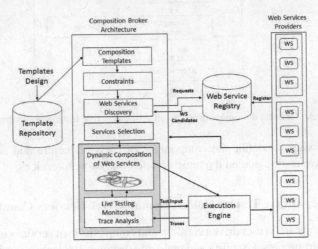

Fig. 2. Broker based architecture for live test guided dynamic composition of web services.

In this architecture we assume that composition templates and constraints exist or can be created by the service developer. The issue that we would like to address is to be able to abort or rollback the dynamic composition if needed after a step in testing. For this purpose, the dynamic composition needs to be guided (validated) by live testing.

The dynamic composition of services guided by live testing algorithm is depicted below (see Fig. 3). We use a composition algorithm that takes a pair of web services that have been selected. Then, monitor the states of services, collect information for possible rollback if needed. Afterwards, test web services invocations in sequence with a set of available inputs. In doing this, we use testing strategy, collect the outputs, and return a verdict by comparing the observed output with the expected one. If the comparison holds, the live testing module will generate the next invocation (composition).

If the observed output is different from the expected one, then the composition can simply abort if there is no damage or rollback, and move to the next pair of services to be composed. Monitoring and testing are under timing constraints to allow real-time dynamic composition.

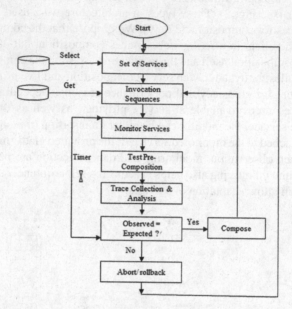

Fig. 3. General dynamic composition guided by live testing algorithm.

In the following we define the components of the architecture and address some challenges of live testing guided dynamic composition of web services.

3.1 Challenges of Live Testing Guided Dynamic Web Services Composition

The open problems are in user driven creation and composition of services in the context of dynamic environments. Usability and real-time discovery, selection, verification and composition of services are important issues. Scalability is becoming an important issue when dealing with large number of services. Proprieties of services are hidden problems such as accuracy, reliability, security and QoS that need to be reviewed and dealt with in the context of dynamicity and real-time composition of services. The following will describe the set of activities that are needed and is specific to live test guided dynamic composition of services.

3.2 Live Composition of Services

The aim is to develop techniques that compose services without stopping their operation. This type of composition faces several challenges, such as their readiness to be composed, how to capture information about services that are in operation and need to be composed, how to capture and isolate components that need to be composed, how to analyze the impact of the composition on services' behavior, properties, and performance, and most importantly, how to foresee it before each step of the composition, how to verify services proprieties in run time, and how to rollback a composition that might impact a services' reliability, security and correctness. Live composition needs a pre-composition phase that is dedicated for instrumentation during the operation of the services to be composed. This step is to be done at runtime. Instrumentation is necessary for information acquisition, run time monitoring or verification, run time testing, and test result analysis for live guided testing.

Live composition is based on specification requires modeling at different levels of abstraction. It requires investigating both cases: (1) shared computation infrastructure between composition and services infrastructures; (2) collaborative computation infrastructure for composition, verification, testing and trace analysis to achieve the required performance and efficiency for runtime activities. The composition of services is a recursive activity that is performed by selecting, monitoring, isolating, pre-testing, integrating, verifying and post-testing all the services and their integration. To perform all the mentioned activities, scheduling of activities plays an important role. Contributions will be in regards to the development and construction of a composition engine of distributed services that is supported by a guided runtime testing, runtime trace analysis and diagnostics.

3.3 Live Testing of Services Composition

The objective of live testing is to be able to test services while they are in operation. This technique is complementary to traditional active and passive testing. Live testing requires instrumentation, monitoring and test results analysis. It can be used in conjunction with runtime verification of proprieties. The published research considers an existing set of test cases and a selection taking place during the execution of the service. This is in order to avoid interference between testing activity and the normal operations of the service and to minimize the impact of the performance. In this case, test cases are generated offline following testing method and test generation algorithm. The challenge in this type of testing is the selection of a minimal subset of suitable test cases that will reveal composition related bugs. This technique requires isolation of the services that are to be tested. A sensitivity analysis is carried out and test architecture is known or deduced. Guided Live Testing generates useful test cases on the fly and applies them in anticipation manner on selected and isolated services. Guided means that the generation of next inputs are based on previous inputs and the analysis of outputs (traces).

The generation algorithms have important performance requirements. Contrary to offline test generation algorithms, the guided live test generation algorithms should have strategies on what to test and why. How to perform distributed testing at runtime while avoiding interferences with the services under test. In addition, the challenge in performance and efficiency will be linked to what to drop and what to test. Guided live test algorithm uses objectives to generate suitable test cases that will detect interaction, and violations of specification and properties. Guided live testing is useful in the case of runtime composition of services, it helps cope with unexpected events and conditions during the composition, and it helps locate the bug by generating additional test cases and performing runtime trace analysis. It can also help rollback the composition if needed.

3.4 Runtime Monitoring

Runtime monitors construction is still a research challenge. It is related to the instrumentation and trace collection at certain locations of the services. The monitors share resources with the monitored services, and have some impact on resource utilization in terms of computation and memory consumption; they may degrade the services performance. The additional challenge is the selection of the location of monitors and their choreography, coordination and possible migration. Monitors can be seen as mobile agents that can migrate according to the tasks and the locality of observation to be gathered. Monitors may be constructed with sort of contract to be preserved. We are going to build on our strengths in verification of mobile agents and their commitments with dynamic setting. Runtime verification of additional properties is known as lightweight verification technique that verifies whether a service execution satisfies or violates a set of given properties. It is partial to avoid state space explosion problem. It also has the capacity to scale with the number of proprieties to verify. Normally, runtime verification is implemented by constructing specific monitors.

3.5 Run-Time Test Results Analysis

Also known as oracle is an analyzer of test results with the intention to check whether the service under test has behaved correctly on a particular test case execution. It is a comparison between the observed behavior and a specified behavior that is assumed to be correct. Runtime test result analyzer is more complex due to time consumption and interferences with services operations and performance. For that particular reason runtime analyzers are very often partial. The challenges are many: how to filter only useful and relevant traces to analyze, existence of a specification, test architecture, computation resources and memory, execution efficiency, and time budgeting strategies. In this proposed research we will address the specific case of live guided test case generation, where a test input is generated based on the analysis of previous traces (outputs) and a model specification. This implies that trace analysis has to be partial and performed at runtime. In addition, not all traces are important to analyze, a selection of what to analyze and it dependency and impact on next operation of the service is important and challenging.

4 Conclusion

The objective of this is the development of broker-based architecture that allow QoS/ guided live test dynamic composition of web services. The goal of the broker is to support live composition of web services with QoS. In addition, we addressed the problem of web services testing. The requirements for the implementation of the proposed architecture are the development of (1) efficient web services discovery methods; (2) dynamic web service selection with QoS constraints and user preferences such as price; (3) dynamic composition and on the fly verification; (4) reliable execution of composite services; (5) approaches and tools for dynamic composition of mobile services; (6) develop a framework that will allow users to create mobile services and compose value added services on the fly; (7) develop a framework for user driven creation and composition of mobile services that include cloud computing (for the back end).

References

1. Ordonez, A., Alcázar, V., Corrales, J., Falcarin, P.: Automated context aware composition of Advanced Telecom Services for environmental early warnings. Expert Syst. Appl. **41**, 5907–5916 (2014)
2. Furno, A., Zimeo, E.: Context-aware Composition of Semantic Web Services. Springer Science + Business Media, New York (2014)
3. Khadka, R., Sapkota, B.: An evaluation of dynamic web service composition approaches, pp. 67–79 (2010)
4. Sheng, Q.Z., Qiao, X., Vasilakos, A.V., Szabo, C., Bourne, S., Xu, X.: Web services composition: a decade's overview. Inf. Sci. **280**, 218–238 (2014)
5. Aslam, M.A., Shen, J., Auer, S., Herrmann, M.: An integration life cycle for semantic web services composition. In: 11th International Conference on Computer Supported Cooperative Work in Design. IEEE, pp. 490–495 (2007)
6. Moghaddam, M., Davis, J.G.: Service selection in web service composition: a comparative review of existing approaches. In: Web Services Foundations. Springer New York, pp. 321–346 (2014)
7. Ran, S.: A model for web services discovery with QoS. ACM Sigecom Exchanges **4**, 1–10 (2003)
8. Zeng, L., Benatallah, B., Dumas, M., Kalagnanam, J., Sheng, Q. Z.: Quality driven web services composition. In: Proceedings of the 12th International Conference on World Wide Web, pp. 411–421. ACM (2003)
9. Kuyoro Shade, O., Frank, I., Awodele, O., Okolie Samuel, O.: Quality of service (Qos) issues in web services. IJCSNS Int. J. Comput. Sci. Netw. Secur. **12**(1), 94–97 (2012)
10. Abowd, G.D., Dey, A.K., Brown, P.J., Davies, N., Smith, M., Steggles, P.: Towards a better understanding of context and context-awareness. In: International Symposium on Handheld and Ubiquitous Computing, pp. 304–307. Springer, Heidelberg (1999)
11. Hafiddi, H., Baidouri, H., Nassar, M., Kriouile, A.: An aspect based pattern for context-awareness of services. Int. J. Comput. Sci. Netw. Secur. **12**(1), 71–78 (2012)
12. Mustafa, F., McCluskey, T.L.: Dynamic web service composition. In: 2009 IEEE International Conference on Computer Engineering and Technology, ICCET 2009, vol. 2, pp. 463–467. IEEE (2009)
13. Qiao, M., Khendek, F., Serhani, A., Dssouli, R., Glitho, R.: Automatic QoS adaptation for composite web services. In: IEEE International Conference on IIT, pp. 180–184 (2008)
14. Valipour, M.H., AmirZafari, B., Maleki, K.N., Daneshpour, N.: A brief survey of software architecture concepts and service oriented architecture. In: IEEE International Conference on ICCSIT, pp. 34–38 (2009)
15. Sun, H., Wang, X., Zhou, B., Zou, P.: Research and implementation of dynamic web services composition. In: Advanced Parallel Processing Technologies, pp. 457–466 (2003)

16. Benatallah, B., Sheng, Q., Dumas, M.: The self-serv environment for web services composition. IEEE Internet Comput. **7**, 40–48 (2003)
17. Kessler, C., Löwe, W.: Optimized composition of performance-aware parallel components. Concurrency Comput. Practice Exper. **24**, 481–498 (2011)
18. Weigand, H., van den Heuvel, W.J., Hiel, M.: Rule-based service composition and service-oriented business rule management. In: Vanthienen, J., Hoppenbrouwers, S. (eds.) Proceedings of the International Workshop on Regulations Modeling and Deployment (ReMoD 2008), pp. 1–12. ACM (2008)
19. Char, A., Mezini, M.: Hybrid web service composition: business processes meet business rules. In: Proceedings of the 2nd International Conference on Service Oriented Computing, pp. 30–38. ACM (2004)
20. Casati, F., Ilnicki, S., Jin, L., Krishnamoorthy, V., Shan, M.: eFlow: a platform for developing and managing composite e-services. Technical Report HPL-36, HPL (2000)
21. Casati, F., Ilnicki, S., Jin, L., Krishnamoorthy, V., Shan, M.: Adaptive and dynamic service composition in eFlow. In: Advanced Information Systems Engineering, pp. 13–31. Springer, Heidelberg (2000)
22. Aggarwal, R., Verma, K., Miller, J., Milnor, J.: Dynamic Web Service Composition in METEOR-S. Technical report, LSDIS Lab, Univeristy of Georgia, Athens (2004)
23. Pires, P., Benevides, M., Mattoso, M.: Building reliable web services compositions. Web, Web-Services, and Database Systems, pp. 59–72 (2002)
24. Pires, P.F.: WEBTRANSACT: A Framework for Specifying and coordinating reliable web services compositions. Technical Report ES-578/02, Federal University of Rio De Janerio (2002)
25. Lécué, F., Silva, E., Ferreira Pires, L.: A framework for dynamic web services composition. In: Emerging Web Services Technology II, pp. 59–75 (2007)
26. Silva, E., Ferreira Pires, L., van Sinderen, M.J.: Supporting dynamic service composition at runtime based on end-user requirements. In: Workshop at the International Conference on Service Oriented Computing (ICSOC) 2009, Stockhome, Sweden, pp. 22–27 (2009)
27. Ordonez, A., Alcázar, V., Corrales, J., Falcarin, P.: Automated context aware composition of advanced telecom services for environmental early warnings. Expert Syst. Appl. **41**, 5907–5916 (2014)
28. Tiwana, A., Ramesh, B.: E-services: problems, opportunities, and digital platforms. In: Proceedings of the 34th Annual Hawaii International Conference on System Sciences (2001)
29. Casati, F., Ilnicki, S., Jin, L.J., Krishnamoorthy, V., Shan, M.C.: An open, flexible, and congurable system for e-service composition. Technical Report HPL-2000-41, HPL (2000)
30. Sheng, Q.Z., Qiao, X., Vasilakos, A.V., Szabo, C., Bourne, S., Xu, X.: Web services composition: a decade's overview. Inf. Sci. **280**, 218–238 (2014)
31. Han, S.N., Lee, M.G., Crespi, N.: Context-aware service composition framework in web-enabled building automation system. In: International Conference on Intelligent in Next Generation Networks, pp. 128–133 (2012)
32. Viswanathan, M.: Foundations for the run-time analysis of software systems. Ph.D. thesis, University of Pennsylvania, Philadelphia, PA, USA (2000)
33. Leucker, M., Schallhart, C.: J. Logic Algebraic Program. A brief account of runtime verification **78**, 293–303 (2009). Elsevier
34. Goodloe, A., Pike, L.: Monitoring Distributed Real-Time Systems: A Survey and Future Directions. NASA/CR, Virginia 23681-2199 (2010)
35. Brenner, D., Atkinson, C., Hummel, O., Stoll, D.: Strategies for the run-time testing of third party web services. In: IEEE International Conference on Service-Oriented and Applications (SOCA 2007), pp. 114–121 (2007)

36. González, A., Piel, E., Grob, H.G.: Architecture support for runtime integration and verification of component-based Systems of Systems. In: ASE Workshops, pp. 41–48 (2008)
37. Suliman, D., Paech, B., Borner, L., Atkinson, C., Brenner, D., Merdes, M., Malaka, R.: The MORABIT approach to runtime component testing. In: 30th COMPSAC, pp. 171–176 (2006)
38. Lahami, M., Krichen, M., Jmaeil, M.: Safe and efficient runtime testing framework applied in dynamic and distributed systems. Sci. Comput. Program. **122**, 1–28 (2016). Elsevier
39. Serhani, M.A., Dssouli, R., Hafid, A., Sahraoui, H.: A QoS broker based architecture for efficient web services selection. In: IEEE International Conference on Web Services (ICWS 2005), pp. 113–120 (2005)
40. Oh, SC., Lee, D., Kumara, SRT.: Effective web service composition in diverse and large-scale service networks. IEEE Trans. Serv. Comput. **1** (2008)
41. Zhao, Y., Oberthür, S., Kardos, M., Rammig, F.J.: Model-based runtime verification framework for self-optimizing systems. Electr. Notes Theor. Comput. Sci. **144**, 125–145 (2006)
42. Lemos, A.L., Daniel, F., Benatallah, B.: Web service composition: a survey of techniques and tools. ACM Comput. Surv. (CSUR), vol. 48 (2016)
43. Bertolino, A.: Software testing research: achievements, challenges, dreams future of software engineering. In: FOSE 2007. IEEE (2007)

Modernization of Legacy Software Tests to Model-Driven Testing

Nader Kesserwan(⊠), Rachida Dssouli, and Jamal Bentahar

Concordia Institute for Information Systems Engineering (CIISE),
Concordia University, Montreal, Canada
n_kesse@encs.concordia.ca,
rachida.dssouli@concordia.ca,
bentahar@ciise.concordia.ca

Abstract. Software has become ubiquitous in healthcare applications, as is evident from its prevalent use for controlling medical devices, maintaining electronic patient health data, and enabling healthcare information technology (HIT) systems. As the software functionality becomes more intricate, concerns arise regarding quality, safety and testing effort. It thus becomes imperative to adopt an approach or methodology based on best engineering practices to ensure that the testing effort is affordable. Automation in testing software can increase product quality, leading to lower field service, product support and liability cost. It can provide types of testing that simply cannot be performed by people.

Keywords: Automation · Model-driven testing · Human factors · Reverse-Engineering · Testing effort

1 Introduction

Proprietary frameworks for software tests are common in industry. The resulting test cases and procedures can be very large, difficult to maintain and hard to compose into complex scenarios involving parallelism. Migration to a standards-based and more efficient software testing environment is appealing to organizations seeking to reduce costs, and to benefit from the continuing advancements in technology. In this paper, we propose to modernize legacy software tests to a model-driven testing methodology, based on formalized test cases. The legacy test procedures are initially translated to Testing and Test Control Notation (TTCN-3) and then abstracted to test cases in the Test Description Language (TDL). The goal here is to study model-driven test procedure generation from TDL, and to evaluate TDL as a formal language for expressing test cases. Software modification is a typical activity in a software system's life cycle and especially in the maintenance phase [19]. During maintenance, the challenges of integration and regression testing are to select a sufficient subset of existing tests to apply and to create new tests. Test automation is highly desirable for regression testing, an activity that is generally tedious and time consuming [8].

After many maintenance cycles, a legacy set of Test Cases and Procedures (TCs and TPs) may become increasingly difficult to adapt to change of the System Under Test (SUT) or difficult to improve using new functionalities related to test automation.

© ICST Institute for Computer Sciences, Social Informatics and Telecommunications Engineering 2018
F. Belqasmi et al. (Eds.): AFRICATEK 2017, LNICST 206, pp. 140–156, 2018.
https://doi.org/10.1007/978-3-319-67837-5_14

This limitation is sometimes exacerbated by the high-cost and the inherent complications of integration with an evolving SUT environment. At some point or another, an organization may wish to modernize its software testing framework. Such a migration is costly, but could bring many benefits: a modern infrastructure that allows better test management and a higher level of test automation [11]. Furthermore, the migrated set of TCs and TPs should be easier to change, enhancing the agility of the organization. Organizations need to be able to integrate additional functionalities seamlessly when new requirements arise. Then, reengineering of legacy TPs could address some of the issues. In this paper, we present a pilot project in reengineering of embedded software TCs and TPs towards a model-driven methodology, whereby executable TPs are automatically generated from TCs. The modernization process has two phases:

i. The first phase is tool-based; it starts with the automatic translation of legacy TPs to functionally-equivalent TPs (test implementation) in the TTCN-3 [9]. The TTCN-3 language was selected for its industrial strength, its ability to enable test automation, and its recognition as a standard.
ii. In a second phase, the TTCN-3 TPs are abstracted into TCs (test specification) written as models in TDL [10]. TDL is a standardized scenario-based approach; it expresses requirements as test objectives and connects them to scenarios that describe the interaction with the SUT. This approach is suitable for automated TPs as tests can be derived from the scenarios and automated.

We use the terminology[1] of the ETSI TDL and TTCN-3 standards, as defined in context, to describe various test artifacts and activities. In this paper, we discuss the modernization of software tests for testing software. The rest of this paper is organized as follows: Sect. 2 surveys related work; Sect. 3 discusses the modernization approach; and Sect. 4 concludes the paper.

2   Related Work

In general, system or software migration is performed in order to increase quality, to manage obsolescence, and/or to satisfy new business requirements. The migration of legacy software tests may involve the hardware platform, the software framework or both. A hardware migration implies switching the hardware platform to a modern one. On the other hand, software migration proposes to change the programing language, the operating system, and the data or the database. For example, data can be migrated from a file system to a database management system. In [4], a migration from a relational to an object-oriented database was implemented to benefit from object-oriented technology. TPs written in programming languages such as Perl, Python, C, C++, etc. are considered to be software programs. Therefore, the migration to a new language is handled as a specific language translation activity. In [15], massive amounts of TPs that were implemented as Excel and Word files were migrated

---

[1] **TDL**: Test Description, Test Objective, Test Configuration, Data Set
TTCN-3: testcase, Test Type, Test Data, Test Component, Test Behavior.

to a centralized test management tool. The authors aimed to achieve better test management of test artifacts— distributed in an ad-hoc manner— by centralizing them in one location. In [12], a medium size software system written in PL/IX was migrated to C++ to respond to new business requirements, such as lower maintenance costs, higher performance and better reliability. In [16], the authors address the potential and risks of migrating the software and the hardware platforms of massive software tests that may require significant computing resources and lengthy execution time to cloud computing. Several tools and strategies to assist in the migration of legacy systems are presented in De Lucia et al. [1, 2]. Reliable analysis of source code is essential for successful software migration. Selecting and comparing analysis tools is usually based on a defined set of criteria. Analysis tools can be used to support a migration, for example, by identifying lines in the test code, analyzing the control flow, and providing information about test data [20]. Our work differs by migrating the software tests to be used in model-driven testing methodology.

3 Reverse-Engineering of Legacy Software Tests

Most companies that provide solutions to organizations in healthcare use Natural Language (NL) to express software requirements. In the Requirements Engineering Management Findings Report [13] several surveys of industry practice are conducted: *"...when asked in what format requirements are being captured, the overwhelming majority of the survey respondents indicated that requirements are being captured as English text, shall statements, or as tables and diagrams"*.

In our pilot project, the original TPs were written in a proprietary test language based on Eclipse Ant/XML [3] software is a PC based verification tool used to execute automated test in order to verify the software. Based on user feedback, manually creating TPs in Ant/XML can be qualified as labor-intensive. The legacy TPs are the starting point of the migration as they convey information about test behavior, test components and test data. In this paper, we propose an approach that starts with the code migration of these TPs to the TTCN-3 language, which in turns will be reverse-engineered into TCs in TDL. Once the reengineering of the software tests is completed, new TCs can be captured directly in TDL, and these TCs can be used to generate TPs in TTCN-3 or in any other desired scripting language. Furthermore, when new requirements emerge to demand the evolution of the software tests, this software evolution can take place at the model level. Figure 1 shows the modernization process of the legacy software tests.

There are some difficulties with the legacy process shown in Fig. 1. The test engineer spends a lot of time transforming TC into TP. There is a large gap in abstraction level between the TC and the TP. The detail level is low in the TC, but very high in the TP. It is an error-prone, time-consuming task to bridge this gap manually. Because resources are always restricted, the software quality engineer has less time for a more intensive TC. For example, Patient Monitors (PM) are electronic medical devices for observing critically ill patients by monitoring their vital signs. The four

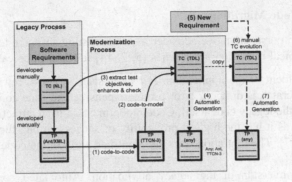

Fig. 1. Modernization of legacy software tests

most important vital signs are the pulse rate, oxygen level, body temperature, and electrocardiogram (ECG) activity. Doctors and nurses are informed by an immediate alarm when a vital sign of a patient such as heart rate falls below a given lower limit or exceeds a given higher limit, so they can provide timely and appropriate treatment. A malfunction of the PM may result in the death of a patient which makes this functionality safety-critical and it must be validated accordingly. Figure 2 shows an example that illustrates a legacy TC for Heart Rate (HR) alarm testing and the transformation to the appropriate TP.

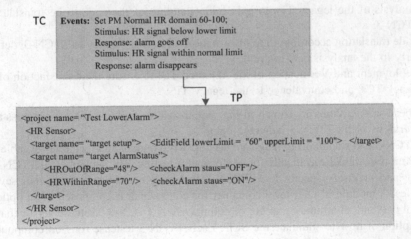

Fig. 2. Develop a TP manually from a TC

The ultimate goal in the modernization process is to enable automatic generation of the TPs and to have them migrate to a more standard testing language to benefit from its important features. The next subsections explain the two activities enclosed in the modernization process, code-to-code migration and code-to-model.

3.1   Code-to-Code Migration

From a migration perspective, we consider a set of existing software tests as software source code. Typical migration approaches [5, 7, 14] fall into three categories:

- New development of the application. For large-scale systems, rewriting an application from scratch is difficult, error prone, expensive and time consuming [6].
- Modernizing the legacy code itself. Code modernization is an attractive approach to organizations as it has the highest probability of success among the three types of approaches [17]. The migration risks are identified early in the code modernization process.
- Automated conversion of the legacy application. Automated conversion is an attractive option when new technology or process improvement initiatives require legacy software tests to be converted to another language, for example to improve the test process itself or its environment. The current technology for legacy migration allows organizations to automate the migration process with lower risk and in a shorter time.

The need for better test management environments grows with the size of the testing effort. Organizing test artifacts and resources is a necessary part of test management and is facilitated in our reengineering process by dispatching elements of the legacy TPs into its new TTCN-3 implementation— in modular style. Our code-to-code migration activity is iterative as it requires a repetition of activities to migrate successfully the code. The process is composed of the following sub-activities:

- Analysis of the legacy TPs to gain understanding of the code to be translated to TTCN-3;
- Code translation according to transformation rules, from legacy to TTCN-3, defined early in the analysis activity; and
- Deployment and Verification of the migrated TPs to ensure their satisfaction of the legacy TCs, and equivalence to the legacy TPs.

These sub-activities are shown in Fig. 3 and will be explained as we progress after an overview of the TTCN-3 language below.

TTCN-3 is a standardized language used to write human and machine-readable test scripts; it is designed specifically for conformance testing. The semantics of TTCN-3 is clearly and precisely specified. A TTCN-3 test suite can be structured into several modules. A module is a top-level container for code which is composed of an optional control part and an arbitrary number of definitions. A TTCN-3 "testcase" is a behavior description of how to stimulate the SUT. Each TTCN-3 testcase runs on components that communicate with each other through ports. A TTCN-3 model is composed of an Abstract Layer and a Concrete Layer. The Abstract Layer can host a test suite that is composed of several modules to describe the test to be executed. The Concrete Layer is responsible for communicating with the SUT, coding and decoding the exchanged messages during the test execution.

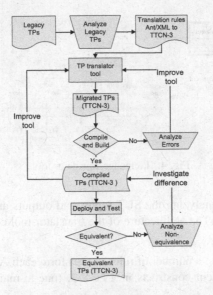

Fig. 3. Code-to-code migration sub-activities

3.1.1 Analysis of the Legacy Code

It is essential to the success of a migration to understand the functionality of the legacy software tests and to know how the SUT interacts via its various interfaces. A typical TP written in Ant/XML is composed of one or more targets where each target may control several interfaces via sending and verifying commands. For example, if a TP needs to sense some data, it specifies the interface to be queried, sends the required commands and reads the result for verification.

After analyzing the legacy TPs, we extracted valuable information that is located exclusively in the TPs; this information helped us to establish principles for code migration from Ant/XML to TTCN-3. We determined that a legacy TP contains instructions pertaining to three aspects: Test Verification, Test Component, and Test Action. This decomposition of a legacy TP can support the translation to TTCN-3 in a modular manner. In our translation scheme, the Test Verification, Test Component and Test Action are respectively translated to Test Data, Test Component and Test Behavior modules in TTCN-3. The transformation rules should convert legacy TP code while preserving the semantics. We found that core TTCN-3 contains equivalent semantics for most Ant/XML language elements, such as sending data, verifying responses, representing regular expression, defining interfaces and connections, etc.; however, since the legacy application did not use an XML schema, the data types of the legacy TP could not easily be rule-transformed. Thus, neither type checking nor value checking could be performed.

3.1.2 Code Migration

We developed a language translator tool to migrate the TPs automatically to three TTCN-3 modules. The resulting modules along with the Type module constitute an executable TTCN-3 TP that is equivalent to the Ant/XML TP. The Type module is

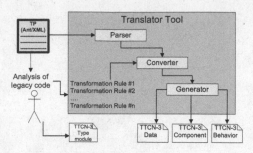

Fig. 4. Language translator tool

produced manually by analyzing the SUT inputs and outputs and the legacy TCs and TPs as shown in Fig. 4. The architecture of the translator tool combines the following elements:

- Transformation Rules: a number of rules to transform each Ant/XML construct to a one or more equivalent constructs in TTCN-3. (one-to-many transformations are possible)
- Parser: reads legacy TP in order to generate syntactic element tokens encountered in the TP.
- Converter: based on transformation rules, it transforms the syntactic element, returned by the Parser, to functionally-equivalent code to the generator.
- Generator: writes the generated TTCN-3 code, produced by the Converter, dispatched in each of the corresponding modules.

Table 1 shows the transformation rules. Third column describes how the TP legacy semantic is preserved using TTCN-3 syntax.

Having a Translator Tool is a key success factor in the migration process. It enables a high degree of automation and meets economic and timeframe objectives, such as lower cost, shorter time-to-market, consistent style, and good quality code. However, the migrated TTCN-3 modules define an abstract test suite, i.e. components residing in the TTCN-3 Abstract Layer. The migrated code lacks any concrete implementation-specific information, such as how messages are encoded or how communication with the SUT actually takes place [21]. In order to execute the TTCN-3 modules, Codecs and SUT Adapters must be provided. These parts reside in the Concrete Layer and allow tests to be encoded into a format understood by the SUT and to be executed by it.

3.1.3   Migrate Real-Time TPs

Real-time embedded applications require testing the functional aspect and the timing aspect of the requirements. The functional aspect of SUT interfaces is concerned with the sending and receiving of the messages; it is verified by checking the message values and their order. On the other hand, the real-time requirements require observing time at the communication ports and associating time with stimuli and responses. Testing real-time behavior remains a challenge as the test system needs to be time-deterministic [18], in order to verify accurately the response time, sending time, latency, delay, jitter, etc.

Table 1. Transformation rules to convert Ant/XML and TTCN-3 languages along with transformation rules.

Legacy code element	Equivalent construct in TTCN-3	Transformation rules
\<project name = "str"\>	module \<str_Template\> { } module \<str_Behavior\> { } module \<str_Configuration\> { }	Rule # 1: **project** element is translated to three **module** constructs which together compose a full TP in TTCN-3. The project name = str is used as a prefix with "Template", "Behavior" or "Configuration" to designate each TTCN-3 module. If the project name contains special characters such as dot or space, they are replaced by underscores.
\<target name = "str"\>	testcase \<target_str\> runs on MTCType system SystemType	Rule # 2: **target** element is translated to a **testcase** construct, and the target name is prefixed with the string target_ The testcase will contain the action and verify constructs (stimulus and response)

\<target name= "all" depends = "str_1, str_2, ..., str_n"/\>	control {
	 execute (target_str_1());
	 execute (target_str_2());
	 execute (target_str_n());
	 }
		Rule # 3: **target** name = all is translated to a **control** construct, and the intermediate targets, str_1, str_2, ... separated by commas, identified in depends are translated to a sequence of **execute** statements such as execute (target_str_1()); in the **control** construct.

interface port = "name"	type port interface_name message {
	 in sending_msg;
	 out receiving_msg; }
	 type component interfaceType {
	 port interface_x interface; }
		Rule # 4: Every interface is mapped to a message-based port and attached to a component.
		
		 The **interface** port = name is translated to a type port message-based construct and attached to a type component construct.

	function action (name, command, str_1, ..., str_n) runs	Rule # 5: **action** elements are translated to **functions** and **function** calls constructs. The action parameters

`<action key = "str_1", "str_2", ..., str_n />`	`on componentType {` `....` `portName.send(command,` `str_1, ..., str_n);` `....` `}`	command, name, str_1, ..., str_n are passed as formal parameters to the function definition. The parameter name represents the interface name where command represents the input to send. Some actions take additional parameters to send the command, they can be represented by str_1, ..., str_n. The parameter portName represents the port via which the input to SUT is sent. The action with its arguments in the legacy TP represent a stimulus to send to the SUT
`< verify query = "str_1" value= "str_2" />`	`template component type` `verifyStep := { str_1 := pattern` `str_2 }` `function matchResult(verify,` `portName) runs on` `componentType {` `alt {` `[] portName.receive(verify) {` `  setverdict(pass);   }` `[] portName.receive {` `  setverdict(fail);    }` `[] replyTimer.timeout {` `  setverdict(inconc, "No` `response from` `SUT")   } }`	Rule # 6: **verification** is translated to **template** construct named verify. One **template** can host several **verifications** for a given step. Then, the construct verify is translated to a function to handle the alternative sequences. In the legacy TP, a comparison between the expected value and returned one is performed: verify query = "str_1" value= "str_2" The TTCN-3 TP migrates the expected values and store them in templates w.r.t to REGEXP used in the legacy. Then, the returned values are matched against the expected ones to issue a verdict.
`< macrodef name = "MacroN" />` `action` `<MacroN interface = "interface_n ame, para_1, para_2, ..., para_n" />`	`function MacroN` `(interface_name, para_1, para_2,` `..., para_n) runs on` `componentType {` `...}` `MacroN( interface_name,` `para_1, para_2, ..., para_n);`	Rule # 7: **macros** elements are translated to **functions** and **function** calls constructs. The macros parameters interface_name, $para_1$, $para_2$, ..., $para_n$ are passed as formal parameters to the function definition. A macro may contain control statement such as looping, if, else. These statements are mapped to their equivalent in TTCN-3

Previously, we transformed Ant/XML TPs, which test the functional behavior of the SUT, to TTCN-3. Now, we discuss how Ant/XML and TTCN-3 handle the real-time. The Ant/XML test system, without any additional mediating devices, is unable to execute precise real-time tests scenarios. The wall clock time is measured at scripting level, i.e. not at the external test adapters. Ant/XML measures time via *tstamp* operation returning time with a millisecond resolution; it controls timing via *sleep* and *waitfor* operations.

Similarly, the core language of TTCN-3 was not originally conceived with real-time focus in mind. The first problem is the precision of time when it is recorded or checked by the test system or when it is associated with certain events. There is the semantic of timers that was not intended for suiting real-time properties, but conceived only for catching (typically long-term) timeouts [19].

A *tstamp* task is mapped to a TTCN-3 timer declaration followed by *start* timer operation. Ant/XML measures duration by computing time difference between two *tstamp* tasks. This can be mapped to TTCN-3 *start* timer and *read* timer operations.

TTCN-3 was extended with set of constructs for real-time testing RT-TTCN-3 [10] that introduces a mechanism to store the arrival time of messages, procedure calls at system adapter level and to control the timing for the stimulation. We have not yet attempted to use RT-TTCN-3. For now, only the core language is used in our pilot project.

3.1.4 Deployment and Testing of a Migrated TPs

As illustrated in Fig. 3, the code migration process is an iterative approach, as the Translator Tool needs improvement and corrections after an unsuccessful attempt to migrate the functionality. The migrated code may not compile or may fail to link to produce a build; in such cases an analysis is performed to improve the tool and fix the problem. It is essential that the legacy and migrated test suites are functionally equivalent and have full consistency in their verdicts that are produced by applying the same stimuli. In order to properly evaluate their conformance, the migrated code should not be manually modified during the process by diverging from the TC. Any enhancement should be added only after a successful migration has been declared. Accordingly, as shown in Fig. 5, testing the functional equivalence can be determined by comparing the original and migrated test verdicts' and the SUT's observable states — actions triggered by SUT in response to events sent by the TP.

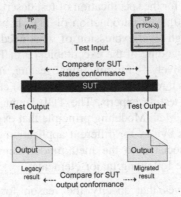

Fig. 5. Validation of legacy and migrated test suites equivalence

The correctness relationship holds when the migrated TPs, for the same test input, make SUT behave the same way as legacy TPs do. In other words, the legacy TPs are used as an oracle version, if the behavior of the SUT differs when stimulated by the migrated TPs, then the correctness relationship breaks and the tester needs to analyze the problem and investigate the difference. Annex 1 shows the TTCN-3 test suite migrated from the legacy TP in Fig. 2. After a successful code equivalence migration to TTCN-3, the second phase starts by reverse-engineering the migrated code in TTCN-3 to abstract models in TDL.

3.2   Code-to-Model

In the second phase of the reengineering process, we obtain the TCs by reverse-engineering the migrated TTCN-3 TPs. In most industrial domains, a test can be conceived at two levels of abstraction: a test specification (or test case) and a test implementation (a test script or procedure). Our goal is to abstract the latter to obtain the former. Here, the test implementation is the migrated TTCN-3 TPs containing concrete information. It is often considered useful to express TPs as stimulus-response scenarios. This is the path that we explore here using TDL.

Let's consider the modules of a TP.

- The *Test Behavior* module is composed of test events (stimuli and responses as interactions) that express the test behavior.
- The *Test Data* module contains information about the test input and the expected test output.
- The *Test Component* module consists of a set of inter-connected test components with well-defined communication ports and an explicit test system interface.

Next we consider a TC. It should use abstract types and instances to refer to test data, and should describe the system components and their actions and interactions with a minimum of details. In our project, to raise the level of test specification, we choose the TDL notation. It has the benefit of being complementary to TTCN-3. For a given test, a description is specified in TDL, whereas TTCN-3 is used to define a detailed implementation. An overview of the TDL concept follows.

TDL is a new language for the specification of test descriptions and the presentation of test execution results [10]. The introduction of TDL is being driven by industry to fill the gap between the high-level expression of what needs to be tested i.e., the test purposes, and the complex coding of the executable TP in TTCN-3 [18]. TDL is used primarily— but not exclusively— for functional testing, its major benefits include: high-quality testing process through scenario design of test cases (test descriptions) that are easy to review by non-testing experts. The TDL language was designed on three central concepts [10]: (1) a Meta-Modeling principle that expresses its abstract syntax, (2) a user-defined Concrete Syntax for different application domains, and (3) the TDL semantics that can be associated to the meta-model elements. Any minimal TDL specification consists of the following major elements:

- A set of Test Objectives that specify the reason for designing either a Test Description or a particular behavior of a Test Description. It can be written as a simple text in NL and it can be complemented with tables and diagrams;
- A Test Configuration, which is a set of interacting components (tester and SUT) and their interconnection;
- A set of Data Instances used in the interactions between components in a test description; and
- A set of Test Descriptions to describe one or more test scenarios based on the interactions of data exchanged between tester and SUT.

In order to obtain the TC (TDL specification) from the TP (TTCN-3 modules), we developed transformation rules to define TC elements from the TTCN-3 TPs'. These rules are meant for human processing; they are based on the equivalence between elements of both languages. The rules aim to remodel the TTCN-3 modules into more abstract TDL elements. The language-sensitive editor understands the concrete TDL syntax, based on the TDL meta-model.

Next, we show how each TDL element is derived from its corresponding TTCN-3 module by applying these rules. However, extracting the TDL Test Objectives cannot be rule-based since the TTCN-3 TPs do not have a concrete representation of the Test Objective. Nevertheless, the test objectives can be extracted from the legacy TCs and copied in TDL corresponding elements.

3.2.1   Remodel Test Data Sets

The concrete data definition, stored in the TTCN-3 *Test Data* module (TestData.ttcn3), is mapped to TDL Data Instances using TDL elements that link the data aspects between TDL and TTCN-3. These Data Instances are grouped in Data Sets and are considered as abstract representation of the corresponding concepts in a concrete type system.

3.2.2   Remodel Test Configuration

In a TDL specification, the Test Configuration element consists of a Tester, SUT components and a Gate. The corresponding TTCN-3 *Component* module contains equivalent objects with many more details. Specifically, it consists of a set of inter-connected test components with well-defined communication ports and an explicit test system interface. TDL does not have a *receive* construct, instead it uses a *send* construct for the interaction between a Tester and the SUT. Therefore, the mapping of TDL Tester and SUT components is validated with the TTCN-3 interaction.

3.2.3   Remodel Test Description

The Test Description element in the TDL specification language defines the TC behavior. The enclosed scenario is mainly composed of actions and interactions between the Tester and the SUT components.

In the TTCN-3 *Test Behavior* module, the action is a function implementation or physical setup. The interaction is represented as a message being sent (from a source) or received (from the target). We remodeled the interaction and the action to their equivalent in TDL by applying the rules listed in Table 2. In the *Test Behavior* module, numerous sequences of events are possible due to the reception and handling of communication timer events. The possible events are expressed as a set of alternative behaviors and denoted by the TTCN-3 *alt* statement. Each TTCN-3 object in the *Test Behavior* is remodeled to an equivalent TDL construct by applying the transformation rules. In our experimentation, we used a TDL Editor to edit and validate the syntax of the TDL specifications.

Table 2. Transformation rules from TTCN-3 to TDL based on the proposed concrete syntax.

TDL Meta-model elements (abstract syntax)	TTCN-3 statements	Our proposed TDL concrete syntax	Description of transformation from TTCN-3 to TDL
TestConfiguration	module <tc_name> { }	Test Configuration <tc_name>	Map to a Test Configuration statement with the name < td_name >
GateType	type port <port_type> message { }	Gate Type <port_type> accepts <Data_Set_name>	Map to a Gate Type statement with the name <port_type> that accepts Data Set elements
ComponentType	type component comp_type{ port <port_type> <port_name>; }	Component Type <comp_type> { gate types : <port_type> instantiate <comp_instance> as Tester of type <comp_type> having { gate <gate_name> of type <port_type> ; }	Map to a Component Type statement with the name <comp_type> and associate a <port_type> to it.
ComponentType	type component system_comp_type{ port <port_type> <port_name>; }	Component Type <comp_type> { gate types : <port_type> instantiate <system_comp_type> as SUT of type <comp_type> having { gate <gate_name> of type <port_type> ; }	Map to a Component Type statement with the name <system_comp_type> and associate a <port_type> as a port of the test system interface to it.
Connection	map (mtc: <comp_type>, system <system_comp_type >)	connect <comp_type> to <system_comp_type >	Map to a connect statement where a test component is connected to test system component.
TestDescription	module <td_name> { import from <dataproxy> all; import from <tc_name> all; }	Test Description(<dataproxy) <td_name> { use configuration: <tc_name>; { } }	Map to a Test Description statement with the name <td_name >. The <DataProxy> element passed as formal parameters (optional) is mapped from an import statement of the <DataProxy> to be used in the module. The import statement of the Test Configuration <tc_name> is mapped to use configuration

TDL Meta-model elements (abstract syntax)	TTCN-3 statements	Our proposed TDL concrete syntax	Description of transformation from TTCN-3 to TDL
			property that is associated with the 'TestDescription'
Alternative Behaviour	alt { }	alternatively { }	Map to alternatively statement
Interaction	<comp_name_source>.send(<concreteData>)	<comp_name_source> sends instance < data_name > to <comp_name_target>	Map to a sends instance statement with respect to the sending component
	<comp_name_source>.receive(<concreteData>)	<system_comp_name_source> sends instance < data_name > to <comp_name_target>	Map to a sends instance statement when the sending source is SUT component
VerdictType	verdicttype <verdict_value>	Verdict <verdict_value>	Map <verdict_value> that contains the values: {inconclusive, pass, fail}to its corresponding value
TimeUnit	time_unit {1E-9,1E-6, 1E-3, 1E0, 6E1, 36E2	Time Unit <time_unit>	<time_unit> contains the following values: {tick,nanosecond,microsecond, miliisecond,second,minute,hour }
VerdictAssignment	setverdict (<verdict_value>)	set verdict to <verdict_value>	Map to a set verdict to statement
Action	function <action_name>()	perform action <action_name>	Map to perform action statement
Stop	stop	stop	Map to a stop statement within alternatively statement
Break	break	break	Map to a break statement within alternatively statement
TimerStart	<timer_name>.start(time_unit);	start <timer_name> for (time_unit)	Map to a start statement
TimerStop	<timer_name>.stop;	stop <timer_name>	Map to a stop statement
TimeOut	<timer_name>.timeout;	<timer_name> times out	Map to a times out statement
Quiescence/Wait	timer <timer_name> <timer_name>.start(time_unit); <timer_name>.timeout	is quite for (time_unit) waits for (time_unit)	Map to is quit for statement or to waits for
InterruptBehaviour	stop	interrupt	Map to interrupt statement
BoundedLoop Behaviour	repeat	repeat <number> times	Map to repeat statement. The repeat is used as the last statement in the alternatively behavior.
DataInstance	type_keyword <data_name>	Data Set <any_name> { instance <data_name> }	Map any <type_keyword> to an instance and group it in Data Set element

3.2.4   Model Real-Time in TDL

Previously, we mapped real-time elements enclosed in legacy TP to TTCN-3 timers' objects. TDL defines time package to express:

- A Time instance or time duration is expressed by a real positive value. The unit of Time instance is described by predefined instances for the TimeUnit. There are two Time Operation that can be applied on Tester components or on Tester gate:
  - Wait: defines the time duration that a Tester waits; and
  - Quiescence: defines the time duration during which a Tester shall expect no input from a SUT;
- A Time Constraint element resides within a test description; it is used to express timing requirements over two or more atomic behavior elements; and
- A Timer element defines a timer that is used by the following Timer Operation:
  - TimerStart: it sets the period property to define the duration of the timer from start to timeout. The Timer changes from idle to running state;
  - TimerStop: it stops a running Timer, the state of the Timer becomes idle; and
  - TimeOut: it specifies the occurrence of a timeout event when the period set by the TimeStart operation has elapsed. The Timer changes from running to idle state.

The TDL time package can be modeled from the TTCN-3 timer operations as shown in Table 2 that illustrates the transformation rules from TTCN-3 to TDL based on the versions in [9, 10].

4   Conclusion

The modernization of software tests to a new platform is often pressured by business requirements to reduce the cost and effort of testing. In this project, we automatically restructured legacy TPs, written as Ant/xml files into the TTCN-3 language that provides strong typing, structured constructs and for modular code. This migration enforced coding standards and offered a more readable, simple to modify and easy to understand test code. Next, we reengineered the code and data to a higher level of abstraction to obtain (model-driven) TPs. Our overarching goal is to support test automation, to reduce the effort involved in testing and to lower maintenance cost while meeting software tests' evolution requirements.

Annex 1

The migrated Heart Rate Test Procedure in TTCN-3

```
1.  module HRDeployTest {
2.    type record HeartRateType {
3.      charstring heartRateSignal    }
4.    template HeartRateType TemplateType := {
5.      heartRateOutOfRangeSignal := "48"  }
6.    template HeartRateType TemplateType := {
7.      heartRateWithinRangeSignal := "70"  }
8.    type record AlarmType {
9.      charstring alarmOFFSignal
10.     charstring alarmONSignal    }
11.   template AlarmType TemplateType := {
12.     alarmOFFSignal := "OFF"
13.     alarmONSignal := "ON"   }
14.   type port defaultGT message {
15.     inout HeartRateType;
16.     inout AlarmType; }
17.   type component Patient {
18.     port defaultGT gPatient ;        }
19.   type component Monitor {
20.     port defaultGT gMonitor ;        }
21.
22.   testcase _TC () runs on Patient {
23.     map (mtc:gPatient, system:gMonitor);
24.     gPatient.send(heartRateOutOfRangeSignal);
25.     alt {
26.         [] gPatient.receive(alarmOFFSignal)
27.             setverdict(pass);
28.         [] gPatient.receive
29.             setverdict(fail);
30.     }
31.     gPatient.send(heartRateWithinRangeSignal);
32.     alt {
33.         [] gPatient.receive(alarmONSignal)
34.             setverdict(pass);
35.         [] gPatient.receive
36.             setverdict(fail);
37.     }
38.   }
39.   control {
40.     execute(_TC());   }
41. }
```

References

1. De Lucia, A., Francese, R., Scanniello, G., Tortora, G.: Developing legacy system migration methods and tools for technology transfer. Softw. Pr. Exp. **38**(13), 1333–1364 (2008)
2. Al-Azzoni, I., Zhang, L., Down, D.G.: Performance evaluation for software migration. In: ACM SIGSOFT Software Engineering Notes, vol. 36, no. 5, pp. 323–328. ACM, March 2011
3. Ant, A.: The Apache Software Foundation (2007). http://ant.apache.org/
4. Behm, A., Geppert, A., Dittrich, K.R.: On the migration of relational schemas and data to object-oriented database systems, pp. 13–33. Universität Zürich. Institut für Informatik (1997)
5. Bisbal, J., Lawless, D., Wu, B., Grimson, J.: Legacy information systems: Issues and directions. IEEE Softw. **5**, 103–111 (1999)

6. Brooks Jr., F.P.: The Mythical Man-Month: Essays on Software Engineering, Anniversary Edition, 2/E. Pearson Education India, Noida (1995)
7. Demeyer, S., Ducasse, S., Nierstrasz, O.: Object-Oriented Reengineering Patterns. Elsevier, New York (2002)
8. Wong, W.E., et al.: A study of effective regression testing in practice. In: The Eighth International Symposium on Software Reliability Engineering, 1997. Proceedings. IEEE (1997)
9. ETSI, E. 201 873-7 V3. 4.5.1 (2013-04): Methods for Testing and Specification (MTS). The Testing and Test Control Notation version, 3. http://www.etsi.org
10. ETSI ES 203 119 (stable draft): Methods for Testing and Specification (MTS); The Test Description Language (TDL), 25 Sept 2013. http://www.etsi.org
11. Fleurey, F., Breton, E., Baudry, B., Nicolas, A., Jézéquel, J.M.: Model-driven engineering for software migration in a large industrial context. In: Engels, G., Opdyke, B., Schmidt, D. C., Weil, F. (eds.) MODELS 2007. LNCS, vol. 4735, pp. 482–497. Springer, Heidelberg (2007). doi:10.1007/978-3-540-75209-7_33
12. Kontogiannis, K., Martin, J., Wong, K., Gregory, R., Müller, H., Mylopoulos, J.: Code migration through transformations: an experience report. In: CASCON First Decade High Impact Papers, pp. 201–213. IBM Corp, November 2010
13. Lempia, D.L., Miller, S.P.: Requirements engineering management handbook. National Technical Information Service (NTIS), 1 (2009)
14. Müller, B.: Reengineering: Eine Einführung. Springer, Heidelberg (2013)
15. Parveen, T., Tilley, S., Gonzalez, G.: A case study in test management. In: Proceedings of the 45th Annual Southeast Regional Conference. ACM (2007)
16. Parveen, T., Tilley, S.: When to migrate software testing to the cloud? In: 2010 Third International Conference on Software Testing, Verification, and Validation Workshops (ICSTW). IEEE (2010)
17. Seacord, R.C., Plakosh, D., Lewis, G.A.: Modernizing Legacy Systems: Software Technologies, Engineering Processes, and Business Practices. Addison-Wesley Professional, Boston (2003)
18. The Design of the Test Description Language (TDL). https://www.swe.informatik.uni-goettingen.de/research/design-test-description-language-tdl-stf-454
19. Wagner, C.: Model-Driven Software Migration: A Methodology: Reengineering, Recovery and Modernization of Legacy Systems. Springer, Wiesbaden (2014). doi:10.1007/978-3-658-05270-6
20. Wagner, C., Margaria, T., Pagendarm, H.-G.: Analysis and code model extraction for C/C++ source code. In: Proceedings of the 2009 14th IEEE International Conference on Engineering of Complex Computer Systems (ICECCS 2009). IEEE Computer Society, Washington, DC (2009)
21. Willcock, C., Deiß, T., Tobies, S., Keil, S., Engler, F., Schulz, S.: TTCN-3 by Example. An Introduction to TTCN-3, Second Edition, pp. 7–24 (2011)

Mobile-Based Applications

Porting the Pay with a (Group) Selfie (PGS) Payment System to Crypto Currency

Ernesto Damiani[1(✉)], Perpetus Jacques Houngbo[3], Joël T. Hounsou[3], Rasool Asal[1], Stelvio Cimato[2], Fulvio Frati[2], Dina Shehada[1], and Chan Yeob Yeun[1]

[1] EBTIC-Khalifa University, UAE Campus, PO Box 127788, Abu Dhabi, UAE
{ernesto.damiani,rasool.asal,dina.shehada,cyeun}@kustar.ac.ae
[2] Dipartimento di Informatica, Università degli Studi di Milano,
via Bramante 65, 26013 Crema, CR, Italy
{stelvio.cimato,fulvio.frati}@unimi.it
[3] Institut de Mathematique et Science Physique Quartier Avakpa, BP 613, Porto-Novo, Bénin
jacques.houngbo@auriane-etudes.com, joelhoun@gmail.com

Abstract. *Pay with a (Group) Selfie* (PGS) is a novel payment system developed at Khalifa University in the UAE, and currently under test at the *Institut de Mathématiques et Science Physique* (IMSP) in Benin. The PGS system uses a *group selfie* to gather all information items needed to encode a purchase: the seller, the buyer, the service/product and the agreed price. Using Visual Cryptography (VC), the photo is then "digitally ripped" into two shares, one for the buyer and one for the seller. In the current version of PGS, these shares are eventually and independently sent to a Bank that cooperates to offer the digital payment service to population living in rural areas. When the purchases of a buyer at a given seller pass a pre-set threshold, the Bank executes a traditional fund transfer between the two. This way, PGS spreads the Bank's transfer fee over multiple purchases, decreasing the financial cost of each purchase. This paper discusses the challenges of *transparently coupling* the PGS payment system with digital wallets holding a crypto currency, bringing the financial cost of each purchase to zero.

Keywords: Payment metaphors, mobile payment systems · Visual Cryptography · Trust · Crypto currency

1 Introduction

Pay with a (Group) Selfie (PGS) [1] is an innovative payment system that uses a *group selfie* to collect all information items behind a purchase: the seller, the buyer, the service/product and the agreed price. Using Visual Cryptography (VC), the selfie is "digitally ripped" into two shares, one transmitted to the buyer's phone and the other kept on the seller's one. In the current version of PGS, these shares are eventually and independently sent to a Bank who accepted to cooperate to offer the PGS service to population living in rural areas. When the purchases of a buyer at a given seller's shop pass a pre-set

© ICST Institute for Computer Sciences, Social Informatics and Telecommunications Engineering 2018
F. Belqasmi et al. (Eds.): AFRICATEK 2017, LNICST 206, pp. 159–168, 2018.
https://doi.org/10.1007/978-3-319-67837-5_15

threshold, the bank executes a traditional fund transfer transaction[1]. While PGS provides an entirely new metaphor for delayed payments (the ripped banknote), its innovation in the back-end consists in splitting the cost of a traditional fund transfer across multiple purchases. In this paper, we discuss backing our PGS payment system with *digital wallets* integrating a crypto currency. We believe that this idea can overcome a number of societal challenges connected with payments in emerging economies. However, here we shall focus on technical challenges only. We start by describing the PGS payment system in Sect. 2. Section 3 will discuss the rationale for putting a virtual currency behind PGS while Sect. 4 will offer a concise overview on digital wallets and crypto-currencies. Among available crypto currencies, Sect. 5 will discuss our choice for the implementation of the next version of the PGS payment system. In Sect. 6 we will discuss the different challenges and ways to overcome them. Finally, Sect. 7 will present the way forward.

2   Pay with a (Group) Selfie Payment System

PGS is a payment system that provides a *virtually costless micro-payment* system suitable for open-air markets in emerging economies. It is based on a powerful, easy-to-understand metaphor and does not require "always on" connectivity: PGS works well in environments where network connectivity is patchy. PGS is based on three key design principles: (*i*) embedding in a simple digital object (a selfie) all information about a purchase: the actors (buyer and seller), the product or service being sold, and the price agreed upon between the parties; (*ii*) producing secure shares of the original selfie, so that each single share has no value, but their combination using the human visual system can reconstruct the original image and provide proof of the purchase; (*iii*) integrating the validation of the selfie with mobile money transfer facilities, or via innovative systems exploiting virtual currencies. In its original design, PGS was *not* intended to replace existing mobile payment infrastructures, but to extend their reach wherever data connections are not guaranteed due to patchy network coverage, cost concerns or usage habits. PGS distributes the cost of a financial transaction (the fund transfer) across arbitrarily many selfie-encoded purchases. The idea of using a selfie as proof of purchase is inspired to the traditional way in which business is conducted in open-air markets. The human visual system has been used for countless years to establish the context of each sale: the purchaser, the supplier, the purchased goods or services, the price to be paid, as well as the time and location of the purchase. PGS's proof of purchase is self-validating, just like a banknote, and like a banknote ripped in two it can be held jointly by the two parties until the money transfer can be finalized. Behind the scenes, PGS uses Visual Cryptography (VC) to split the selfie, generating two random-looking shares. VC provides unconditional security [2]: owning a single share gives no possibility to reconstruct the original image, and tampering with it makes the reconstruction impossible. PGS fully supports the metaphor of putting back together the two parts of a ripped banknote. Indeed, the reconstruction of the selfie could be even performed without a

---

[1] The Bank alerts the sellers if the buyer's funds become insufficient for the eventual transfer. Each seller can decide whether to block or allow further purchases.

computer, simply by stacking the shares printed on two transparencies. In the current implementation, reconstruction is performed by a desktop application that stacks the shares provided by the parties, using the mobile applications (Fig. 1), to validate the transaction.

Fig. 1. The interfaces of the three components of PGS. The pictures of the modules are identical on purpose to let users feel the same environment.

Another important aspect of PGS design is that no "always on" assumption is made: when no network coverage is available, money exchange is deferred until shares have been independently and securely delivered to a payment service provider, who will stack them and validate the transaction.

3   Rationale for a Virtual Currency Behind PGS

As mentioned above, PGS original design relied on (*i*) a single Bank to accept selfie shares as proofs of the buyer's obligation to pay the seller, and (*ii*) mobile telco operators' network services to deliver the shares to the Bank. This design is distinct from (though related to) the design of so-called *mobile money* systems, which are bound to a specific mobile telecommunication operator who plays also the role of the Bank. All mobile money users are required to hold accounts with the same operator to be able to transfer their mobile money (often, in the form of minutes of conversation) between each other. In the case of PGS, any mobile telco provider can be used to deliver the selfie shares to the Bank, but all PGS users (sellers and buyers alike) are supposed to hold accounts at the same Bank, as it is the latter that executes fund transfer[2]. A first attempt to alleviate this constraint is adding a "Broker" module. The PGS design will then operate as

---

[2] Of course, inter-bank arrangements could be made to support account holders from other banks. This would however increase the financial cost of the transactions.

described in Fig. 2. This solution relies on the trusted Broker to act as a store-and-forward transport layer (where trust in the broker plays the role of security controls [3]), pushing selfies between PGS users on one side and multiple Banks on the other side.

The PGS implementation being tested in Benin is based on this design [1]. In this paper, we discuss how to dispense with the Banks entirely, by integrating PGS and *digital currencies* in a fully transparent way. Users will see cash transfers, possibly unaware that a virtual currency is used behind the scenes. This way, PGS will get close to catching the so-called "*mobile money unicorn*": an electronic purchase whose cost is the communication one only. The coming section aims at presenting a summary of the concepts related to virtual currency and it will then open way to the selection of one of them for implementation.

4   Crypto Currencies and Digital Wallets

Virtual currencies, e-money, digital wallets, crypto currencies, payment technology, distributed ledger and block chain are terms that often popup in conversations, many people using them loosely. This section will present some clarifications so that the rest of this work can accurately use these terms when and where needed. *Electronic money*, or *e-money*, is a fund balance expressed in a traditional currency but recorded electronically, e.g. on a stored-value pre-paid card. To generate e-money, the real currency (e.g., in form of cash) is handed over to banks and financial institutions who, in turn, load the corresponding e-money balance into microprocessors embedded in the cards. *Digital currency* has been proposed as an Internet-based form of currency. Any amount denominated in a digital currency is called *digital money*. The same way traditional physical money, such as banknotes and coins, is used in transactions, digital money can be used for digital transactions. Digital currency has its own generation and distribution mechanisms that prevent double-spending and inflation of digital money. Financial institutions worldwide tend to stress on the difference between digital currency/money and e-money. In 2012, the European Central Bank (ECB) has defined digital currency as "a type of unregulated, digital money, which is issued and usually controlled by its developers, and used and accepted among the members of a specific virtual community" [4]. Digital currency is a digital representation of value. Even though it functions as a medium of exchange, as a unit of account and as a store of value, it does not have legal tender status [5]. The Committee on Payments and Market Infrastructures (CPMI) of the Bank for International Settlements (BIS), a financial entity cooperatively owned by the world's Central Banks, asked a working group to draft a report on digital currencies. That report, published in November 2015, defines digital currency as an *asset represented in digital form and having some monetary characteristics* [6, p. 5]. Unlike today's traditional currencies, which are managed by Central Banks[3], a digital currency can be centralized or decentralized. When centralized, the virtual currency has a single administrating authority that controls the system. That authority issues the currency, establishes the rules for its use, maintains a central registry of ownership,

---

[3] This was however not always the case. Some traditional currencies managed by multiple authorities have survived until the late 1800 s.

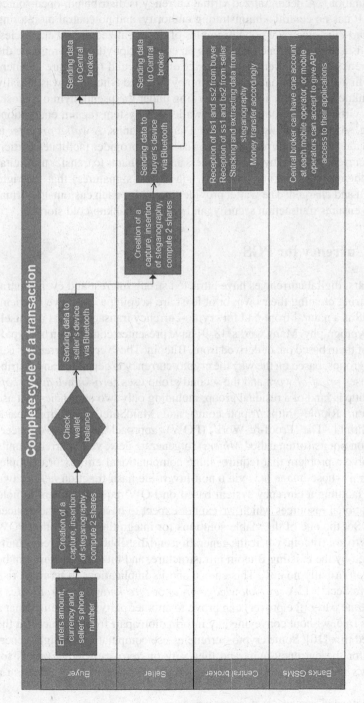

Fig. 2. PGS transaction cycle including a Central Broker, where bs1: share 1 created at buyer's side, ss2 share 2 created at buyer's side,
ss1: share 1 created at seller's side

maintains a central payment ledger, and has authority to redeem the currency (i.e., withdraw it from circulation). A decentralized virtual currency is distributed, open-source and peer-to-peer. It has no central administrating authority, and no central monitoring or oversight. *Crypto-currencies* are good examples of decentralized digital currencies. A cryptocurrency is a digital currency that relies on cryptography to *(i)* to regulate the generation of currency units *(ii)* verify the transfer of funds, and *(iii)* secure payment transactions. The first fully functional cryptocurrency is called Bitcoin. It was initially proposed by an unknown group or individual writing under the pseudonym of Satoshi Nakamoto [7]. A virtual- (or crypto)-currency wallet is a system (again, encryption-based) for holding, storing and transferring virtual currency units. A *wallet provider* is an entity that provides a digital currency wallet. The wallet provider facilitates participation in a digital currency system by allowing users and merchants to transfer the digital currency among themselves, making sure (e.g., via digital signatures) that the right parties are credited and charged. The wallet provider maintains each customer's virtual currency balance, ensures transaction security, and performs backup/cold storage.

5 A Digital Currency for PGS

In the last few years, digital currencies have attracted strong interest and even Central Banks are considering creating their own, or at least are keeping a close eye on them. We claim that PGS is a natural front-end for crypto-currency transactions, as it is itself based on visual cryptography. Many works[4] [8, 9] have presented comparison of crypto-currencies, most of them based on, or derived from, Bitcoin. Those cryptocurrencies can be split into three groups, based on the way the crypto-currency is generated and distributed. One group uses *proof-of-work* and the second group uses *zero-knowledge proofs* [10]. The third group is kind of a residual group, including only two currencies that use central distribution: Ripple (https://ripple.com/) and MaidSafeCoin (https://maid-safe.net/safecoin.html). The Proof-of-Work (POW) approach allows (volunteer) currency generation points (often called *Miners*) to generate new, valid currency units each time they solve a problem that requires huge computational effort (for example, "finding a number x whose image $h(x)$ via a non-invertible hash function $h()$ has two leading zeros"). Handling a currency system based on POW requires Miners to hold powerful computational resources which we cannot expect to have among the devices targeted by PGS. So, the one of the viable solutions for integrating PGS with a POW crypto-currency is to use Bitcoin, where the generation and distribution of currency units are already handled by the existing Bitcoin infrastructure, and bitcoin transfers can be used as a service at virtually no cost. This choice and its implications in terms of risk will be discussed in Sect. 5.1. A *zero-knowledge proof* or *zero-knowledge protocol* is a method by which one party (the prover) can prove to another party (the verifier) that a given statement is true, without conveying any information apart from the fact that the statement is indeed true [10]. Some crypto-currencies use computationally light generation techniques for the currency units and then rely on zero-knowledge proofs for proving each unit's uniqueness and single ownership at transaction time. Albeit at a

---

[4] https://en.bitcoin.it/wiki/Comparison_of_cryptocurrencies.

different time with respect to POW, managing this type of currencies also requires huge computational resources that mobile devices cannot currently afford. For the sake of conciseness, in this paper we shall not elaborate further on this group of currencies. Both Ripple and MaidSafeCoin belong to the residual group of digital currencies that use central distribution. Ripple's solution is built around an open, neutral protocol (Inter-ledger Protocol or ILP) while MaidSafeCoin is issued to the users of the decentralized Internet called the SAFE (Secure Access for Everyone). These special users, appropri-ately called *Farmers*, make their unused computing resources available to perform many of the protocols of collective interest (e.g., the Domain Name System) for running the Internet. In our opinion, farming looks a very interesting idea, as it envisions to use proof-of-availability to share unused resources (i.e., proof of setting aside resources for *potential* work) as a value generation mechanism rather than Bitcoin's *real* work, computing a difficult problem. Also, we find it attractive to couple PGS with a digital currency whose generation and distribution functionalities can require limited compu-tational effort, and therefore can be entirely handled by standard mobile devices looks attractive. We shall discuss this idea in Sect. 5.2.

5.1   Integrating PGS with Bitcoin

Let us first consider a scenario where some *trusted third party* (in our case, the PGS back-end server) holds digital wallets for both PGS buyers and sellers. We assume the organization running the PGS back-end has collected cash advance payments from PGS buyers (or, alternatively, has obtained an initial cash pool from a donor organization). The advance money/cash pool is used to purchase bitcoins, which are stored in the buyers' digital wallets. Whenever the proof of a PGS purchase (i.e., the two VC shares of the group selfie containing item, parties and agreed-upon price) reaches the PGS back-end, the corresponding bitcoin transfer is triggered between the buyer's and the server's digital wallets. Periodically, PGS sellers can request to withdraw money from their digital wallets. The PGS back-end handles these requests by exchanging bitcoins held in the sellers' wallets into cash. We claim that, although very simple, this scenario has many interesting features. First of all, it is transparent: buyers and sellers incur into little additional costs with regard to traditional cash transactions[5] and may even not be aware of the digital currency used by the PGS back-end. Secondly, the ecosystem includes no financial institution but the digital currency community, so there will be no intermedia-tion costs. Let us now consider the PGS back-end's profit model as if the back-end was a fund manager trading in and out the digital currency on behalf of investors. In the simplest case, we consider a single purchase. The PGS back-end receives the advance money from the buyer and invests it into bitcoins. Later it cashes out bitcoins to pay the purchase amount out in cash to the seller. Neglecting the cost of running the back-end in terms of hardware and bandwidth, and assuming no financial costs for the users[6], the

---

[5] Here, we neglect both the cost – for the buyer – of having/carrying a mobile terminal and the saving – for the seller – due to not having to handle cash.

[6] Ideally, the only costs PGS users will have are the ICT ones, coming close to the "digital unicorn" of no-financial-cost payments.

profit (or loss) of the PGS back-end will depend on the difference in the bitcoin-to-cash exchange rate at the moment when the cash was advanced by the buyer and at the moment when it was withdrawn by the seller. Due to the absence of transaction costs, it is difficult to make general statements about bitcoin exchange rate's statistical properties [11]. However, a general remark can be made. The Proof-of-Work bitcoin Miners must provide in order to obtain a currency unit is monotonically increasing, due to a built in mechanism that cuts the POW-to-reward ratio [7]. This suggests a long-term appreciation trend of Bitcoin with regard to traditional currencies. Looking at available empirical evidence, [12] discusses volatility of bitcoin exchange rate against six major currencies. Using raw annualized and adjusted data over a four year period from 2010 to 2014, the authors found that bitcoin had the highest annualized volatility in daily exchange rates. However, after accounting for the (low) volume of Bitcoin trades, the bitcoin exchange rate looks much more stable. Using data for the period 2010–2013, [13] showed that "Bitcoin investment exhibits very high volatility but also very high returns. In addition, for holders of well diversified portfolios, high risk is compensated by low correlations with other assets". So, depending on the actual timings of buyers' cash-ins and sellers' cash-outs, the notion of the PGS back-end as an intermediary for investing in bitcoin may provide a sensible business model. We plan to verify this experimentally.

5.2   Implementing a Digital Currency for PGS

Of course, we can also envision setting up a digital currency system specifically designed for PGS, including currency generation and distribution functionalities. Due to the context of the PGS application (payments in open air markets in developing countries) we need to dispense with approaches based on proof-of-work or zero-knowledge proofs. Luckily, other notions are available. Dimitris Chatzopoulos et al. have suggested that the computational hardness of the proof of ownership be replaced with "*the social hardness of ensuring that all witnesses to a transaction are colluders (users assisting the malicious user to double spend)*" [9]. They have then suggested LocalCoin, "*an alternative cryptocurrency that requires minimal computational resources, produces low data traffic and works with off-the-shelf mobile devices*".

LocalCoin perfectly suits the environment of mobile devices, it is a nice candidate for *PGS credits* as its generation mechanisms is based on the notion of proof of availability to do something useful [8] introduced by Stefan Dziembowski. We focus on the design presented by Dominic Wörner and Thomas von Bomhard [14]. They suggests that people can earn digital currency by making their devices available to share data of public interest, including early warnings of severe droughts and rains, products prices on local markets, traffic information, providing evidence to support credibility checks of scoops in social media, as part of the fight against gossip, rumor and hoax. We can assume our community will coincide with PGS buyers and sellers. Our proposed system is hybrid: "normal" buyers will buy credits in exchange of cash, as discussed in Sect. 5.1. Some special buyers, called *Sharers*, will get PGS credits by provably making their devices (or themselves) available for some *pro bono* activity. Once a seller holds PGS credits in her digital wallet, she can either cash them out or take advantage of the Sharers' resource pool. As far as implementation is concerned, we remark that creating a crypto-currency is no longer a big deal, as every crypto-currency on the market today is based on the open source bases like Lite-coin, available on GitHub (https://github.com/bitcoin). The main features to customize are:

- Creating blocks corresponding to new currency units based on Proof of Sharing Obligation (POSH) rather than Proof of Work (POW), or by implementing a hybrid version.
- How many credits Sharers receive when they submit a POSH block (*sharing reward*);
- The hashing algorithm to be used when creating the POSH blocks;
- The time duration between POSHs creation;
- The rate at which the sharing reward cuts in half (this is needed to ensure the appreciation trend w.r.t. traditional currencies, see Sect. 5.1).

6   Challenges

Many of the challenges that PGS-plus-digital-currency system will face are societal in nature: building a community to use the new crypto-currency, setting up a robust and capable team to handle development and bug fixing, marketing the new cryptocurrency for Sharers to keep adding value and other users to reinforce trust, bringing merchants onboard so that users can have a place where they spend their PGS credits, educating the community on the promises of the new tool and on the risks it bears so that users will have what they need to secure their wealth. The challenges this work wants to focus on are basically the technical ones. As PGS is already available on mobile devices using Android, we need to show the feasibility of a crypto-currency back-end, including (*i*) the POSH notion and (*ii*) a single wallet for PGS and Bitcoin currencies.

7   Conclusions

Traditional purchase of goods and services online are dominated by credit and debit cards, or PayPal. PGS provides a much simpler alternative to these systems which is based on a powerful metaphor (ripping a banknote in two) and requires virtually no technology training. Also, PGS allows to spread the cost of a fund transfer over multiple purchases. Field experience in Benin [1] has shown that PGS is suitable for low value purchases typical of open-air market in developing countries. As the relative cost of processing low value transactions is much greater for traditional payment methods than for digital money, the latter looks an ideal companion for PGS, further increasing its competitive advantage [15]. We discussed direct interfacing between PGS as Bitcoin, as well as the design of a LocalCoin-style digital currency based on the notion of Proofs of Sharing obligations (POSH). Implementation of the PGS Back-end is currently underway.

Acknowledgements. This work has been partly funded by the Bill & Melinda Gates Foundation under the grant n. APP198273.

References

1. Cimato, S., Damiani, E., Frati, F., Hounsou, J.T., Tandjiékpon, J.: Paying with a Selfie: A Hybrid Micro-payment Framework Based on Visual Cryptography. In: Glitho, R., Zennaro, M., Belqasmi, F., Agueh, M. (eds.) AFRICOMM 2015. LNICSSITE, vol. 171, pp. 136–141. Springer, Cham (2016). doi:10.1007/978-3-319-43696-8_15
2. Naor, M., Shamir, A.: Visual cryptography. In: Workshop on the Theory and Application of Cryptographic Techniques, 1–12 (1994)
3. El Zarki, M., Mehrotra, S., Tsudik, G., Venkatasubramanian, N.: Security issues in a future vehicular network. Eur. Wirel. **2**, 270–274 (2002)
4. European Central Bank: Virtual currency schemes. European Central Bank Internal report, Frankfurt-on-Main (2012)
5. Financial Action Task Force (FATF). Virtual currencies key definitions and potential AML/CFT Risks (2014)
6. Bank für Internationalen Zahlungsausgleich and Committee on Payments and Market Infrastructures: Digital currencies (2015)
7. Nakamoto, S.: Bitcoin: a peer-to-peer electronic cash system. https://bitcoin.org/bitcoin.pdf (2009)
8. Dziembowski, S.: Introduction to cryptocurrencies. In: 22nd ACM SIGSAC Conference on Computer and Communications Security, pp. 1700–1701 (2015)
9. Chatzopoulos, D., Gujar, S., Faltings, B., Hui, P.: LocalCoin: an ad-hoc payment scheme for areas with high connectivity. In: 17th ACM International Symposium on Mobile Ad Hoc Networking and Computing, pp. 365–366 (2016)
10. Krantz, S.G.: Zero knowledge proofs. Expeditions in Mathematics, 249–260 (2011)
11. Chu, J., Nadarajah, S., Chan, S.: Statistical analysis of the exchange rate of bitcoin. PLoS One **10**(7), e0133678 (2015)
12. Sapuric, S., Kokkinaki, A.: Bitcoin Is Volatile! Isn't that Right? Lecture Notes Bus. Inf. Process. **183**, 255–265 (2014)
13. Brière, M., Oosterlinck, K., Szafarz, A.: Virtual currency, tangible return: portfolio diversification with bitcoin. J. Asset Manag. **16**(6), 365–373 (2015)
14. Wörner, D., von Bomhard, T.: When your sensor earns money: exchanging data for cash with Bitcoin. In: 2014 ACM International Joint Conference on Pervasive and Ubiquitous Computing: Adjunct Publication, pp. 295–298 (2014)
15. Grinberg, R.: Bitcoin: an innovative alternative digital currency. Hast. Sci. Technol. Law J. **4**, 160–207 (2011)

Security

Cloud Digital Forensics Evaluation and Crimes Detection

Raja Jabir[(✉)] and Omar Alfandi

College of Technological Innovations, Zayed University, Abu Dhabi, UAE
{M80006379,Omar.Alfandi}@zu.ac.ae

Abstract. Cloud computing is one of the significant topics of today's era; due to the enhancement it brings to the Information Technology world. This transformation lead to its rapid adoption by different sectors, ranging from enterprise to personal usage. Organizations are constantly looking for ways to increase productivity with optimum cost; which derived the need for Cloud environments and its underlying virtualized infrastructure. With the increase usage of Cloud based infrastructure, criminals utilized its anonymity factor to hide their criminal activities; escaping from legal actions. This paper highlights the obstacles experienced during Cloud virtual layer forensics acquisition and analysis, due to lack of specialized forensics tools. We have developed a framework to aid in assessing the virtual environment readiness for forensics investigation and examine the applicability of existing state-of-the-art forensics tools to Cloud environment. The paper reveals the need for having specialized forensics tools for Cloud infrastructure forensics.

Keywords: Cloud computing · Virtual layer · Digital forensics · Cloud forensics · Forensics analysis · Dropbox

1 Introduction

Cloud computing has significantly transformed the way Information Technology (IT) services are being perceived. This advancement of technology has changed the traditional (IT) resource utilization and consumption, enabling IT service providers to meet organizations needs for high-end solutions with optimum cost. Cloud is built on the concept of resource sharing, where a pool of resources are accessed over the network on demand [1]. Cloud characteristics, as defined by National Institute of Standards and Technology (NIST), are an on demand self service, resource pooling, wide network access, and rapid elasticity [1]. The fundamental part of Cloud computing is the virtual layer; that serves as a platform to optimize resource utilization, transforming a single physical server into multiple virtual servers, thus increasing return on investment by reducing the overhead costs.

This growth in Cloud usage has raised concerns about security, integrity and privacy of data residing in a Cloud environment. With the diverse usage of Cloud environment and its unique nature, it enables additional functionalities such as IT computational outsourcing and sharing of resources, the concern of using Cloud as a platform for cybercrimes is increasing. From a security standpoint, it is critical for law enforcement

© ICST Institute for Computer Sciences, Social Informatics and Telecommunications Engineering 2018
F. Belqasmi et al. (Eds.): AFRICATEK 2017, LNICST 206, pp. 171–180, 2018.
https://doi.org/10.1007/978-3-319-67837-5_16

and digital forensics investigators to detect and solve criminal cases conducted using Cloud platforms. Unfortunately, the field of Cloud forensics is still immature with limited support from specialized digital forensics tools. This is possibly due to unavailability of standardization and interoperability between different Cloud vendors and deployed infrastructures.

This paper proposes a framework to examine the current state of Cloud virtual layer forensics. Experiments are conducted using three VMware ESXi Servers; due to its wide deployment across various enterprises. Servers hard disk images are acquired and examined using different forensics analysis tools. Anti-forensics activities, such as detecting deleted artifacts, is performed. Cloud Storage applications (exemplified using Dropbox) analysis is conducted to analyze traces availability. As a result of this research, we were able to highlight the tools that are applicable for Cloud forensics analysis.

2   Background

During the experiments we used a cluster of three Servers with VMware ESXi installation, a popular proprietary enterprise hypervisor provided by VMware. ESXi is installed on the physical servers to create a virtualization layer between the server and the operating systems [2]. This proprietary hypervisor utilizes the physical server 'host' resources such as memory, processor, network and storage, and virtually present them to several instances of virtual machines 'guest' [2]. The created virtual machines (VM) can run different operating systems independently of the host operating system and independently of each other; as each VM has its own operating system, memory, BIOS, network and storage. The hypervisor is responsible for this segregation between 'guests' and 'host' by the implementation of virtualization layer. VMware ESXi was chosen as the experiment environment due to its wide deployment and increasing market margin.

3   Literature Review

Cloud computing is rapidly being implemented in different domains from enterprise to personal usage. Due to its capability and cost efficiency organizations are moving toward Cloud infrastructure, aiming to reduce their operation expenses. Despite Cloud wide implementation across the world and the increase usage of Cloud in criminal activities, there is limited research on the area of Cloud forensics, leading to lack of awareness about Cloud issues [3]. Ali et al. [4] explained the different available Cloud models today; stressing on the associated security threats targeting the different Cloud components. Some of the threats discussed are virtual network vulnerabilities, threats on the communication layer, and privacy concerns due to user inadequate control on their data. The Authors discussed important security measures such as applying identity management and access control technologies. Pichan et al. [5] also provided a broad explanation of Cloud challenges and the different solutions; highlighting Cloud issues such as unknown geographical location, jurisdiction, encryption, and decentralized data. The Authors used the traditional digital forensics framework as a platform for assessing and analyzing the current Cloud issues.

From the security perspective, understanding the security threats and exploits in a Cloud environment is imperative to take proactive protective actions. Khorshed et al. [6] identified that the main Cloud challenges are trust issues, security risks and security threats. Other Cloud challenges [7] included application security, information leakage, data segregation, and privacy due to exploits of data confidentiality. To address these issues the Authors proposed applying fine grained access control and RSA encryption mechanism to avoid data disclosure; however this increases the complication of the Cloud forensics investigation process.

One of the main obstacles facing digital forensics examiners is data acquisition, that is critical to be conducted efficiently [8]. Preservation of possible evidentiary data during the acquisition and collection process is crucial; to ensure its integrity and admissibility in the court of laws. Quick and Choo [9] addressed the data integrity challenges during the evidence collection process, by utilizing public cloud storage providers such as Google Drive and Dropbox. The Authors findings presented that files metadata remains unchanged during the process of uploading, storing and downloading. This is applicable for unaltered files, which is difficult to control in a Cloud environment where files are shared and modified by different individuals. The Authors also illustrated changes in downloaded files timestamps when compared to the original file, which may hinder the forensics investigation process.

With Cloud forensics being a relatively immature domain it is important for a forensics examiner to understand the nature of artifacts stored in a Cloud environment; to support the forensic examination and analysis process. Martini and Choo [10] examined the artifacts available in Storage-as-a-Service Cloud model 'ownCloud' on both the client and server sides, categorized them and assessed their relevance to the forensics investigation process. The Authors assessed the stored files metadata and the authentication artifacts, highlighting their importance in identifying the Cloud instance used in any criminal activities and linking those acts to Cloud users.

This research will discuss the current state of Cloud environment, customizing traditional digital forensics framework and tools to meet Cloud unique requirements. Moreover this research will also determine detection of anti-forensics activities such as intentionally deleting artifacts. The research will exemplify Cloud readiness for forensics investigations and the experienced challenges.

4 Experimental Setup

The purpose of the experiments was to imitate real life scenarios and study the type of artifacts most likely to be involved in a Cloud environment crime scene. The presented framework is applicable to forensically analyze various Cloud environments. It consists of the following main sections:

(1) *System Preliminary Assessment*: Host examination for any virtual instances traces and artifacts was conducted by performing manual search and analysis; in order to collect any available artifacts and identify their location in the Cloud virtual layer.
(2) *Host Forensics Analysis*: Acquisition and forensics analysis of the selected ESXi Servers was conducted using commercial and open source digital forensics tools.

This is to determine the applicability of the current digital forensics process and tools to Cloud virtual environment.

(3) *Cloud Storage Forensic Analysis*: Forensics examination and analysis for the artifacts created on a Host during the installation and usage of a Cloud Storage Application was performed. This aims to identify and study the type of evidence created when such storage applications are used, and to assess the level of security implemented by these applications.

A. ESXi Servers

During the experiments we used a cluster of three Servers with VMware ESXi installation, a popular enterprise hypervisor provided by VMware. Each server had five physical internal SATA hard drives, each with a storage capacity of 500 GB. The servers were managed using vCenter server which was used to create new virtual machines and allocate storage space. In addition the system was connected to a VNX storage system, in which created virtual machines configurations and data files were stored.

B. Performed activities

The experiment was designed to simulate real life scenarios that will be utilized for subsequent investigations. Virtual Machines were created and assigned to users to perform certain activities such as log-in/log-off from the assigned machines, accessing the internet, creating and deleting files; which is important to investigate anti-forensics actions. In addition Dropbox Cloud Storage application was installed and used to upload and delete files from the Cloud storage service application. The objective is to investigate the artifacts that are created when users perform these activities.

C. Forensics Acquisition

To acquire the ESXi Servers hard disk images, each hard drive was removed and using an ATA serial cable we connected the hard disk to a Tableau SATA bridge, which also functions as a write-blocker. This is critical to avoid contaminating and tampering the original servers hard drive while performing the image acquisition. FTK Imager software was used to physically acquire the images, in raw format, and validate them by generating two checksums MD5 and SHA1; to ensure their integrity and detect any errors. The image acquisition process was a lengthy process that consumed approximately eight hours for each Hard Disk.

D. Forensics Analysis

We used the best available digital forensics tools throughout our experiments. The selection was based on the popularity and relevance. The tools used are as follows:

(1) *X-Ways forensics*: The tool did not allow exploring the disk images file systems. However it was able to display the disk images in chunks (318 chunks), which means the investigator should manually open each chunk separately and perform the analysis. It was also used to perform keyword search for server name, usernames and used applications. We were able to locate the server name, type and public key token. This is a tedious process if the search keywords are not known in advance; being the case in a criminal case investigation.

(2) *Autopsy*: We used Autopsy 4.0 to perform keyword search. It was more effective then X-Ways, as it displayed the entire image in a single window rather than dividing it into 318 chunks and having to analyze each chunk individually. The tool detected the system partition, as it supports internal file system structure. Utilizing the keyword search feature in Autopsy, it displayed details about the volume. The details are: full volume name, type as 'File system', it being an allocated space, date of creation, modification and access, Internal system ID, and finally the volume MD5 hash value. Furthermore the search also displayed information about the VMware ESXi boot details and configuration file. In addition Autopsy also displayed details about a deleted file, which was placed in the disk unallocated space. This file contained information about a deleted virtual machine configuration and the guest operating system as 'windows 7-64', the vCenter unique ID, ethernet card address, guest and host CPU ID. Theses information can be useful during the investigation process.

(3) *Magnet Internet Evidence Finder (IEF)*: version 6.7 was used as it is known to support artifacts analysis from different computer domains such as gaming consoles and Cloud storage applications. The image parsing consumed about three hours, after which the results were displayed. The software provided information about the file system type, number of available sectors, volume name and number, and source details. In addition information about system identifiers were retrieved. The Security User ID was displayed for accounts that accessed the ESXi Server, with a corresponding 'Artifact ID'. We then used this ID to map it with an entry in the Windows Event Logs; in order to associate an action with a specific user security ID. The information retrieved are the Event ID, the associated Security User ID, date and time the event occurred, and finally events description. Another interesting detected information is details about users login and log-off actions on the ESXi server. This is important for audit trailing, and associating an activity to a particular user.

(4) *ProDiscover*: Version 7 was used as it includes options to view registry entries and to retrieve deleted files and images. Details retrieved are image type 'DD image', total sectors size, total image size, the volume name 'ESXi', volume serial number (only ProDiscover and IEF Magnet detected this information), File System type, total clusters and sectors per cluster, the image starting and ending sectors. However, unlike Autopsy it did not detect the deleted system files.

E. Cloud Storage Application Forensic

These applications popularity is increasing, with shifts from the standard home users to businesses who are utilizes them for file sharing, document backups and other various activities. Cloud storage service providers are competing to supply additional features and even developing mobile applications to allow users to access their files, that were uploaded to the service website, on the go without geographical restrictions. These services allowed automatic data synchronization for any modification performed using any of the installed application connected to the cloud storage account. For example, when you upload a new document from your laptop, this file will be available when logging from your mobile device.

For this experiment, we studied the Cloud storage forensics implications, Dropbox was used to exemplify Cloud Storage applications; in order to examine the nature of artifacts produced once the application is installed and used. Initially signed-up for the Dropbox service and then downloaded the application on a virtual machine. The application created a directory under the used user's profile, and contained all user's Dropbox documents, which is considered as an offline cache of the Dropbox account documents. This is important to synch accounts data, and so it was reflected in the user's local 'Dropbox' folder.

5   Experimental Results

5.1   System Manual Examination

This phase addresses the major challenge of audit trailing in a virtual environment. In this aspect, artifacts that can be linked to virtual machine users were investigated. We found that when a virtual machine is launched, several files were created in the host machine under the virtual machine home directory. These files are used to allow the communication between the host and guest operating system. Artifacts that can associate actions to users of a virtual machine instance 'guest VM' were searched. In the investigation we focused on identifying artifacts about the virtual machine instance users, installed/used applications, and other metadata such as date and time of mentioned actions.

In this experiment, we used VMware, which created a directory called 'caches' in the host machine under the virtual machine home directory. Inside 'caches' folder, another directory was created called 'GuestAppsCache' which included two main subdirectories 'appData' and 'launchMenu'. On browsing the 'appData' folder contents, several files were found each named with a 32 character hex format. Each name was repeated twice with two different file types 'APPICON' and 'APPINFO'. The file information such as modification date, time, and size were available. For example, a files called '0e469eee0c8567ed0659732027f7ce54.appicon' of size 52 KB and a its corresponding file called '0e469eee0c8567ed0659732027f7ce54.appinfo' were created on the same time, with the preceding being of 1 KB size. We then extracted the files and viewed them using a Hex editor. The '0e469eee0c8567ed0659732027f7ce54.appicon' file contained information about VM users and launched applications and the corresponding file '0e469eee0c8567ed0659732027f7ce54.appinfo' contained information about the appicon file in a human readable format. As part of our observation, it was noticed both 'APPINFO' and 'APPICON' file types were created when the virtual machine users launch any application.

The second folder was called 'launchMenu', and contained a file called 'launch-Menu.menudata'. This file had information about the virtual machine Start Menu shortcuts. By associating the date and time of the file, an audit trail was established. This is important for activity monitoring and audit trailing, as it helps in associating an action on a virtual machine to the right user. Using these information we were able to establish a chain of events; aiding in crime detection.

In addition deleted artifacts were examined in attempt to determine anti-forensics activities. An experiment included deleting an application from a virtual machine and checking if the corresponding files '.APPICON' and '.APPINFO' on the host were deleted or not. Interestingly, these files existed and were not removed. This is important during a crime scene investigation in which criminals attempt to delete their traces as a form of anti-forensics activity.

5.2 Image Forensics Analysis

VMware ESXi Server 'Host' forensics analysis and examination was conducted utilizing the most reliable traditional digital forensics software in the market. It is imperative for a forensics investigator to be able to validate the forensics software outcome; to ensure results reliability and integrity. This was achieved by utilizing different tools and performing a comparison of their outcome, detecting any inconsistency and error rates. These tools also save effort by automating the process of searching for artifacts of evidentiary nature located across the forensic image. We used four different forensics software X-Ways Forensics, Autopsy, Magnet Internet Evidence Finder and ProDiscover. These tools were used to conduct a thorough and exhaustive analysis on the forensically acquired image of the ESXi Server using FTK Imager and a write blocker; to prevent original evidence contamination.

Most of the tools detected the ESXi partitions but failed to parse them and retrieve evidentiary information. Magnet IEF was the best out of the investigated tools. However it failed to retrieve deleted files like Autopsy. Each tool retrieved different information making it difficult to validate their accuracy and error rate. This indeed proved the incompatibility of current available digital forensic tools to parse and analyze Cloud virtual layer image. This requires vendors to develop specialized digital forensics tools customized to meet the Cloud environment needs (Table 1).

Table 1. Artifacts summary

Forensics tool	Retrieved artifacts
X-Ways forensics	Keyword search: server name, server type, public key token
Autopsy 4.0	Keyword search: server name, server type, volume name and type of space (allocated), date of creation/modification/access, Internal system ID Deleted files: Information about guest OS, vCenter ID, guest & host CPU ID
Magnet IEF 6.7	File system type, number of available sectors, volume details, security user ID, events details (such as login/logoff actions)
ProDiscover 7	Total sectors/image size, volume name, volume serial number, File System type, total clusters and sectors per cluster, the image starting and ending sectors

5.3   Cloud Storage Application Forensics

Several files were retrieved from the Dropbox directory, and have been investigated to detect useful artifacts. The investigated files and directories are [12]:

- **config.dbx**: This is an SQLite file that included information about the associated Dropbox account, email address, and installation related information.
- **filecache.dbx**: This file is consisted of tables. It includes information about the files inside the users' Dropbox directory.
- **bin**: This folder includes the executable files that are used by Dropbox application.

Further analysis was performed using Magnet IEF tool that allowed the decryption of both config.dbx and filecache.dbx file.

- Config.dbx file displayed the Dropbox associated email address 'xxx@gmail.com'.
- filecache.dbx file displayed records of all the available folders, files and images in the Dropbox account under investigation. The information obtained are file name, file path, creation date and time, modification date and time, file size, file version ID; this is used by Dropbox to avoid data duplication optimizing storage space utilization. All entries were located in the 'file_journal' table.

5.4   Countermeasures

As a security measure, we applied encryption to all confidential files before uploading them to the Cloud storage application. Boxcryptor application was installed on the our virtual machine. This software created a drive that is connected to the user's Cloud Storage application. By saving the files in this drive we can encrypt and decrypt them instantly. All files saved to the drive were found to be reflected in the Dropbox folder; which were then synchronized to the Dropbox account.

6   Analysis and Discussion

The conducted experiments' outcome demonstrated the limitation of the specialized state-of-the-art digital forensics analysis tools. This is clearly due to Cloud being a relatively new domain, with limited research and knowledge. The retrieved artifacts were a result of our preceding knowledge such as system type and sequence of conducted events, which is not applicable to traditional crime investigations.

From the vendor perspective, they are competing to deploy enhanced high level security mechanisms in an attempt to combat criminal attempts to invade Cloud users confidentiality and privacy. This study aims at directing the focus of forensics investigation to Cloud environment, due to its increasing large deployment scale, and its future of being a rich source of digital evidences.

7   Challenges and Limitations

Despite the advantages introduced with the implementation of Cloud setup, there are drawbacks to this technology, that affects the digital forensics investigation process:

- Limited documentation about Cloud setup and virtualization layer specifically.
- Inadequate knowledge and lack of trained and expert digital forensics investigators in Cloud environment.
- Vendors implementation of proprietary file systems and hypervisors, which is an unsupported format by most of the existing digital forensics tools.
- Lack of specialized Cloud forensics tools that are specialized in virtual systems and distributed systems.
- Limited control on the data stored in Cloud environment.
- Multiply users, so it is difficult to identify system users and data owners.
- It is difficult to retrieve evidences that are stored in Cloud, as its might involve breaching the confidentiality of other Cloud users.
- Hard to produce a forensically sound evidence to be accepted in court.
- Legal restrictions, as systems hosting Cloud infrastructure reside on different geographical locations (can be different countries) each with its own laws and regulations.
- Service providers are not cooperative, with each Cloud provider having different Cloud computing setup and approaches.

8   Recommendations

Enhancing the process of Cloud forensics, involves cooperation between all stakeholders to contribute to Cloud and its underlying components readiness for digital forensics investigations. Below are some of the recommendations:

- Introducing legal regulations, that enforces cooperation between all countries hosting cloud infrastructure.
- Training digital forensics investigators and examiners, to be Cloud experts.
- Educating users on the risks of Cloud systems, such as data privacy and confidentiality.
- Cooperation of Cloud service providers with digital investigations, providing information about the implemented systems and proprietary hypervisors.
- Developing specialized tools, policies, and procedures for Cloud forensics, that is customized to meet Cloud requirements.

9   Conclusion

In this paper, we assessed the current state of Cloud computing forensics, to evaluate its readiness for digital forensics analysis and investigation. The most reliable digital forensics applications were utilized to test their applicability to Cloud environment needs. During the experiment, all four used tools detected the ESXi Server system partition.

Manual host examination provided useful information that can be used for audit trailing, which is one of the major Cloud issues today. This research directs the spotlight to the need of specialized Cloud tools that are virtualization compatible, and it also aims at increasing awareness about the significance of establishing partnerships with Cloud Service Providers for forensics investigators to be up to date with the advancement of technology and establish understanding about the type of Cloud artifacts.

References

1. Mell, P., Grance, T.: The NIST definition of cloud computing (2011)
2. VMware, E.S.X., ESXi, V.: The market leading production-proven hypervisors. vmware. Disponível em: http://www.vmware.com/files/pdf/VMware-ESX-and-VMware-ESXi-DS-EN.pdf. Data de Acesso 11(11) (2009)
3. Harichandran, V.S., Breitinger, F., Baggili, I., Marrington, A.: A cyber forensics needs analysis survey: revisiting the domain's needs a decade later. Comput. Secur. **57**, 1–13 (2015)
4. Ali, M., Khan, S.U., Vasilakos, A.V.: Security in cloud computing: opportunities and challenges. Inf. Sci. **305**, 357–383 (2015)
5. Pichan, A., Lazarescu, M., Soh, S.T.: Cloud forensics: technical challenges, solutions and comparative analysis. Digit. Invest. **13**, 38–57 (2015)
6. Khorshed, M., Ali, A., Wasimi, S.: A survey on gaps, threat remediation challenges and some thoughts for proactive attack detection in cloud computing. Futur. Gener. Comput. Syst. **28**(6), 833–851 (2012)
7. Rao, R., Velumadhava, K.: selvamani: data security challenges and its solutions in cloud computing. Proced. Comput. Sci. **48**, 204–209 (2015)
8. Rozanski, S.: Using cloud data to accelerate forensic investigations. Netw. Secur. **2015**(9), 19–20 (2015)
9. Quick, D., Choo, K.K.R.: Forensic collection of cloud storage data: does the act of collection result in changes to the data or its metadata? Digit. Invest. **10**(3), 266–277 (2013)
10. Martini, B., Choo, K.K.: Cloud storage forensics: owncloud as a case study. Digit. Invest. **10**(4), 287–299 (2013)
11. Kent, K., Chevalier, S., Grance, T., Dang, H:. Guide to Integrating Forensic Techniques into Incident Response. NIST Special Publication, pp. 800–886 (2006)
12. vmware. https://www.vmware.com/support/ws55/doc/

Detecting Malware Domains:
A Cyber-Threat Alarm System

Khalifa AlRoum[1], Abdulhakim Alolama[1], Rami Kamel[1],
May El Barachi[2], and Monther Aldwairi[1(✉)]

[1] Zayed University, Khalifa City B, Abu Dhabi, United Arab Emirates
{M80006834, M80006863, M80006762,
monther.aldwairi}@zu.ac.ae
[2] University of Wollongong Dubai, Knowledge Village, Dubai, U.A.E
MaiElbarachi@uowdubai.ac.ae

Abstract. Throughout the years, hackers' intentions' varied from curiosity, to financial gains, to political statements. Armed with their botnets, bot masters could crash a server or website. Statistics show that botnet activity accounts for 29% of the Internet traffic. But how can bot masters establish undetected communication with their botnets? The answer lies in the Domain Name System (DNS), using which hackers host their own domain and assign to it changing IP addresses to avoid being detected. In this paper, we propose a multi-factor cyber-threat detection system that relies on DNS traffic analysis for the detection of malicious domains. The proposed system was implemented, and tested, and the results yielded are very promising.

Keywords: DNS analysis · Cyber-threat · Malicious domains' detection · Botnets

1 Introduction

With the rapid increase in the newly registered domains around the world, the challenge of identifying the malicious domains from the legitimate ones becomes more complicated. It is well known that without the domain name system (DNS), surfing the Internet would become nearly impossible. Hackers around the world use the DNS to direct the traffic coming from their botnets, so if a system admin of a specific network blocks a traffic from flowing to a suspicious IP address, the hacker still can get the traffic by updating his domain with a new IP address. Blocking the traffic flowing to suspicious IP addresses would solve the problem in the past, but nowadays using the frequent DNS entry change feature, this technique is less effective. Therefore, there is a need for building a system for the detection of malicious domains rather than suspicious IP addresses.

Many cyber-attacks have been launched using botnets, - a botnet consisting of a group of machines controlled by a hacker, via a command and control center. Such botnets cannot only be used to launch cyber-attacks, but also to collect a variety of useful information for hackers. The importance of botnets is such that some hackers may lease their botnets to other hackers in the dark-net.

© ICST Institute for Computer Sciences, Social Informatics and Telecommunications Engineering 2018
F. Belqasmi et al. (Eds.): AFRICATEK 2017, LNICST 206, pp. 181–191, 2018.
https://doi.org/10.1007/978-3-319-67837-5_17

In response to such malicious activities, various companies have taken the responsibility to detect and stop any botnet reporting to command and control servers. The key to achieving this role lies in the development of an efficient multi-factor botnet detection and alarm mechanism.

In the next section of the paper, we give some background information about the DNS system as well as botnets. This is followed by the methodology we followed to develop a cyber-threat alarm system. In Sects. 4 and 5, the results obtained are analyzed and our conclusions are drawn.

2 Botnets and the Domain Name System

2.1 What are Botnets?

A botnet is defined as a group of computers connected to the Internet, which are controlled by a hacker without the awareness of their users/owners [1]. For a machine to be controlled by a hacker, it must be first turned into a zombie. This typically occurs through an Internet port that was left open and was used by the hacker to plant a Trojan horse or a malicious code with a backdoor on the machine – this backdoor can be used for later attacks. Whenever needed, the zombie botnet can be used to obey a command sent by the hacker. The hacker can use botnets to simultaneously send a very large number of bogus requests to a specific server causing it to crash [1].

2.2 How do Botnets Work?

Typically, botnets wander the Internet looking for exposed computers to quickly infect them and remain discrete waiting for the right time to perform a task given to them by their master. Tasks performed by the botnet can be classified into four categories (Table 1):

Table 1. Types of Botnet Activities

Sending	Botnets are used to send spams, viruses, and malware to different systems through the Internet
Stealing	Botnets are used to steal sensitive information from the infected computers - information such as credit card numbers, passwords
DoS attack	Botnets are used to perform a denial of service attack through redirecting transmissions to a specific server in the effort of crashing that server and blackmailing the owners
Click fraud	Botnets can be used to click on Internet ads to boost web advertisement

- **Internet Relay Chat (IRC) signals:** This concentration on IRC ports by the bot masters guided some information security specialist to block all IRC communications when setting up a business network environment. This has led bot masters to search for new ways of communicating with their bots, such as the following:

- **JPG files:** A more advanced way a bot herder can communicate with his bots is through the metadata in JPG file. Because those files are transmitted through HTTP port 80, most computers will allow them.
- **Microsoft Word 2007 files:** Microsoft Word 2007 files contain XML metadata and by using this metadata, the bot master can send commands to the bots, which will not raise any suspicion as the traffic is being passed through port 80.
- **LinkedIn.com Status:** bots can be programmed to use the LinkedIn API to receive commands by periodically checking the status message of a dummy account.

2.3 Botnets and DNS

It is obvious that the command and control server must be able communicate with its zombies. Thus, the perfect way in which a bot master can communicate with its zombies is a way that can assure that the communication remains undetected and discrete. Due to this, bot masters tend to use DNS as a communication channel to send the commands needed to carry out a specific malicious task, because of the following reasons: First, the fact that there is no effective mechanism to differentiate between the legitimate DNS queries from the malicious ones. Moreover, DNS as a protocol is left untouched in terms of firewalling and securing a system in most environments. Another advantage is the ability to change DNS records frequently, as DNS was built initially as a distributed system that assures resilience [2]. Fast Flux Networks (FFN) are a subset of botnets that changes IP and domain name association frequently to pose as Content Distribution networks (CDNs) in an effort to avoid detection [3]. This helps hackers in case the C&C IP address was blocked, as changing DNS record will allow botnets to continue communicating with the bot master.

3 Literature Review

According to Hao, Feamster and Pandrangi, malicious domains can be detected using certain parameters such as number of queries performed after the domain registration, the fraction of IP addresses associated with those domains, and the ACs containing the domains' records [4]. However, those conclusions were reached based one month of monitoring using locally installed probes – a technique which presented temporal and scope related limitations.

Based on Bilge's work presented in [5], Exposure (a system introduced in the paper) was scalable enough for detecting malicious domains using passive DNS analysis. The system was unique because of the 15 behavioral features it uses to detect malicious domains. The limitation associated with the paper, is that an attacker can avoid detection by Exposure if he studied the features it looks for and tries to avoid them. Another limitation of Exposure that was highlighted by Antonakakis et al. [6], is that it relies on monitoring traffic that is initiated from some local recursive DNS servers.

Konte et al. [7] focused on the monitoring of URLs associated with scan campaigns, in order to better understand the behavior of fast flux networks as their associated rapid changes in DNS mappings. Nevertheless, this work was concerned with the study of scam websites, not addressing the issue of malware detection. Spring [8] presented an anti-phishing black listing can contribute to limiting the lifetime of a phishing website. Moreover, using specific DNS information may help in the automated detection method of fast flux networks.

Choi et al. [9] proposed to monitor DNS traffic in order to detect a group activity of resolving a domain by sending simultaneously DNS queries where this indicate a distributed botnets trying to resolve a bots' master domain. This approach was found to be effective for the detection of botnets. Its main limitation remains its large processing time. Furthermore, botnets can evade this algorithm if they use DNS only in the initialization stage. Finally, botnets can paralyze this algorithm by intentionally generating DNS queries that spoof their source addresses.

Another work that addresses botnets and C&C detection by monitoring the time period between the domain registration and its first DNS activity is presented by Spring et al. [10]. In this work, the authors propose a pattern for botnet detection in which legitimate domain activity will not take a long time to start DNS activity. The main limitation in this case is that this solution relies on passive DNS sources.

While all the mentioned algorithms tackled DNS activity at the low level of the hierarchy, Kopis [6] is more interested in the upper DNS hierarch, which ensures global visibility. The main advantages of Kopis are its use of real data for a period of six months, in addition to the ability to detect newly created and previously unclassified malware domains several weeks before their appearance in any blacklist.

Another botnet detection method consists in detecting illegal fast fluxing that ensures for a bot master a reliable hosting with high availability. In the paper presented by Holz et al. [11], an automated mechanism for the detection of new fast fluxing domains is proposed. Although the proposed approach yields low false positive and false negative rates, the algorithm needs enhancement to be more reliable and detect complex botnet communities. Freiling et al. [12] proposed approaches to prevent botnet attacks by observing the communication flow within the botnet and detecting the IP address that it resolved. Another approach is by terminating the infrastructure hosting the C&C server, by manipulating DNS replies.

4 Research Methodology

In this work, we propose a multi-factor cyber-threat detection system that relies on DNS traffic analysis for the detection of malicious domains. In order to achieve this goal, a simulated network was built. In this network, a computer acts as a bot trying to communicate with a specific Command and Control (C&C) server through DNS queries. The DNS queries are passed to a specific DNS server, which we have configured. An IDS implementing a DNS multi-factor detection mechanism is placed in the network to enable the differentiation between legitimate domains and malicious ones. In addition to the DNS traffic retrieved from our own DNS server, we also relied on AUE DNS records obtained for the last month from Etisalat (the main ISP in the UAE). The retrieved DNS records are analyzed to explore botnet activity in the UAE cyber space.

4.1   The Simulated Network Components

As depicted in Fig. 1, the main components of the built simulated network consist of the following:

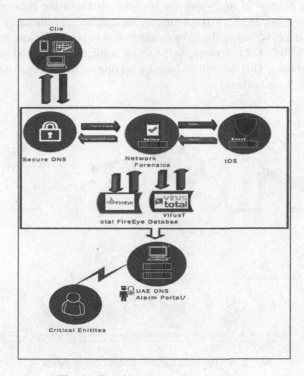

Fig. 1. Simulated network components

1. **Domain Name System (DNS) Server**: To build our DNS server, we choose the bind9 open source tool because it has the capability to operate on multiple platforms, nevertheless, adding the feature of forwarding the DNS queries to a real DNS server. Another reason why bind9 is being chosen is the friendly interface associated with the tool.
2. **Infected Machine:** A script to manipulate the cron tab will be planted in the infected machine, in which it will schedule a malicious communication with our C&C server. This way, we will ensure that malicious activities will take place in our environment, using which we can test the effectiveness of our intrusion detection system [13].
3. **Cyber Threat Alarm System:** Different applications and network components were optimized to ensure effective collaboration malicious domains detection. Figure 2 illustrates the applications used to build our cyber threat alarm system. Some applications may have features, which other applications do not. For instance, Snort lacks the ability of showing the geo location while Xplico, a network forensics analysis tool, provides this information [14]. Snort will be placed online,

thus all traffic will be passed through it. This ensures that all traffic will be examined and matched to our pre-defined rules [15], which would enable the flagging of any suspicious traffic. On the other hand, Xplico will provide us with additional analysis of the traffic where it will reflect a live acquisition of the network. This tool will automate the process of analyzing the traffic throughout the network, which will reduce the time needed to inspect suspicious queries. Additionally, the findings, which are extracted from sniffing the monitored network traffic can be compared to a list of well-known C&C servers, well-known malicious ports, and owners of other malicious websites. This list will be built by relying on trusted third party databases, such as FireEye and others.

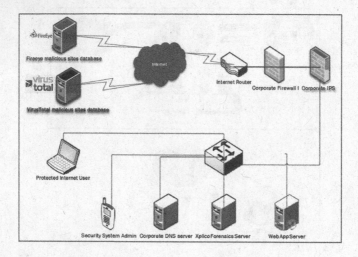

Fig. 2. Cyber threat alarm system components

To achieve effective results, a multi-factor malicious domain detection mechanism was developed and integrated with the IDS, to raise alarms in case of malicious activity detection. The developed mechanism relies on the seven factors listed in Table 2 for the detection of malicious domains.

Table 2. Malicious domains detection factors

Factors	Definition
Reputation	Domain reputation can indicate the suspiciousness of the domain as it reported from different entities/antivirus/security research center
Geo location	Geo location can be used as a factor on detecting suspicious traffic based on risk rating of the most countries hosting/generating such traffic (attacks/)
Destination port	Many suspicious traffic can be detected based on a well-known suspicious port it use as a destination (since it communicate to the bot master) adding to this, some ports which is not included in the list but is from the range of not allocated ports (1-1024) can also show a suspicious traffic

(continued)

Table 2. (*continued*)

Factors	Definition
Known C&C	Some leading organization are publishing any new botnets with their associated C&C. in this project we will refer to one of these organization (FireEye)
Domain owner	In a domain was owned by the same person who owned a well-known C&C, this also indicate that the new domain is most probably a suspicious one
Frequent DNS changes	Changing domain information/record should not be a frequent thing. Some organization (domain tools and others) keep record of these changes and raise an alert in case changes were very frequent
Behavior	In case that a client resolve a suspicious domain and then establish a communication with it followed by a misbehaving traffic (such as generating a DoS attack) then it raise a concern of being infected

All the factors mentioned are assigned weights and calculated as a weighted sum, which if it reached a certain threshold would trigger an alarm at the IDS level. Weight categories were distributed in a way to cover all possible scenarios that might happen and require the activity to be flagged. The weighted sum of the different detection factors is expressed as follows:

$$S = 1 - (0.4(r + g + b + f)) + k + o + p \qquad (1)$$

If $S \leq 0$, flag it as Suspicious DNS record
If $S \leq 0$, flag it as good DNS record
S: DNS flag; r: Site DNS reputation.
g: DNS Geolocation; b: Suspicious traffic behavior.
f: frequent DNS changes; k: Known botnet command & control center
o: Blacklisted domain owners; p: Known blacklisted port

Our factors are divided into two categories; the first category contains the must-stop factors while the other category contains the partial-stop factors. The point where an alarm flag must be raised is when either one of the must-stop factors is met or if three of the partial-stop factors are met. Having the three partial-stop factors meet doesn't guarantee that the domain being flagged is a suspicious domain, however flag this domain for further inspection can eliminate the risk of a botnet being deployed in the network. The weight categories associated with each factor along with the reason of assigning that much weight is shown in Table 3 below.

Table 3. IDS factors to completely or partially block investigated DNS name

Factor	IDS Decision	Reason
Known C&C servers	Must stop	Already being flagged as a known C&C by a trusted third party leaves no doubt that this factor is a must-stop factor
Known C&C ports	Must stop	Communicating through an already known port as a preferred random port by C&C is a must-stop activity

(*continued*)

Table 3. (*continued*)

Factor	IDS Decision	Reason
Known Owners	Must stop	The name of known C&C servers' owners when associated with a new domain raise a must- stop flag
Reputation	Partial stop	Some domains may have a bad reputation although they are legitimate however others are surely malicious. The key phrase here is "no smoke without no fire"
Behavior	Partial stop	When a non-ordinary traffic behavior is experienced toward a domain a partial-stop flag should be raised
Frequent- change in DNS entries	Partial stop	A frequent change in DNS entries is a popular action done by bot masters, however other legitimate domains do that to achieve redundancy that leaves us with a partial-stop flag
Geo- location	Partial stop	Some geolocation unfortunately is well known for malicious activity, however that doesn't mean that anything coming from this location is malicious, but in the other sided it deserves a partial-stop category flag

5   Data Collection and Data Analysis

In this project, we will use primary data source in order to get accurate results. Our primary data will be the internal network is another primary source for data. These data will be analyzed as explained in the methods where this project will consider a domain as a malicious domain based on the final score that is assigned to it. The score is calculated based on several criteria such as the domain registrar information and when it was register, the review of this domain in the online reputation service as well as the IP reputation that is assigned to that domain, the behavior of the traffic generated toward this domain and the port is used for such communication. If most of these criteria were flagged, then this domain is suspicious. To test and check how accurate our solution is we compare the results with some ATP solutions such as FireEye. After verifying the accuracy of our solution, we can then detect C&C in real time.

Tables 4 and 5 depict the test results obtained, as well as the analysis of those results.

Table 4. Obtained Results

	Real threat	*Algorithm decision*
ftp.idm.ae	No Threat	Blocked
office.ontimedata ~ soluitions.com	Suspicious DNS	Blocked
zu.ac.ae	No Threat	Allowed
d99q.cn	Suspicious DNS	Blocked
datatoad.iptime.org	Suspicious DNS	Blocked

(*continued*)

Table 4. (*continued*)

	Real threat	*Algorithm decision*
doubleclick.net	Suspicious DNS	Blocked
fbcdn.net	Suspicious DNS	Blocked
gstatic.com	Suspicious DNS	Allowed
aptuslearning.com	Suspicious DNS	Blocked
Lucydriver ~ translations.com	Suspicious DNS	Blocked
rgmechanics.ru	Suspicious DNS	Blocked
eri.edu.pk	Suspicious DNS	Blocked
icet-logistics.ro	Suspicious DNS	Blocked
samdriver.com	Suspicious DNS	Blocked
www.kareenas.com	Suspicious DNS	Allowed
www.elderology.net	Suspicious DNS	Blocked
abrico.info	Suspicious DNS	Blocked
powervoice-2.tk	Suspicious DNS	Blocked
esportskart.com	Suspicious DNS	Blocked
www.lagunasderuidera.net	Suspicious DNS	Blocked
emazkid.ghettohost.tk	Suspicious DNS	Blocked
hank-moody2.tk	Suspicious DNS	Blocked
www.motorfliegen.ch	Suspicious DNS	Blocked
southwest.icims.com	Suspicious DNS	Blocked
www.stylenstitch.com	Suspicious DNS	Allowed
www.tamilkamadesam.in	Suspicious DNS	Blocked
google.bi	Suspicious DNS	Allowed

Table 5. Results' analysis

		Suspicious DNS records	
		True (23 records)	*False (two records)*
Algorithm Decision	*Positive (22 records)*	21	1
	Negative (5 records)	4	1

The malicious domains' detection accuracy % can be represented by Eq. (2) below:

$$a = 1 - \frac{tp + fn - fp - tn}{t} \cdot 100\% \qquad (2)$$

a: detection accuracy; tp: True positive decisions.
fn: False negative decisions; fp: False positive decisions.
tn: True negative decisions

Based on the obtained results, we conclude that our system yields the following accuracy:

$$a = 1 - \frac{21 + 1 - 1 - 4}{27} \cdot 100\% = 62.9\%$$

6 Conclusions and Future Work

In this work, we presented a multi-factor cyber-threat detection system that relies on DNS traffic analysis for the detection of malicious domains. The conducted experiments show that our system yields a malicious domains' detection accuracy rate of 62.9%. This performance in terms of accuracy level can be improved by considering more factors for the detection. One of the additional factors that can be considered is the domain owner – a factor that may lead to the detection of malicious domains in advance and in some cases before that domain starts its malicious activities. This value comes with an overhead as it requires the tracking of not only the malicious domains but also their owners, in addition to the monitoring of owners to determine if they registered any new or existing domains, and if these domains actively change. Domain monitoring tools such as a domain service provider can assist in detecting dynamic changes but for the premier users and this is offered as well in their APIs. This will help detecting the fast fluxing in malicious domains as they depend on frequent changing in their records. On the other hand, the IDS rules were implemented in order to detect any suspicious domains by comparing all DNS content with the list of well-known C&C domains. This list can be obtained from FireEye as they publish all the newly detected ones. Adding to this, detecting known bad ports as well as any misbehaving traffic are implemented in IDS rules, which alert the network admin of the existence of a botnet in the network.

Acknowledgements. This work was supported by Zayed University Research Office, Research Cluster Award # R17079.

References

1. Dietrich, C.J., Rossow, C., Freiling, F.C., Bos, H., Steen, M.V., Pohlmann, N.: On Botnets that use DNS for command and control. In: 2011 Seventh European Conference on Computer Network Defense (EC2ND), Gothenburg (2011)
2. Botnet (zombie army) definition. http://searchsecuritytechtarget.com/definition/botnet (2012)
3. Al-Duwairi, B., Al-Hammouri, A., Aldwairi, M., Paxson, V.: GFlux: a Google-based system for fast flux detection. In: IEEE Conference on Communications and Network Security (IEEE-CNS 2015), Florence, Italy, 27–29 Sept 2015 (2015)
4. Hao, S., Feamster, N., Pandrangi, R.: Monitoring the initial DNS behavior of malicious domains. In: Proceedings of ACM SIGCOMM Conference on Internet Measurement Conference, New York, NY, USA (2011)

5. Bilge, L., Kirda, E., Kruegel, C., Balduzzi, M.: EXPOSURE: finding malicious domains using passive DNS analysis. In: Proceedings of 18th Annual Network and Distributed System Security Symposium (NDSS), San Diego, CA, February 2011

6. Antonakakis, M., Perdisci, R., Lee, W., II, N.V., Dagon, D.: Detecting malware domains at the upper DNS hierarchy. In: Proceedings of 20th USENIX Security Symposium, San Francisco, CA, August 2011

7. Konte, M., Feamster, N., Jung, J.: Dynamics of online scam hosting infrastructure. In: Proceedings of Passive and Active Measurement (PAM), Seoul, South Korea, April 2009

8. Spring, J.M.: Large Scale DNS Traffic Analysis of Malicious Internet Activity with a Focus on Evaluating the Response Time of Blocking Phishing Sites, Master's Thesis, School of Information Science, University of Pittsburgh, Pittsburgh, PA, p. 26 (2010)

9. Choi, H., Lee, H., Kim, H.: Botnet detection by monitoring group activities in DNS traffic. In: 7th IEEE International Conference on Computer and Information Technologies (2007)

10. Spring, J.M., Metcalf, L.B., Stoner, E.: Correlating domain registrations and DNS first activity in general and for malware. In: Proceedings of Securing and Trusting Internet Names (SATIN), Teddington, United Kingdom, April 2011

11. Holz, T., Gorecki, C., Rieck, K., Freiling, F.C.: Measuring and detecting fast-flux service networks. In: NDSS (2008)

12. Freiling, F., Holz, T., Wicherski, G.: Botnet tracking: exploring a root-cause methodology to prevent distributed denial-of-service attacks. In: 10th European Symposium on Research in Computer Security (2005)

13. Aldwairi, M., Khamayseh, Y., Al-Masri, M.: Application of artificial bee colony for intrusion detection systems. Secur. Commun. Netw. **8**(16), 2730–2740 (2015)

14. Kharbutli, M., Aldwairi, M., Mughrabi, A.: Function and data parallelization of Wu-manber pattern matching for intrusion detection systems. Netw. Protocols Algorithms **4**(3), 46–61 (2012)

15. Aldwairi, M., Alansari, D.: Exscind: Fast pattern matching for intrusion detection using exclusion and inclusion filters. In: Proceedings of the 2011 7th International Conference on Next Generation Web Services Practices, pp. 24–30 (2011)

Intrusion Detection Using Unsupervised Approach

Jai Puneet Singh[(⊠)] and Nizar Bouguila

CIISE Department, Concordia University, Montreal, Canada
jaipuneet.singh@mail.concordia.ca,
nizar.bouguila@concordia.ca

Abstract. The process of detecting intrusion on network traffic has always remained a key concern for security researchers. During the previous years, intrusion detection had attracted many researchers to find anomaly on NSL-KDD data set. Hence, most of the approaches applied on NSL KDD data set were supervised approaches. We had conducted statistical analysis on this data set using Dirichlet Mixture model. We have seen initialization using Aitchison distance fits better for proportional data. The feature selection highly affects both the performance and results into an improved evaluation of anomaly detection by an unsupervised approach.

Keywords: Mixture models · Intrusion · Aitchison distance · Feature selection

1 Introduction

With an emerging growth of networks and rate of transfer of data through networks has increased the demand for network security. There is a significant literature on Anomaly detection. Anomaly detection deviates from normal traffic and it is important to find an anomaly in an era of communication. Although, there are a lot of articles on intrusion detection, feature selection, and unsupervised learning approach is often underrepresented. There are very limited publicly available data sets for network-based anomaly detection. Earlier KDDCup99 was used heavily for all kind of intrusion detection through machine learning methodology. KDDCup99 has a huge number of redundant records [24]. It was found that around 78% of records in KDDCup99 were duplicated. Mchugh [21] gave many critics on KDDCup dataset and DARPA data set of 1998 as it was not good for applying statistical approaches to learning. The new NSL KDD data set was proposed [2] to overcome the problems present in KDDCup99 and DARPA data sets [1]. NSL KDD data set does not have redundant and duplicates records. There is the lot of work which has been done on NSL KDD data set to find an intrusion [3]. All existing approaches are supervised learning approach. The author in [18] had used Principle component analysis for feature extraction followed by SVM for finding intrusion in NSL KDD data set. The author in [22] had used a combination of classifiers or clusters which are followed by supervised or unsupervised data filtering. The author in [26] had used feature selection technique for a specific group and then comparing corrected KDD data set of feature selection with NSL KDD data set.

© ICST Institute for Computer Sciences, Social Informatics and Telecommunications Engineering 2018
F. Belqasmi et al. (Eds.): AFRICATEK 2017, LNICST 206, pp. 192–201, 2018.
https://doi.org/10.1007/978-3-319-67837-5_18

In our paper, we have used unsupervised approach using Dirichlet Mixture Model. The initialization of mixture model is done with K-means using different distance metrics. Aitchison distance metrics shows better results than Euclidean distance for proportional data. It is followed by feature selection on NSL KDD data which reduces features from 41 to 16 features. The comparative analysis has been drawn which, shows that how feature selection and proper initialization increases the detection rate in NSL-KDD data set.

In Sect. 2 of our paper, we have discussed the feature selection approaches and results are showed in form of graph. In Sect. 3, Dirichlet Mixture model is discussed with Aitchison distance being applied on K-means as a distance metrics. Section 4, gives the result of an experiment performed and comparison table. Finally in Sect. 5 concluding remarks are drawn.

2 Feature Selection

There is a subtle difference between feature selection and feature extraction where feature selection performs removal of features which are not relevant when computed with labels during its posterior processes. There are various feature selection methods, popular are being: Stepwise Regression, Stability Selection, Significance Analysis for Microarrays, Weight by Maximum relevance, Least Absolute Selection and Shrinkage Operator (LASSO) etc. Feature extraction transforms the attributes and transformed attributes are a combination of the original attributes. In this process, linear dependence between the features are minimized and projection of original data is on new space. The common feature extraction methods are PCA (principal component analysis), ICA (independent component analysis), Multifactor dimensionality reduction, Latent semantic analysis etc. The novel methods of feature extraction on proportional data were proposed by an author in [20] which extracts features of proportional data using data separation by Dirichlet distribution. In our paper, we have concentrated upon feature selection which is different from feature extraction.

2.1 Weight by Maximum Relevance

It has been proposed by Blum et al. [4], is a filter that measures the dependence between every feature x and the classification feature y (i.e., the label) using Pearson's linear correlation, F-test scores, and mutual information [4, 19]. The high score by mutual correlation reveals the features which are important. The NSL KDD Dataset has 41 features and in order to reduce the complexity and finding an optimal solution we have reduced to 16 features taking into an account that Weight by Maximum Relevance score of the feature is $f \geq 0.05$. The output obtained can be shown by the Fig. 1.

Weight by Maximum Relevance correlation vector can be defined by Pearson Correlation coefficient as:

$$R(i) = \frac{cov(X_i, Y)}{\sqrt{Var(Xi)Var(Y)}} \tag{1}$$

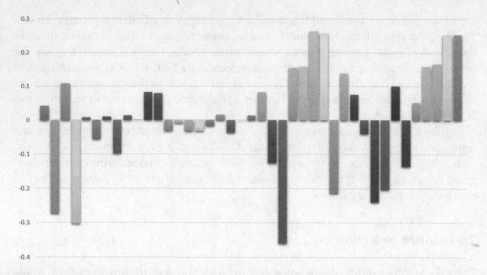

Fig. 1. Score obtained after applying weight by maximum relevance feature selection technique

The equation can be written as:

$$R(i) = \frac{\sum_{k=1}^{M} (x_{k,i} - \bar{x})(yk - \bar{y})}{\sqrt{\sum_{k=1}^{M} (x_{k,i} - \bar{x})^2 \sum_{k=1}^{M} (yk - \bar{y})^2}} \tag{2}$$

This can only detect the linear dependency between variable and target [17].

2.2   Least Absolute Selection and Shrinkage Operator (LASSO)

Tibshirani Robert [25] explains feature selection by checking vector β which is a coefficient vector. It minimizes the residual sum of squares which is related to coefficient being less. It shrinks coefficients and set others to zero, therefore tries to retain the good features of both subset selection and ridge regression. It is given $(x_1, x_2, \ldots, x_D)$ and an outcome be y, the LASSO should fit linear model. The computation of LASSO is a quadratic problem and can be solved by standard numerical analysis algorithms. LASSO does shrinkage and variable selection whereas ridge regression only shrinks. The initial idea is to start working with the large value of λ and slowly start decreasing it. The minimization for LASSO can be expressed as follow:

$$\sum_{i=1}^{n} (y_i - \sum_{j} x_{ij}\beta_j)^2 + \lambda \sum_{j=1}^{p} |\beta_j| \tag{3}$$

In this equation yi is the outcome variable, for cases $i = 1, 2, \ldots, n$ features $x_{ij}, j = 1, 2, \ldots, p$. Figure 2 represents feature selection by LASSO and reducing features to 16 features by taking into an account $f \geq 0.0053$.

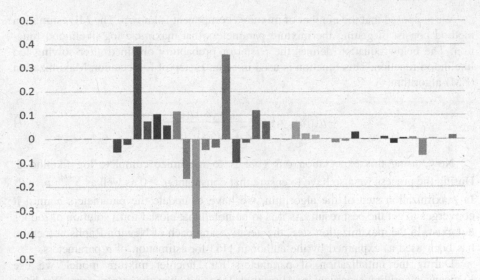

Fig. 2. Score obtained after applying LASSO feature selection technique

3 Proposed Method

Let $X = \{\mathbf{X}_1, \mathbf{X}_2, \ldots, \mathbf{X}_N\}$ be the data set with N D-dimensional such that Dirichlet mixture model being applied on it. The density function of Dirichlet mixture model can be given by

$$p(X_i|\theta) = \sum_{j=1}^{M} p_j p(X_i|\alpha_j) \tag{4}$$

where α_j is the parameter vector of component j, p_j is the mixing proportion which should be positive and always sum to 1. $\theta = \{p_1, p_2, \ldots, p_M; \alpha_1, \alpha_2, \ldots, \alpha_M\}$ is the complete set of parameters fully characterizing the mixture $M \geq 1$ is the number of components. Each Dirichlet distribution can be written in the form

$$p(X_i, a_j) = \frac{1}{\beta(\alpha)} \prod_{d=1}^{D} X_{id}^{\alpha_{jd}-1} \tag{5}$$

$$\beta(\alpha) \frac{\prod_{d=1}^{D} \Gamma(\alpha_{jd})}{\Gamma(\sum_{d=1}^{D} \alpha_{jd})} \tag{6}$$

where $x_{id} > 0 \; d = 1, 2, \ldots, D, X = \{X_{i1} + X_{i2}, \ldots, + X_{id} = 1\}$ and $\alpha_j = (\alpha_{j1}, \alpha_{j2} \ldots \alpha_{jD})$ represents parameter vector for j^{th} population. Let N D-dimensional vector be $\mathcal{X} = \{X_1, X_2, \ldots, X_N\}$ a data set of with a common, but unknown, probability density function $p(\mathbf{X}_i|\theta)$ as given in above equation.

We supposed that the number of mixtures component is known. The ML estimation method consist of getting the mixture parameters that maximize log likelihood function. The below equation defines the posterior probability obtained after solving log likelihood function. This function is used in as an E-step of Expectation Maximization (EM) algorithm.

$$p(j|X_i, \alpha_j) = \frac{p_j p(X_i|\alpha_j)}{\sum_{k=1}^{K} p_{ik} p(X_i|\alpha_k)} \tag{7}$$

Now, using this expectation our goal is to maximize complete log likelihood. During the process we also have to ensure that constraint $p_j \geq 0$ as well as $\sum_{j=1}^{M} p_j = 1$. In maximization step of the algorithm, we have to update the parameters α until it converges to get the best result. As it is to be noted that closed form solution of α does not exist. In the maximization step, the iterative approach of Newton Raphson method has been used as explained by the author in [11] for estimation of α parameters.

During the initialization of parameters for Dirichlet mixture model, we use K-means algorithm as given in Algorithm 1 to initialize the parameters. We have compared our results by changing K-means algorithm using different distance metrics. We have used Euclidean distance and Aitchison distance inside K-means for initialization of parameters for Dirichlet mixture model. As we know that Aitchison distance outperforms euclidean distance metrics when proportional data is in question. In order to increase the performance of an algorithm, we have used feature selection methodology [5, 7, 9, 15, 16]. In order to perform feature selection, the first step we have taken to normalize the NSL KDD data set using Eq. 8.

$$x_i = \frac{x_i}{x_1 + x_2 \dots + x_D} \tag{8}$$

After obtaining proportional data, which act as an input for Weight by Maximum Relevance (*WMR*) proposed by Blum et al. [4] and Least Absolute Selection and Shrinkage Operator (*LASSO*) for selection of features from a data set.

Normalization of data leads vector to $(X_{i1} + X_{i2}, \dots X_{iD} = 1)$ unit sum constraint and each $X_i \geq 0$. After normalization, we have used Dirichlet Mixture Model with an initialization of parameters using K-means with Aitchison and Euclidean distance metrics.

In Algorithm 1, the distance metric which has been used is Aitchison Distance metric which can be given as:

$$d_{AD}(x,y) = \frac{1}{D} \sum_{i<j} \left(\log\frac{x_i}{x_j} - \log\frac{y_i}{y_j} \right) \tag{9}$$

Algorithm 1. K-Means Algorithm

1: Set the Initial number of centroids randomly or sequentially
2: Calculate the distance between each data point and cluster centers
3: **repeat**:
4:     Assign the minimum **distance data points** to cluster center whose distance is minimum to that point.
5:     Recalculate the cluster center using:
6: $c_i = \frac{1}{m_i} \sum_{j=1}^{m_i} x(i)$; m_i represents total number of data points in a cluster
7:     Re-calculate the distance between each data point and newly obtained cluster center
8: **until** : No data point is reassigned.

Algorithm 2. EM Algorithm Dirichlet Mixture Model

1: **Input:** Data set $(\mathbf{X}_1 + \mathbf{X}_2 ... \mathbf{X}_N)$ and specified number of components M.
2: Apply the k-means algorithm as given in Algorithm 1 on N D-dimensional vectors to obtain initial M clusters.
3: calculate $p_j = \dfrac{\text{Number of elements in class j}}{\text{N}}$
4: Apply moments method to obtain α parameters.
5: **Expectation-Maximization step** after Initialization
6: E-Step: Compute the posterior probability $p(j|\mathbf{X_i}, \boldsymbol{\alpha})$
7: M-Step:
8: **repeat**:
9:     Update priors p_j using equation 7 .
10:     Update the parameters α using Newton Raphson method.[11].
11: **until** : $p_j \leq \epsilon$, discard j and go to E-Step.
12: if convergence test is passed then terminate, else go to E-Step.

$$d_{AD}^2(x,y) = \sum_{k=1}^{D} \left(\log \frac{x_i}{g(x_j)} - \log \frac{y_i}{g(y_j)} \right) \tag{10}$$

The methodology used in our experiment is as follows:

4 Experiment with NSL KDD Data Set

We have taken NSL KDD 2009 data-set for performing Intrusion detection. The NSL KDD data set contains 41 features and data set contains normal and attack sets. The attacks can be divided into four parts which are: Denial of Service Attack (DoS), User to Root attack (U2R), Remote to local attack (R2L) and probing attack and rest are normal sets. In our experiment, we have taken only normal and attack sets into consideration without finding different types of attacks. In our methodology, we have used Dirichlet Mixture Model for clustering of a data set which contains 41 features. While performing clustering using Dirichlet mixture model results into 51.12% of accuracy which was relatively increased to 53.44% when clustering was performed with initialization of k-means using Aitchison distance $d_{AD}(x,y) = \frac{1}{D}\sum_{i<j}\left(\log\frac{x_i}{x_j} - \log\frac{y_i}{y_j}\right)$ instead of Euclidean distance in k-means algorithm. In our experiments, we have done feature selection using the methodology of Weight by maximum relevance where features were reduced to 16 features. The experiment on 16 features using Dirichlet Mixture model with euclidean distance in K-means during initialization results into 52.54% of accuracy and 56.37% was obtained when initialization was done with K-means using Aitchison distance in Dirichlet mixture model as seen in Table 1 and Fig. 3. To depict our results, we have used confusion matrix as shown in Figs. 4 and 5. to show the accuracy of our results. Accuracy is defined as the percentage of correctly classified vectors. The accuracy of results can be written as:

Algorithm 3

1: **Input:** The Data (X_i) with labels.
2: To Normalize the data using equation 8
3: To find the correlation between data and labels using Weight by Maximum Relevance **or**
4: To find least square regression coefficients using set of regularization coefficients Lambda.
5: To select attributes from data set by using figure 1 or figure 2.
6: **Output:** Dimensionally reduced data set (X_i)
7: **Next Process**
8: **Input** To input obtained data without using Labels to Algorithm 2 with number of mixtures.
9: **Output**: We get clusters of normal data and anomaly data.

$$Accuracy = 100 \times \frac{\text{Correctly identified vector}}{\text{total vectors}} \qquad (11)$$

Table 1. Accuracy, Precision and Sensitivity obtained after applying different methods

S.No.	Process	Accuracy	Precision	Sensitivity
1.	DMM (Euclidean Distance)	51.12%	0.78	0.55
2.	DMM (Aitchison Distance)	53.44%	0.76	0.56
3.	FS WMR DMM (Euclidean Distance)	52.54%	0.78	0.58
4.	FS WMR DMM (Aitchison Distance)	56.37%	0.80	0.57

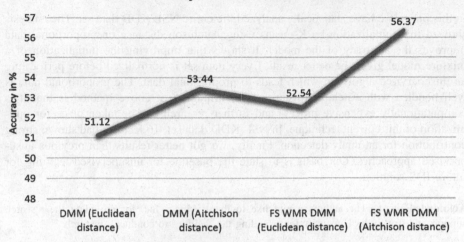

Fig. 3. Accuracy of DMM models using different techniques

	Yes	No			Yes	No
Yes	5386	1492		Yes	4953	1564
No	4300	672		No	3953	1380

DMM (Euclidean distance)   DMM (Aitchison distance)

Fig. 4. Confusion matrix of DMM, initialization with K-means euclidean and Aitchison distance

	Yes	No			Yes	No
Yes	5587	1513		Yes	5128	1285
No	4111	639		No	3884	1553

FS WMR DMM (Euclidean distance)   FS WMR DMM (Aitchison distance)

Fig. 5. Confusion matrix of DMM after feature selection, initialization with K-means Euclidean and Aitchison distance

In our case, we have used only test data without labels. Our results are better than SVM approach where accuracy determined is 51.90% [19] where the model was trained before determining the intrusions. The author in [14] obtained results in one of the clustering method was 47% which is comparably less than our approach.

5   Conclusion

In this paper, we have statistically analyzed the entire NSL KDD data set. The analysis showed that initialization by K-means using Aitchison distance on proportional data improves the accuracy of the model. It shows that improving the initialization of a mixture model gives the better result. Every data set is normalized before performing an unsupervised algorithm which leads to proportional data. The proportional data is well handled with Aitchison distance. The limitation of above method is that it is computationally expensive process and further research can be taken place for optimization of this current technique. In NSL KDD data set, 16 features had shown strong contribution for anomaly detection. Finally, we got better results than previous unsupervised approaches. Our basis is to state the baseline for unsupervised learning for future IDS solution.

Acknowledgment. The authors would like to thank Mitacs Inc. for providing the research support and Concordia University for providing the facilities to conduct a research.

References

1. Darpa intrusion detection evaluation. http://www.ll.mit.edu/IST/ideval/data/dataindex.html. Accessed 05 Nov 2016
2. NSL-KDD data set for network-based intrusion detection systems. http://nsl.cs.unb.ca/KDD/NSLKDD.html. Accessed 05 Nov 2016
3. Al-Yaseen, W.L., Othman, Z.A., Nazri, M.Z.A.: Multi-level hybrid support vector machine and extreme learning machine based on modified k-means for intrusion detection system. Expert Syst. Appl. **67**, 296–303 (2017)
4. Blum, A.L., Langley, P.: Selection of relevant features and examples in machine learning. Artif. Intell. **97**(1), 245–271 (1997)
5. Bouguila, N.: Bayesian hybrid generative discriminative learning based on finite Liouville mixture models. Pattern Recogn. **44**(6), 1183–1200 (2011)
6. Bouguila, N., ElGuebaly, W.: Discrete data clustering using finite mixture models. Pattern Recogn. **42**(1), 33–42 (2009)
7. Bouguila, N., Ziou, D.: MML-based approach for finite Dirichlet mixture estimation and selection. In: Perner, P., Imiya, A. (eds.) MLDM 2005. LNCS, vol. 3587, pp. 42–51. Springer, Heidelberg (2005). doi:10.1007/11510888_5
8. Bouguila, N., Ziou, D.: On fitting finite Dirichlet mixture using ECM and MML. In: Singh, S., Singh, M., Apte, C., Perner, P. (eds.) ICAPR 2005. LNCS, vol. 3686, pp. 172–182. Springer, Heidelberg (2005). doi:10.1007/11551188_19
9. Bouguila, N., Ziou, D.: A countably infinite mixture model for clustering and feature selection. Knowl. Inf. Syst. **33**(2), 351–370 (2012)
10. Bouguila, N., Ziou, D., Hammoud, R.I.: On Bayesian analysis of a finite generalized Dirichlet mixture via a metropolis-within-gibbs sampling. Pattern Anal. Appl. **12**(2), 151–166 (2009)

11. Bouguila, N., Ziou, D., Vaillancourt, J.: Novel mixtures based on the Dirichlet distribution: application to data and image classification. In: Perner, P., Rosenfeld, A. (eds.) MLDM 2003. LNCS, vol. 2734, pp. 172–181. Springer, Heidelberg (2003). doi:10.1007/3-540-45065-3_15

12. Elguebaly, T., Bouguila, N.: Finite asymmetric generalized Gaussian mixture models learning for infrared object detection. Comput. Vis. Image Underst. **117**(12), 1659–1671 (2013)

13. Epaillard, E., Bouguila, N.: Proportional data modeling with hidden Markov models based on generalized dirichlet and beta-liouville mixtures applied to anomaly detection in public areas. Pattern Recogn. **55**, 125–136 (2016)

14. Eskin, E., Arnold, A., Prerau, M., Portnoy, L., Stolfo, S.: A geometric framework for unsupervised anomaly detection. In: Barbará, D., Jajodia, S. (eds.) Applications of Data Mining in Computer Security. Advances in Information Security, vol. 6, pp. 77–101. Springer, Boston (2002)

15. Fan, W., Bouguila, N., Ziou, D.: Unsupervised anomaly intrusion detection via localized Bayesian feature selection. In: 2011 IEEE 11th International Conference on Data Mining (ICDM), pp. 1032–1037. IEEE (2011)

16. Fan, W., Bouguila, N., Ziou, D.: Unsupervised hybrid feature extraction selection for high-dimensional non-gaussian data clustering with variational inference. IEEE Trans. Knowl. Data Eng. **25**(7), 1670–1685 (2013)

17. Guyon, I., Elisseeff, A.: An introduction to variable and feature selection. J. Mach. Learn. Res. **3**, 1157–1182 (2003)

18. Heba, F.E., Darwish, A., Hassanien, A.E., Abraham, A.: Principle components analysis and support vector machine based intrusion detection system. In: 2010 Proceedings of the 10th International Conference on Intelligent Systems Design and Applications, pp. 363–367. IEEE (2010)

19. Iglesias, F., Zseby, T.: Analysis of network traffic features for anomaly detection. Mach. Learn. **101**(1–3), 59–84 (2015)

20. Masoudimansour, W., Bouguila, N.: Dimensionality reduction of proportional data through data separation using Dirichlet distribution. In: Kamel, M., Campilho, A. (eds.) ICIAR 2015. LNCS, vol. 9164, pp. 141–149. Springer, Cham (2015). doi:10.1007/978-3-319-20801-5_15

21. McHugh, J.: Testing intrusion detection systems: a critique of the 1998 and 1999 DARPA intrusion detection system evaluations as performed by Lincoln laboratory. ACM Trans. Inf. Syst. Secur. (TISSEC) **3**(4), 262–294 (2000)

22. Panda, M., Abraham, A., Patra, M.R.: A hybrid intelligent approach for network intrusion detection. Procedia Eng. **30**, 1–9 (2012)

23. Singh, S., Singh, M., Apte, C., Perner, P.: Pattern Recognition and Data Mining: Third International Conference on Advances in Pattern Recognition, ICAR 2005, Bath, UK, 22–25 August 2005, vol. 3686. Springer, Heidelberg (2005)

24. Tavallaee, M., Bagheri, E., Lu, W., Ghorbani, A.A.: A detailed analysis of the KDD CUP 99 data set. In: 2009 Proceedings of the Second IEEE Symposium on Computational Intelligence for Security and Defence Applications (2009)

25. Tibshirani, R.: Regression shrinkage and selection via the lasso. J. Roy. Stat. Soc. Ser. B (Methodol.) **58**, 267–288 (1996)

26. Zargari, S., Voorhis, D.: Feature selection in the corrected KDD-dataset. In: 2012 Third International Conference on Emerging Intelligent Data and Web Technologies (EIDWT), pp. 174–180. IEEE (2012)

Short Papers

Cloud Computing and Virtualization in Developing Countries

Yness Boukhris[✉]

School of Engineering, ESPRIT, Z.I. Chotrana II B.P. 160,
Pôle Technologique El Ghazela, 2088 Aryanah, Tunisia
ines.boukhris@esprit.tn

Abstract. Cloud computing has emerged since almost a decade as a paradigm for hosting and delivering services over networks. A growing number of business owners and organizations worldwide has adopted Cloud computing as it enables users to access a scalable and elastic pool of data storage and computing resources, as and when required. To build cloud based architectures, virtualization should be ensured as well. It plays a key role for providing flexibility and consolidation of the underlying resources. Despite the cloud computing is witnessing a fast and wide spread across the globe, this technology is not as trendy for some other states, especially for developing countries. The purpose of this theoretical study is to explore a new way for developing countries to benefit from cloud computing use cases and to deal with its challenges and obstacles.

Keywords: Cloud computing · Virtualization · Developing countries · Cloud services · Cloud benefits · Cloud prerequisites

1 Introduction

People in developing countries are facing every day several challenges including poverty, hunger, health calamities and even wars. There is no better way to enhance life facilities than involving technologies in daily life, as it was the case in the developed world. Obviously, the advance of technologies cannot solve all these difficulties but it is worth to say that it should be part of the solution.

Cloud computing provides a relatively new business model and is one of the hippest buzzy word of the last decade. When we mention cloud, virtualization is often mentioned too. These technologies are not interchangeable but virtualization is fundamental for a better cloud usage. Developing world should have the urge to embrace these technologies as it will help them to increase flexibility, accessibility and cost effectiveness. However, due to all the instabilities that are hampering investment capacity in infrastructure, Cloud computing still only on its early stage in these countries.

This paper will start by introducing and differentiating both of virtualization and cloud computing concepts. Then, it will highlight the opportunities of cloud utilization for developing countries. In further sections, cloud infrastructure prerequisites will be detailed in order to boost developing world to challenge these adoption factors. Finally, this paper will close with a conclusion.

© ICST Institute for Computer Sciences, Social Informatics and Telecommunications Engineering 2018
F. Belqasmi et al. (Eds.): AFRICATEK 2017, LNICST 206, pp. 205–213, 2018.
https://doi.org/10.1007/978-3-319-67837-5_19

2   Cloud Computing and Virtualization Concept

2.1   Cloud Computing

We can find several cloud computing definitions over the internet, but the most commonly used is the NIST[1] definition as it involves all the approved aspect of this technology. According to this institute, [1] "cloud computing is a model for enabling ubiquitous, convenient, on-demand network access to a shared pool of configurable computing resources (e.g., networks, servers, storage, applications and services) that can be rapidly provisioned and released with minimal management effort or service provider interaction". The NIST describes Cloud Computing as being based on:

– Five characteristics: On-demand self-service, broad network access, Resource pooling, rapid elasticity and measured service.
– three service models: Infrastructure as a Service (IaaS), Platform as a Service (PaaS), Software as a service (SaaS)
– four deployment models: Private clouds, Community clouds, Public clouds, Hybrid clouds

2.2   Virtualization

Virtualization is a technique that provides a layer of abstraction on top of the underlying hardware or software and allows users to divide computer resources into multiple isolated execution environments. The main goal of using virtualization is running multiple operating systems or applications on the same physical server. Virtualization is ensured by a software called the Virtual Machine Monitor (VMM) also known as hypervisor. It is generally running on top of hardware to manage and allocate the required resources.

2.3   Virtualization Versus Cloud Computing

Many non-IT folks have issues to distinguish between virtualized data centers and cloud-based architecture. In fact, virtualization is a fundamental technique in cloud computing but it is not the cloud either. There is a weighty gap between these technologies capabilities.

The term Cloud computing refers to a business model using the paradigm as a service while virtualization only abstracts physical resources to create various dedicated ones. Although, virtualization provides a more efficient way to consume hardware resources, it stills always too far from the level of elasticity, self-service, and automation of cloud. Moreover, Virtualization offers multiple advantages and benefits that make it plays a key role in delivering a flexible, scalable, and cost effective cloud services, especially in computing service.

The first virtualization advantage is consolidation. It means that hardware resources usage will be optimized by running multiple virtual machines on the same physical

---

[1] NIST: National Institute of standards and technology.

server. Thus, not only hardware utilization percentage may reach 80% in each server instead of leaving it shiftless but also this practice reduces considerably hardware investments and energy consumption.

Besides, Virtualization offers a higher level of security by running each service in an isolated container on a single physical server. This method is known as "jailing of services".

Then, virtualization provides a greater flexibility by running several types of applications and operating systems on the same server. So it facilitates building testing environments and labs.

To summarize, Cloud and virtualization should not be confused but it does not mean that they could not be combined. And what about building cloud without virtualization? Let's say it is also possible but it will be with a lower level of efficiency.

3   Cloud Computing and Virtualization for Developing Countries

3.1   Actual State in Developing Countries

In developing countries, Cloud computing has already taken a major part in daily life. People often use a wide range of cloud provided applications such as Google Maps[2], Facebook[3], Microsoft's Hotmail[4], and so on...

In order to enhance the economic growth through cloud services, what is expected from these nations is almost adopting, exploiting and why not offering this technology in both of their own states and worldwide rather than a simple consumption of public cloud services. To do so, developing countries requires at least a bit of awareness of cloud computing impact in their economic models, and some expertise to plan for an adoption strategy.

According to a Gartner survey conducted among large enterprises in 2009, half of the respondents in emerging markets either had not heard of cloud computing or didn't know what it meant [2].

Otherwise, since then developing countries are more conscious of cloud computing benefits and consequently markets are getting wider every day.

3.2   Cloud Computing Impact in the Economic Model

– Increase the Economic Investment

Cloud computing is actually a weighty shift in both of business and economic model. One of its major impact in the economic model is to decrease business investment by acquiring a minimum amount of modern IT infrastructure, and then increase corporate profitability by serving maximum IT resources requests. Balancing these factors not only leads to a noticeable cost saving percentage in hardware resources but also drives investment through the reinvestment of retained profits.

---

[2] Google Maps. Find local businesses, view maps and get driving directions.
[3] Facebook. online social media and social networking service.
[4] Microsoft's Hotmail. free, personal email service from Microsoft.

When implemented properly [4], the cloud economic model can drastically reduce the operations and maintenance cost of IT infrastructures (Fig. 1).

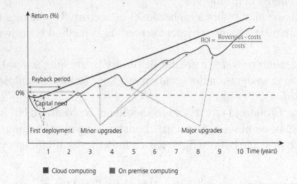

Fig. 1. A Deloitte (Deloitte is the brand under which tens of thousands of dedicated professionals in independent firms throughout the world collaborate to provide audit, consulting, financial advisory, risk management, tax, and related services to select customers) study confirms that cloud deployments delivered greater investment returns with a shorter payback period when compared to the traditional on premise delivery option [4]

– CapEx and OpEx Savings

Developing countries have the possibility to improve their economic evolution not only through private deployments but also within public cloud services. When public cloud model is used, it can play a key role for companies to transform IT expenses from CapEx[5] to OpEx[6] through purchasing the use of the service rather than having to own and manage the resources of that service. Thus, they can eliminate long-term investments in favor of pay-as-you-go costs.

Besides, the OpEx approach can also provide a suitable level of flexibility which allows companies to scale up or scale down depending on their needs and save up money for other investments.

– New Business Creation and Employment

Cloud computing is meant to increase and to have a relevant macroeconomic impact. This technology has changed the market structure of many sectors thanks to cost savings, reinvestment of profits and an improved level of competitiveness. This change in the market induces business expansion or creation and a re-allocation of jobs in developing countries.

---

[5] CapEx. Capital Expenditures creating future benefits. it is incurred when a business spends money either to buy fixed assets or to add the value of an existing asset with a useful life that expend beyond the tax year.

[6] OpEX. Operational Expenditures refers to expenses incurred in the course of ordinary business.

3.3   Benefit of Cloud Usage for Developing Countries

Rather than its economic and socio-economic advantages, cloud can offer other benefits like elasticity and multitenancy. This section will detail how developing nations can take profit from cloud computing environmental and technical advantages.

– Green IT

The traditional data centers running Web applications are often provisioned to handle sporadic peak Loads [8], which can result in low resource utilization and wastage of energy. Thanks to virtualization, Cloud datacenter can reduce the energy consumption through server consolidation. Thus, multiple workloads can use the same physical server and idle servers can be turned off. A recent research by Accenture [9] shows that moving business applications to Cloud can reduce carbon footprint of organizations.

Developing countries, suffer from pollution due to some local factors such as over-population. In this context, government should induce cloud utilization as it represents a green technology initiative which most businesses should adopt. Thus, Cloud computing and virtualization will reduce energy costs as well as it will offer a lower carbon emission.

– Scalability

Scalability is one of the most important advantage. In fact, in traditional on-premise IT infrastructure, consumers are always tied up to the physical constraints limitation such us hard-drive space, CPU, memory and bandwidth. But with [10] Cloud computing resources should look limitless and can be purchased at any time and in any quantity.

When Public Clouds are used by development countries, a pool of unrestricted resources is offered to simple consumers or business. This provide more flexibility and cost effective resources usage, reduce capital investment in business creation, decrease or even eliminate the need of hardware resources acquirement.

– Remote Access

With cloud computing, [11] instead of connecting to the network server, a mobile phone or device connects to the cloud service provider. All services are available from wherever we are, as long as there is a connection to the network. Armed with such portability and flexibility in the computing environment, businesses can reach their customers 24/7 anywhere in the world. Students can study online courses from anywhere in the world, and individuals can socialize on their mobile phones, SMS and do whatever they want from wherever they are, whenever they want [11].

– Improvement of Life Facilities

According to Kshetri's report (2010), cloud has several applications in daily life, such as E-health, E-education, E-commerce, E-business, and supply chain... If applied properly, people in developing countries could take a lot of profits from this technology even in daily life. It will not only build a new generation of skilled ICT professionals, but it will eliminate repetitive burdens in private or public establishment. The table below analyses the possible advantages in each application area (Table 1).

Table 1. Benefits of cloud computing application in different sectors in Developing Countries

Cloud applications	Examples
E-education	- Enable Academic Cloud based programs in engineering schools to enhance expertise level in developing countries - Provide unrestricted resources to students for development and testing purpose - Enables education for poorer country by offering remote courses
E-health	- Implement healthcare data-sharing and analytics technologies (example of china) - Develop insurance platform, to claim and follow up refund - Use cloud to build next generation medical research
E-commerce/ E-business/supply chains	- Offer local/worldwide shopping platform - Automating business processes - Improve performance and quality of Telecommunication, banking and IT hosting customer services
E-governance	- collaboration with industry and tertiary institutions to ensure the development of skilled and cloud-aware ICT professionals - Implementation of a cloud based platform to deliver more efficient government services - Delivering all the services on the web too in an easy fast and reliable way regardless to the distances and time - Reduce costs by reducing repetitive operations and increase the effective use of resources
E-environment	- Access powerful computer to analyze and predict climate changes
Telecommuting	- Build highly available call centers

3.4   Prerequisites and Limitations of Cloud Adoption in Developing Countries

Technical shortcomings and regulatory difficulties are inhibiting fast adoption of Cloud. This makes it imperative to comprehend the adoption barriers and to find ways to overcome them. Barriers can be divided into two main categories: internal and external barriers.

3.4.1   Internal Barriers

Internal barriers can be summarized in different attitudes towards cloud computing. In developing countries, there is no regulatory rules that ensure personal data protection and data transfer security in cloud environments.

That's why CEO's and decision makers are always anxious about their data privacy and security, the location of data and reliability of their services.

3.4.2   External Barriers
– Government Incentives and Regulations
As cloud adoption stills at a nascent stage in developing countries, governments should waste no time for defining new policies based on an assessment of cloud solutions and be rooted in a full understanding of existing ICT and cloud use within countries. Governments need to be aware of the diversity of cloud use cases and services, the huge number of cloud users.

To accelerate the adoption process, a governmental cloud strategy should be implemented in the general national development plan. Governments should ensure the execution of this strategy by continuous supervision and evaluation. Policy approaches should be then tailored to the circumstances of individual economies, and be consistent with the overall strategic framework for national economic development and for leveraging ICTs [13].

Among developing countries, let's take the example of Vietnam and China [2] which are notable examples of economies that have meaningful government interventions in the cloud sector. Cloud computing in Vietnam is driven fundamentally by the government's belief that this technology would help the country build a skilled workforce. A government agency uses the cloud to link the government, universities, private-sector research, startups, and other organizations [14].

– Inadequate Infrastructure
The feasibility of cloud computing depends to a great extent on the availability of reliable, affordable, high-quality communications networks. In practice, this means broadband networks that link all parties in the supply chains [13]. Developing countries suffer from limited or inadequate access to high-quality and affordable broadband infrastructure. Another important environmental factor for cloud adoption is reliable and redundant power suppliers. It is essential for maintaining large data centers and ensuring continuous service providing.

Multiple countries, like Tunisia have only one national power supplier which is insufficient since at least two distinct ones are mandatory in order to be compliant with the basic standards for cloud oriented data centers.

– Lack of Adequate Legal and Regulatory Frameworks for Electronic Commerce and Cybersecurity
Online transactions are the most important pillar to benefit from the pay as you go business model. Except that, there is a prerequisite for conducting commercial transactions online, including electronic payments, is that there is legal equivalence between paper-based and electronic forms of exchange, which is the goal of e-transactions laws. E-transactions laws have already been adopted by 143 countries, of which 102 are developing countries (UNCTAD, 2015). Another 23 have produced draft legislation in this area. That leaves nine developing countries with no e-transactions laws and 18 for which data are lacking. While four out of five countries in Asia and in Latin America and the Caribbean have adopted such laws, Eastern and Middle Africa countries are lagging behind the most [15].

Furthermore, laws may require the establishment of a national certification authority. However, due to the human and financial costs involved, certification authorities, especially in developing countries, have sometimes not been set up, or have been set up only after an extended period of time. In such cases, e-transactions may lack legal recognition when the intervention of the national certification authority is required to give legal validity to the transaction. In addition, a requirement to use cryptographic systems when conducting e-commerce or e-government operations can represent a barrier to online transactions [15].

4   Conclusion

Through this study we managed to detail factors and KPIs (key performance indicators) regarding cloud and virtualization adoption impact on the developing countries and show the actual state of this adoption is some of them.

Looking deeply in such experiences we managed to extract the main difficulties and breaks to such a change and we draw process draft that could by involving people, companies and governments overcome and accelerate such an adoption.

Even though the benefits are undeniable, meticulous planning and long term strategies are still key elements to successfully achieve the goals behind such a revolution along with a lot of change management.

References

1. Mell, P., Grance, T.: The NIST Definition of Cloud Computing. National Institute of Standards and Technology, Information Technology Laboratory (2011)
2. Ksherti, N.: Cloud computing in developing economies. IEEE Comput. **43**(10), 47–55 (2010)
3. Maaref, S.: Cloud computing in Africa situation and perspectives (2012). http://www.itu.int/ITU-D/treg/publications/Cloud_Computing_Afrique-e.pdf
4. Jackson, K.L.: The Economic Benefit of Cloud computing. NJVC white paper (2011)
5. Pandey, P.K., Agarwal, A., Tiwari, A.K.: Variance of increasing cloud computing technology on SMEs in India. Int. J. Adv. Res. Comput. Sci. Softw. Eng. **5**, 495–500 (2015)
6. Ahmad, T., Waheed, M.: Cloud computing adoption issues and applications in developing countries: a qualitative approach. Int. Arab J. e-Technology **4**(2) (2015)
7. Tornatzky, L.G., Fleischer, M.: The Process of Technology Innovation. Lexington Books, Lexington (1990)
8. Garg, S.K., Buyya, R.: Green cloud computing and environmental sustainability (2011). http://www.cloudbus.org/papers/Cloud-EnvSustainability2011.pdf
9. Accenture Microsoft Report: Cloud computing and sustainability: the environmental benefits of moving to the cloud (2010). http://www.wspenvironmental.com/media/docs/newsroom/Cloud_computing_and_Sustainability_-_Whitepaper_-_Nov_2010.pdf
10. Sosinky, B.: Cloud Computing Bible. Wiley, New York (2011)
11. Goundar, S.: Cloud computing: opportunities and issues for developing countries. DiploFoundation (2011). https://www.diplomacy.edu/sites/default/files/IGCBP2010_2011_Goundar.pdf
12. Afshari, M.: Cloud computing adoption in developing countries (2014). http://cloudtweaks.com/2014/06/cloud-computing-adoption-developing-countries/

13. United Nations: The Cloud Economy and Developing Countries (2013). http://unctad.org/en/PublicationsLibrary/ier2013_en.pdf
14. Cleverley, M.: Viewpoints: emerging markets: how ICT advances might help developing nations. Commun. ACM **52**(9), 30–32 (2009)
15. United Nations: Cyber laws and regulations for enhancing e-commerce: Case studies and lessons learned (2015). http://unctad.org/meetings/en/SessionalDocuments/ciiem5d2_en.pdf

Analysis and Effect of Feature Selection Over Smartphone-Based Dataset for Human Activity Recognition

Ilham Amezzane[1(✉)], Youssef Fakhri[1], Mohammed El Aroussi[1], and Mohamed Bakhouya[2]

[1] Faculté des Sciences, Université Ibn Tofail, Kenitra, Morocco
ilhammaj@gmail.com, fakhri@uit.ac.ma,
mohamed.elaroussi@ieee.org
[2] International University of Rabat, Sala Aljadida, Morocco
Mohamed.bakhouya@uir.ac.ma

Abstract. The availability of diverse and powerful sensors that are embedded in modern smartphones has created exciting opportunities for developing context-aware services and applications. For example, Human activity recognition (HAR) is an important feature that could be applied to many applications and services, such as those in healthcare and transportation. However, recognizing relevant human activities using smartphones remains a challenging task and requires efficient data mining approaches. In this paper, we present a comparison study for HAR using features selection methods to reduce the training and classification time while maintaining significant performance. In fact, due to the limited resources of Smartphones, reducing the feature set helps reducing computation costs, especially for real-time continuous online applications. We validated our approach on a publicly available dataset to classify six different activities. Results show that Recursive Feature Elimination algorithm works well with Radial Basis Function Support Vector Machine and significantly improves model building time without decreasing recognition performance.

Keywords: Human Activity Recognition · Smartphone sensors · Feature selection

1 Introduction

Human Activity Recognition (HAR) using Smartphones has been widely studied during recent years mainly because Smartphones are not intrusive and widely used in everyday life. Researchers are developing many new challenging application scenarios based on mobile phone sensors in various fields such as in healthcare (e.g., fitness, diabetes, elderly and obesity assisted surveillance), in smart buildings (e.g., context aware automatic indoor air quality and thermal comfort control) and in smart cities applications (e.g., traffic congestion). Actually, modern Smartphone devices have great capacity for collecting and classifying large amounts of multiple sensor readings. However, for real-time online implementation, data pre-processing and training steps

© ICST Institute for Computer Sciences, Social Informatics and Telecommunications Engineering 2018
F. Belqasmi et al. (Eds.): AFRICATEK 2017, LNICST 206, pp. 214–219, 2018.
https://doi.org/10.1007/978-3-319-67837-5_20

are required to be achieved under hardware resource constraints, such as memory and battery life. Many solutions have been studied so far in literature to overcome these limitations [1], for example, by reducing the amount of training data needed in the learning phase.

In this paper, we present a comparison study based on feature selection approaches in order to reduce the dimensionality of the training dataset while maintaining high recognition performance. The remainder of this paper is organized as follows. A brief overview of the related work is presented in Sect. 2. Section 3 presents the dataset, the experimental methodology and simulation results. Section 4 presents the conclusions and future work.

2 Related Work

Many research efforts have been done to implement HAR process on different Smartphone devices using various data sets. However, for real-time online implementation, data pre-processing and training steps are required to be achieved under hardware resources constraints. Recently, researchers focus mainly on mobile phone's onboard sensors for real-time online applications. For example, authors in [1] have reviewed research studies in this domain and stated that only few of them focused on online training in which classifiers can be trained in real time on mobile phones [2–5]. Authors, in [2], introduced "hardware friendly" adaptation of the classification algorithms in order to overcome the resources constraints. In [6], authors used dynamic and adaptive sensor selection to save battery energy. Other studies used adaptive sampling techniques [7] for the same goal.

Classifiers could play a key role in HAR process regarding energy consumption depending on their simplicity or complexity. Nonetheless, some of them have proven their suitability for Smartphone implementation, such as K-nearest neighbor (KNN), Support Vector Machine (SVM) and Decision Tree (DT) [1]. In fact, in the pre-processing phase, various features (aka. predictors or variables) are extracted from sensors readings. These features are used by the classifier later during training (aka. learning), validation (optionally) and testing phases. Moreover, in online activity recognition, two main types of features are generally used: time or/and frequency domain features. It has been shown in [8] that time domain features are cheaper than frequency domain features in terms of computation and storage costs. In practice, large feature sets may significantly slow down the learning process [9]. In addition, the "dimensionality curse" phenomenon states that the number of training data needed grows exponentially with the number of dimensions used [10]. Subsequently, the online training requires further intensive computation if locally undergone on Smartphones [11]. For this reason, the goal of Feature Selection (FS) methods is to select optimal subsets of variables in the pre-processing step. The main benefits are reducing the computation cost and storage requirements as well as training time [9].

There are three main approaches for feature selection in literature: (i) *Wrapper* methods for measuring the "usefulness" of the features guided by a classifier performance, (ii) *Filter* methods for measuring the "relevance" of the features independently of the classifier, and (iii) *Embedded* methods that are implemented by algorithms having their own built-in FS methods for performing variable selection implicitly while the model is being trained.

Regarding the performance, an important source of influence on the HAR process is the classifier itself as stated in [11]. For this reason, in our comparison study, we have evaluated different classifiers belonging to different categories before and after feature selection. Our final selection included four classifiers: Linear Discriminative Analysis (LDA), Radial Basis Function Support Vector Machine (RBF SVM), K-nearest neighbors (KNN), and Random Forest (RF). In order to discriminate test data into labeled classes, the classifiers need to be trained first. Thus, we trained our selected classifiers using a 10-fold cross validation technique. The parameters of the best final models were preserved for testing on holdout data.

3   Experimental Methodology and Results

In this work, we used a publicly available dataset: "Human Activity Recognition Using Smartphones Data Set" [12], which has been used by the authors to conduct experiments using Support Vector Machine (SVM) classifier [13]. The latest update (15-Feb-2015) includes labeled data collected from 30 subjects who engaged in six different activities (standing, sitting, laying down, walking, walking downstairs and walking upstairs), while wearing Smartphones that embed accelerometer and gyroscope sensors. The list of all the measures applied to the time and frequency domain signals are available in [13]. A total of 561 features were extracted to describe each activity window (2.56 s) in the dataset. Two files for activity labels and subjects ID numbers are also available. The classification results of the original work [13] show an overall accuracy of 96% for the Test data. In our comparison study, we have used the same "Test" data. In addition, we partitioned the original "Training" data (7352 observations) into "Training/Validation" subsets to avoid overfitting during learning phases.

In the comparison study, we tried one wrapper algorithm called Recursive Feature Elimination (RFE) and one embedded algorithm specific to Random Forest (RF) classifier called Variable Importance (varImp). After running calculations, 20 variables have been selected with the latter while 50 have been selected with the former. After looking at the names of those features, we first noticed that the "50 features subset" include almost all the variables of the "20 features subset" except one. Moreover, we noticed that only 5 variables in the latter are of frequency domain, against 10 variables in the former. In both cases, this reduction in the number of frequency domain features is beneficial in terms of computation cost, because the original feature set contains many frequency domain features based on Fast Fourier Transform (FFT) [13] which demands extra computation [8]. Finally, we constructed two new data sets with the features selected from both methods before applying different classifiers, and conducted a comparison study in order to select the feature subset that works well regarding the recognition performance and the training time.

Because balanced class proportions assumption is verified in our data sets, good performance of each classifier can be measured by accuracy metric only, and good performance of each activity is obtained if that activity can be classified with high precision (PR), recall (RC), and F-measure (F1) metrics. As shown in Table 1, we examined 20, 50 and 561 features datasets for the comparative performance for each classifier, in terms of classification accuracy (see Table 1 on Left side) and time taken to build the model in seconds (see Table 1 on Right side). Overall, LDA offered the highest performance, yielding 96% accuracy for the original feature vector. However, SVM is the best performing classifier for the "50 features subset" with 93% accuracy. However, for the sake of concision, we do not show the detailed metrics for each activity per classifier. Instead, Table 2 shows the averaged precision (macro-PR), recall (macro-RC) and F-measure (macro-F1) for the "50 features subset" classifiers.

Table 1. Comparison of classifier performance for different number of features (N.F): Left side: overall accuracy; Right side: model building time (in seconds).

N.F	LDA	KNN	SVM	RF	N.F	LDA	KNN	SVM	RF
20	0.90	0.87	0.90	0.84	20	1.5	1.6	4.7	10.7
50	0.92	0.91	0.93	0.91	50	2.0	1.8	6.9	23.4
561	0.96	0.90	0.93	0.91	561	21.1	3.0	43.0	276

Table 2. Averaged evaluation metrics for the "50 features subset" classifiers.

N.F (50)	Macro-PR	Macro-RC	Macro-F1
LDA	0.91	0.92	0.91
KNN	0.91	0.92	0.91
SVM	0.94	0.94	0.93
RF	0.92	0.92	0.92

Table 3. Confusion matrix of best performing classifier on test data: (Predicted activities *(P)* vs Actual activities)

Activities	Laying	Sitting	Standing	Walking	Walking-downstairs (T)	Walking-upstairs (T)
Laying *(P)*	537	0	0	0	0	0
Sitting *(P)*	0	397	35	0	0	0
Standing *(P)*	0	94	497	0	0	0
Walking *(P)*	0	0	0	488	12	37
Walking-downstairs *(P)*	0	0	0	6	370	10
Walking-upstairs *(P)*	0	0	0	2	38	424

We have also tested our final SVM model on unseen and unlabeled data, which we kept strictly apart. We noticed that the accuracy has slightly decreased (92%), which means that there was almost no overfitting in the training phase. In Table 3, the confusion matrix is presented. We first notice a perfect classification between "moving" and "non-moving" activities. However, the classifier sometimes confuses and mis-classifies one activity from another when there are inter-class similarities. Actually, it confuses little bit between all types of walking activities, but little more between "Sitting" and "Standing". On the contrary, the "Laying" activity is perfectly classified.

Furthermore, in order to figure out how well they perform over different sized versions of the training set, we have also simulated the learning curves of the final SVM models obtained before and after feature selection (see Fig. 1). For this purpose, the original Training data (7352 instances) was partitioned into Training set (75%) and Test set (25%), and 10-fold cross validation was used for resampling. As expected, reducing the feature space helped reducing the amount of training data needed to reach the same classification performance. For example, in order to reach 90% of accuracy, approximately 5000 instances were needed before feature selection (Fig. 1, Left side), while only 3500 instances were needed after feature selection (Fig. 1, Right side).

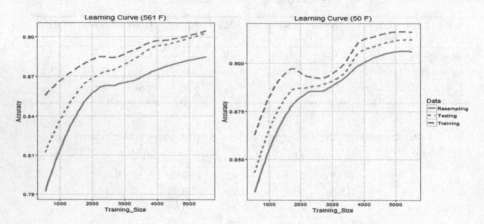

Fig. 1. Learning curves of the RBF SVM final models obtained: before feature selection (Left side), after feature selection (Right side).

4   Conclusions and Future Work

In this paper, we have conducted a comparison study using Smartphone accelerometer and gyroscope sensors data obtained from a publicly available HAR dataset. As the dimensionality of the original feature set is very high, we used feature selection approaches in order to reduce the feature space before classifying activities. Results show that, with RFE algorithm, only around 9% of the original feature set is needed to achieve the best tradeoff between classification accuracy, model building time, and confusion matrix. This comparison study is our starting point towards finding energy efficient techniques for real time HAR based on Smartphone sensors. Further research would involve an accelerated implementation of the proposed model, which might take advantage of specific computation platforms, alongside with energy consumption and performance analysis. HAR over smartphones is also under development for diabetic control and prediction of hypoglycemia [14].

References

1. Shoaib, M., et al.: A survey of online activity recognition using mobile phones. Sensors **15**(1), 2059–2085 (2015)
2. Anguita, D., Ghio, A., Oneto, L., Parra, X., Reyes-Ortiz, J.L.: Energy efficient smartphone based activity recognition using fixed-point arithmetic. J. UCS **19**, 1295–1314 (2013)
3. Frank, J., Mannor, S., Precup, D.: Activity recognition with mobile phones. In: Gunopulos, D., Hofmann, T., Malerba, D., Vazirgiannis, M. (eds.) ECML PKDD 2011. LNCS, vol. 6913, pp. 630–633. Springer, Heidelberg (2011). doi:10.1007/978-3-642-23808-6_44
4. Ouchi, K.; Doi, M.: Indoor-outdoor activity recognition by a smartphone. In: Proceedings of the 2012 ACM Conference on Ubiquitous Computing, Pittsburgh, PA, USA, pp. 600–601, 5–8 September 2012
5. Kose, M., Incel, O.D.; Ersoy, C.: Online human activity recognition on smart phones. In: Proceedings of the Workshop on Mobile Sensing: From Smartphones and Wearables to Big Data, Beijing, China, pp. 11–15, 16 April 2012
6. Wang, Y., Lin, J., Annavaram, M., Jacobson, Q.A., Hong, J., Krishnamachari, B., Sadeh, N.: A framework of energy efficient mobile sensing for automatic user state recognition. In: Proceedings of the 7th International Conference on Mobile Systems, Applications, and Services, Krakow, Poland, pp. 179–192, 22–25 June 2009
7. Yan, Z., Subbaraju, V., Chakraborty, D., Misra, A., Aberer, K.: Energy-efficient continuous activity recognition on mobile phones: an activity-adaptive approach. In: Proceedings of the 2012 16th International Symposium on Wearable Computers (ISWC), Newcastle, Australia, pp. 17–24, 18–22 June 2012
8. Figo, D., Diniz, P.C., Ferreira, D.R., Cardoso, J.M.: Preprocessing techniques for context recognition from accelerometer data. Pers. Ubiquitous Comput. **14**, 645–662 (2010)
9. Kotsiantis, S.B.: Feature selection for machine learning classification problems: a recent overview. Artif. Intell. Rev. **42**, 157 (2014). https://doi.org/10.1007/s10462-011-9230-1
10. Verleysen, M., François, D.: The curse of dimensionality in data mining and time series prediction. In: Cabestany, J., Prieto, A., Sandoval, F. (eds.) IWANN 2005. LNCS, vol. 3512, pp. 758–770. Springer, Heidelberg (2005). doi:10.1007/11494669_93
11. Bulling, A., Blanke, U., Schiele, B.: A tutorial on human activity recognition using body-worn inertial sensors. ACM Comput. Surv. (CSUR) **46**, 33 (2014)
12. UCI Machine Learning Repository: Human Activity Recognition Using Smartphones Data Set (2012). http://archive.ics.uci.edu/ml/datasets/Human+Activity+Recognition+Using +Smartphones
13. Anguita, D., Ghio, A., Oneto, L., Parra, X., Reyes-Ortiz, J.L.: A public domain dataset for human activity recognition using smartphones. In: ESANN, April 2013
14. De Florio, V., Bakhouya, M., Elouadghiri, D., Blondia, C.: Towards a smarter organization for a self-servicing society. In: Proceedings of the 7th International Conference on Software Development and Technologies for Enhancing Accessibility and Fighting Info-exclusion, pp. 1–6 (2016)

Empowering Graduates for Knowledge Economies in Developing Countries

Maurice Danaher[1(✉)], Kevin Shoepp[2], Ashley Ater Kranov[3], and Julie Bauld Wallace[4]

[1] Zayed University, Dubai, UAE
maurice.danaher@zu.ac.ae
[2] Jumeria University, Dubai, UAE
[3] Washington State University, Pullman, USA
[4] Higher Colleges of Technology, Abu Dhabi, UAE

Abstract. Professional, transferable, or 21st century skills such as life-long learning, problem solving and working in a multi-disciplinary team are vitally important for graduates entering knowledge economies. Students in the developing MENA countries have been identified as weak in these skills, which are challenging to both teach and assess. This paper describes the creation and application of the Computing Professional Skills Assessment (CPSA) in the United Arab Emirates (UAE), an IT specific instrument to assess students' abilities in the professional skills, administered using a Learning Management System (LMS). As part of this research students were surveyed on their perceptions and the results revealed a positive response regarding the benefits of the CPSA. It is suggested as an effective and applicable blended learning method in developing countries to better enable students to learn and apply 21st century skills. The use of this method in regions with limited IT infrastructure is discussed.

Keywords: Professional skills · Learning outcomes · Performance task · Online discussion · Assessment · Learning management system

1 Introduction

Learning Management System (LMS) supported e-learning initiatives in developing nations have been shown to face specific challenges due to the digital divide [1]. These include ineffective maintenance strategies, insufficient user/technical support, usability issues of learning management systems and poor internet connectivity. In this paper we present a method that is implemented in an LMS and that we believe can be effectively used in a developing nation despite the challenges mentioned above.

The engineering and computing disciplines around the world place importance nowadays on graduates being enabled with 21st century non-technical skills, also known as professional or transferable skills. These skills include teamwork, communication, critical thinking, ethical and social considerations, and have become a focus of university programs as measurable learning outcomes. They have also become critically important as developing countries make the transition to knowledge economies, and studies show

© ICST Institute for Computer Sciences, Social Informatics and Telecommunications Engineering 2018
F. Belqasmi et al. (Eds.): AFRICATEK 2017, LNICST 206, pp. 220–225, 2018.
https://doi.org/10.1007/978-3-319-67837-5_21

employers value them more than disciplinary knowledge [3]. Globally, graduates are weak in professional skills, particularly in the MENA region [4].

Teaching and assessing these critical skills is challenging and even questionably impossible [2, 5]. Within engineering and technology disciplines, the technical learning outcomes are more confidently met by programs [2]. To address the difficulties of integrating professional skills, accreditation bodies such as ABET, the international Accreditation Board for Engineering and Technology, have sought to improve program quality to increase student attainment of learning outcomes, with some success. A 2006 study found that graduates from 2004 were better prepared than their 1994 predecessors due to the emphasis on professional skills [5].

There are six non-technical outcomes which have been identified by ABET as key graduate skills:

- Ability to analyse a problem and identify solutions;
- Ability to function on multidisciplinary teams;
- Understanding of professional and ethical responsibility;
- Ability to communicate effectively;
- Understanding of the local and global impact of technology;
- Recognition of, and ability to, engage in life-long learning.

To assess these skills simultaneously, the Engineering Professional Skills Assessment (EPSA) was developed by a team in Washington State University's College of Engineering led by Ater Kranov, one of the authors [6]. The EPSA is based on the performance assessment model, which is an effective way to measure student performance on simultaneous learning outcomes in an interdependent way [2]. Prior to the CPSA the EPSA was the only method in the literature which could assess all of these learning outcomes directly and concurrently for engineering programs, thereby increasing the validity of the assessment [7]. The various methods used to assess professional skills previously, such as e-portfolios and internships, were found to be limited in their efficacy to assess all of the skills in an integrated and rigorous way. The EPSA consists of a real world engineering scenario to generate discursive analysis in forty-five minutes, and these responses are then recorded and evaluated using a rubric.

Inspired by the concept of EPSA, Zayed University (ZU) conducted a study in the ABET accredited College of Technological Innovation (CTI) to develop a method for assessing computing programs in the Gulf region in terms of professional skills. (Zayed University is a federal English-medium institution for Emirati Nationals with gender-segregated campuses in the UAE). The ABET key learning outcomes for computing were adopted and the scope of the project included the development of appropriate region-specific scenarios, a rubric named the CPSA and an implementation strategy which utilized blended learning with an LMS and asynchronous online discussion forums as the platform of the performance task. The use of discussion forums in a LMS is a significant enhancement to the method over the earlier EPSA.

We believe that this method can be used effectively in the developing world as it does not require a sophisticated level of technology. Provided there is access to the internet and access to a discussion board, the method may be employed. While we used the Blackboard LMS any system that provides a discussion board may be used. Minimal bandwidth is required and intermittent dropouts are acceptable as there is no synchronous communication. During the connection to the internet the user just needs to read the posts of others and upload a post, which could be composed offline. As the users of the CPSA will have an IT background not much technical support should be required by the students or instructors.

2   CPSA Method

CPSA was conceived in 2014 for computing related disciplines with the writing of technology related scenarios, development of the CPSA rubric and the use of asynchronous online discussion forums as the delivery strategy and main platform for student interactions and production. The adoption of online discussion technology was due to its strengths as a communication tool and stage for students to utilise the ABET professional skills. Online discussion has become widely integrated in education, and has been shown to allow for discourse in a more reflective way than oral discussion [8]. The skills of working in a team and co-constructing knowledge develop strongly through online discussion, and it's particularly important in a non- native learning environment to allow time for reflective responses [9]. There are three stages to the CPSA; a discipline related scenario, student analysis of the scenario, and a rubric to grade the analysis, which will be explained further.

The scenarios consist of approximately 700 words regarding a current issue in technology and were created by the research team using criteria from EPSA to maintain reliability and validity, and conform to a Level 12 Flesch-Kincaid Readability Scale for students working in a second language. The scenarios include local and global technology related content, the perspectives of various stakeholders, and overriding issues such as security or privacy, and use credible news sources and academic articles. Each scenario has a set of question prompts, which are crafted to guide the students' thinking process in alignment with ABET's professional skills. It's imperative that the scenarios contain sufficient facets and complexity to generate analysis according to these prompts. Examples of successful scenarios which have generated meaningful discussion may be found in a previous paper [10].

As the method and the use of asynchronous online discussion is new to the students, the CPSA process is supported by an in-class presentation and walk-through and then a trial run to familiarize students. During the presentation and walk-through the method is explained and groups of 5–6 students discuss a scenario. This is followed by a 12-day semi-guided online discussion board facilitated by the instructor to ensure participation and on-task responses. Students are given instructions on how to interact within the online discussion, and regular readings and postings are required for task fulfilment. During the trial run the instructor provides guidance in the online discussion, with the aim of facilitating an independent student-led discussion. Students become conversant with the process and the expectations of this performance task. To ensure participation by all students the activity is a mandatory graded course requirement.

Following the trial run a new scenario is presented to students and the method runs over 12 days with the instructor monitoring rather than participating. The forum responses are then evaluated using the CPSA rubric, which has been developed in an iterative process over a two year period, and is now a reliable and valid tool. The first version of the CPSA rubric was developed from the EPSA model as this was proven in terms of validity and reliability. Deployment of the rubric involves a team who work towards calibration through norming sessions, initially with a discussion of the rubric, aiming for levels of consensus between raters of 70% or greater [11]. Raters work towards standardisation of rubric use by analysing student responses and comparing ratings in groups against the criteria, and detailed examples from the discussion text to support ratings. To arrive at the final ratings, scores from individual raters are calculated for the mean, with rounding applied, to generate overall scores. An example of the results from a rating session may be found in a previous paper [12]. The CPSA was run with a number of student groups and the results are given in a previous paper [10]. The results showed that we were able to identify areas of strength and weakness for those student groups in relation to the six ABET outcomes. As the assessment is for program level the data we obtained showed that the areas of problem solving, impact of computing and professional development needed considerable improvement; the areas of teamwork and ethics needed improvement to a lesser degree; and the area of communication was on target.

3   Survey

During the implementation of CPSA, the efficacy of the scenario and online discussion forum as a valuable learning activity emerged. The use of a scaffolded asynchronous online discussion forum as a tool for students to respond to the technology specific scenarios and utilize their 21st century skills was highlighted as a valuable teaching method. Students were afforded the opportunity to participate in group problem solving from mobile devices and various locations, with the benefit of time to create reflective responses. As the research team has decided to trial adapting the method for teaching input was sought from the students on their perceptions of the educational value of this performance task. The particular class of students surveyed consisted of 29 native Arabic-speaking females, in their early 20's, who were studying a 3rd year core course.

Once the online discussion board had closed, students received an anonymous online questionnaire with eight closed-response Likert scale items and three open- ended items. The open-ended questions asked respondents what they liked about the activity, what they didn't like and how it could be improved. The closed-response items were adapted from the Australian Course Experience Questionnaire (CEQ), a survey addressing quality in tertiary education. These CEQ questions align with the ABET professional skills. On a scale of (1) Strongly Disagree to (5) Strongly Agree students evaluated if the activity helped to develop their ABET transferable skills, and responses were ranked from highest to lowest according to the mean shown in Table 1 below.

Table 1. Analysis of survey responses

Question	Mean	SD
The activity helped to develop my ability to analyse problems	4.21	0.68
The activity helped to develop my problem-solving skills	4.11	0.63
The activity helped to improve my skills in written communication	4.03	0.78
The activity helped me to develop my understanding of ethical, legal and social issues	3.97	0.50
The activity helped me to develop the ability to analyse the impact of computing on the world	3.93	0.59
The activity helped me to recognize the limits of my knowledge and the need to continue to learn more	3.79	0.68
As a result of the activity, I feel more confident about tackling unfamiliar problems	3.75	0.75
The activity helped me develop my ability to work as a team member	3.55	1.02

The results clearly indicate that respondents felt the CPSA method offered a valuable opportunity to develop and practice the professional skills. The respondents were particularly positive about the benefit of the method for developing their analytical and problem solving skills, and communication skills. The open-ended items also generated positive responses related to the opportunity to develop skills for team work, and the use of online discussion forums, pointing particularly to the allowance for reflection. The comments included: *it gave us time to think before we talk which resulted in great discussions; it helped us as a team to engage one another and understand different points of view; my group was going deep into problems; I like the whole idea of a discussion board because it gave us time to think before we talk which resulted in great discussions.* (The comments have been edited for grammar and spelling to enhance readability). With a number of comments such as *everything was good and helpful, I liked this activity*, the overall response was confirmatory and pointed to developing the CPSA method as a teaching strategy in addition to assessment.

4   Discussion

Observations of the CPSA method, and positive responses on the survey demonstrated that CPSA offers a rich opportunity for students to practice and improve their use of transferable skills simultaneously. The period of 12 days worked well in allowing students adequate time to collate and share ideas, to conduct further research, to explore the issues presented in the scenario in depth, and to reflect upon and formulate written responses. The strength of the method is in its ability to offer the students a means to utilise and develop all of the six ABET identified professional skills in relation to their discipline.

To address the gap between workplace requirements in the knowledge economy and the transferable skill abilities of graduates, CPSA is suggested an innovative blended delivery performance task for teaching the professional skills at all levels of the curriculum, with the possibility of development for other disciplines. Additional LMS features allow for the mining of response data which can be used for both accreditation and continuous improvement reporting purposes. The refinement and improvement of the CPSA is an ongoing process and it will be made freely available.

Acknowledgement. This research work is being funded by grants from the Abu Dhabi Education Council Award for Research Excellence and the Zayed University Research Incentive Fund.

References

1. Ssekakubo, G., Suleman, H., Marsden, G.: Issues of adoption: Have e-learning management systems fulfilled their potential in developing countries? In: Proceedings of the South African Institute of Computer Scientists and Information Technologists Conference (2011)
2. Besterfield Sacre, M., Mcgourty, J., Shuman, L.J.: The ABET professional skills - Can they be taught? Can they be assessed? J. Eng. Educ. **94**(1), 41–55 (2005)
3. Arab Thought Foundation: Enabling job creation in the Arab world: A role for regional integration? (2013). http://www.pwc.com/m1/en/publications/enabling-job-creation-in-arab-world.pdf
4. Organisation for Economic Co-operation and Development: PISA 2012 results in focus (2014). http://www.oecd.org/pisa/keyfindings/pisa-2012-results-overview.pdf
5. Barakat, N., Plouff, C.: A model for on-line education of ABET-required professional aspects of engineering. In: Global Engineering Education Conference (2014)
6. Girardeau, L., Hauser, C., Kranov, A.A., Olsen, R.G.: A direct method for teaching and assessing professional skills in engineering programs. In: Proceedings of the 2008 ASEE Annual Conference and Exposition, Pittsburgh (2008)
7. Suskie, L.: Assessing student learning: A common sense guide. Jossey- Bass, San Francisco (2009)
8. Anderson, T., Archer, W., Garrison, D.R.: Critical inquiry in a text-based environment: Computer conferencing in higher education model. Internet High. Educ. **2**(2–3), 87–105 (2000)
9. Salmon, G.: E-Moderating: The Key to Teaching and Learning Online, 3rd edn. Routledge, New York (2011)
10. Schoepp, K., Danaher, M., Kranov, A.A.: The computing professional skills assessment: An innovative method for assessing ABET's student outcomes. In: IEEE Global Engineering Education Conference, Abu Dhabi (2016)
11. Brualdi, A.C.: Implementing performance assessment in the classroom. Pract. Assess. Res. Eval. 6(2) (1998)
12. Danaher, M., Schoepp, K., Ater Kranov, A.: A new approach for assessing ABET's professional skills in computing. World Trans. Eng. Technol. Educ. **14**(3), 1–6 (2016)

Designing an Electronic Health Security System Framework for Authentication with Wi-Fi, Smartphone and 3D Face Recognition Technology

Lesole Kalake[✉] and Chika Yoshida

Graduate School of Technology, Kobe Institute of Computing,
Kano-cho 2-7-7, Chuo-ku, Kobe 6500001, Japan
Lesole.kalake@gmail.com, cyoshida@kic.ac.jp

Abstract. Information technology for development is the tool that has been around for ages and it is now mainly focusing on making people lives easy including of those in a health sector. However, health practitioners and patients are somehow had not fully experienced this benefits due to sensitive information distribution and security concerns around the distribution of electronic health records. There have been various issues and challenges on security breaches, leakage of confidential patient records and computer attacks which have been raised on security and privacy concerns in electronic health records. The unauthorized access, denial of services, lack of standardization of the system increases mistrust on electronic health record system and makes it very difficult for the parties involved in handling and transmission of patients' record. Therefore the aim of this paper is to propose an efficient and cost-effective face recognition security framework through Wi-Fi to enable the monitoring and access control on patient record in developing countries.

Keywords: 3D face recognition · Biometric · Mobile device encryption · Patient electronic health record · Wi-Fi · Mac address · Serial number · International mobile station equipment identity · Authentication and security

1 Introduction

Healthcare process in developing countries is hierarchy structured based on the type of service, specialization and location. This means a patient have to carry a paper file or card with sensitive information and move from one place to a referral practitioner at the another side of a Health Institution or region [1]. This poses a huge risk for files been easily accessed by unauthorized persons or fall into the wrong hands and deprive patient privacy rights. The electronic patient health record is the ideal system that healthcare professionals around the globe believe it will offload work and help in making work and patient health record distribution easy by enabling information sharing over the network. However, electronic patient health record is faced with security threats and challenges as to how to secure the patient record and who should have what rights on which section of the electronic health record [2, 6].

© ICST Institute for Computer Sciences, Social Informatics and Telecommunications Engineering 2018
F. Belqasmi et al. (Eds.): AFRICATEK 2017, LNICST 206, pp. 226–232, 2018.
https://doi.org/10.1007/978-3-319-67837-5_22

There have been lots of security protocol and framework proposals for e-health authentications and security improvement but most of them sound time consuming, expensive and exposes negative impact on the practitioner's daily work coverage. They also seem to contribute to health record distribution path error and have a huge potential on information management risk. The patients are very much worried about their information control access and risks such as information leakage and disclosure. They do not want everybody at Health Institutions to have access to their information without their consent [3]. Therefore, they want a full control, tight security and activity log on their health records of the authorized individuals. On the other hands, both health professionals and patients don't like to spend too much time waiting for system authentication or have to go through lots of hectic authentication processes. Therefore, there is a need for a more secure, quick, hygienic and accurate authentication technology method. Hence, this paper proposes a cost-effective and efficient facial recognition technology method through Wi-Fi for e-health security system to enable the system administrators to have easy access control on authorized individuals. It is also intended to improve the distribution of patient record in a securely and efficiently technological environment.

1.1 Objectives and Scope

Electronic patient health record system is the place where everybody wants to go but the limitation is the best security technologies. Hence, sharing sensitive information over the network needs tight security. Nowadays smart phones have cameras and this is the boost for face recognition authentication procedures and can be used to scan the face on live and authenticate the user within less than five seconds. The proposed e-health system in this paper will use the mobile device, biometric and network technologies to strengthen authentication and eliminate security threats.

1.1.1 User Login Credentials
User shall register to creating a profile over the internet using work computers and notebooks. Use a 3D face recognition application installed on a smartphone to scan a face.

1.1.2 Device Information Storage
The Smartphone's information retrieval and verification shall be done by the system through a request sent via an email or SMS to the user for the account activation. During a user profile creation process the system solution will link the user, personal computer and smartphone device information that has been retrieved from Wi-Fi, and then encrypt and store it on the Web server for future authentication process and auditing.

2 Related Work

Biometric technologies have been used in the different fields but mostly where the confidentiality matters most such as in army, hospital, finance and intelligence agencies.

The facial recognition is one of the biometrics that is mostly used in the market today. The United Services Automobile Association has deployed the face recognition authentication technology for its members to login to mobile banking with the blink of an eye literally [4]. ZoOm™ has developed the 3D facial authentication smartphone application which use the front-facing camera on any smartphone to capture a selfie video and instantly process frames on the device and compare against previously stored biometric data [5] (Table 1).

Table 1. Biometric technologies comparisons

Facial recognition (3D)	Voice recognition	Signature recognition	Finger print	Iris recognition
Very high accuracy	Low accuracy	Medium-Low accuracy	Very high accuracy	Very high accuracy
Verification time is generally less than 5 s	Verification time is generally less than 6 s	Verification time is generally more than 5 s	Verification time is generally more than 5 s	Verification time is generally less than 5 s
No face picture or video can be used	Voice pitch not always exactly the same due to flue and surrounding environment	Signature not always exactly the same	Can be chopped off or damaged	No eye from a dead person can be used
Non intrusive	Non intrusive	Non intrusive	very intrusive	Intrusive
Medium storage required	Small storage required	Small storage required	Small storage required	More memory storage needed
Economical	Very cheap	Very cheap	Economical	Expensive

Facial recognition 3D technology is indeed the highly accurate, nonintrusive and economical biometric technology that can be incorporated in e-health security framework to improve the authentication and security.

3 System Solution Overview

Everybody is sensitive about their health status disclosure that is why carrying the files to the referred practitioner is always in a massive protected route. Hence, proposes a cost-effective e-health system to ensure that patient information is highly secured over the internet in developing countries. It shall be an integrated multi-authentication with a Web application for transactions, Web servers, Wi-Fi, smartphone, database and facial recognition applications for authentication.

3.1 Web Authentications

The patients, hospital receptionists, health practitioner assistance, pharmacists or health practitioners (like Drs and Specialists) are always using the smartphone for different tasks every day, but this paper proposes the use of the same mobile device with Wi-Fi switched on for both registration and authentication process. This will enable the system to register the device and store the information such as serial number, MAC address and IMEI on the background linked with the user profile for authentication process.

3.2 Device Role

A device used for profile creation or to activate a user account is the primary device that will be used in the future to authenticate and link with other devices if the users have multiple devices. All devices must be on the same network during the process. The user will need to type in the e-health URL and the device information will be mapped and linked with the information stored. A web server will reply with a face recognition application request to user's smartphone for an auto login authentication process. In a case of a loss or theft of one of the devices, the system administrator can easily disable the device from the database at the backend to enable the user to register a new device.

3.3 User(s) Role

The roles will be created based on the levels such as patient, hospital receptionist, health practitioner assistance (nurses), pharmacist and health practitioner (like Drs and Specialists), whereby the patient have the full control of his or her electronic health record. Doctors and Specialists will have full view and edit of the records while others will have row or table level view permission only.

3.4 Face Recognition Application

Smartphone's front face camera shall be used to capture face live via 3D face recognition application, processed and sent to the backend for storage. The face recognition application shall also be used for face scanning and a quick user authentication without login credentials been required.

3.5 Wi-Fi and Smartphone Roles

A smartphone always sends a signal when the Wi-Fi is turned on regardless of connections to the network. Therefore, the smartphone information shall be easily retrieved and used for user identification, matches, face and frame instant processing; and analysis of activity logs or communication packets. Instead of using computers for authentication, smartphone on the same Wi-Fi with the computer will be used for login and access onto e-health system.

4   Proposed System Architecture

When devices are on the same network their information can uniquely be retrieved, paired and stored. They can also establish an easy and fast communication channel to distribute packages over the network amongst themselves. Hence, it can be told which device was used and by whom, when and for what purpose.

The proposed system architecture includes several devices and components that contribute to the effectiveness of a solution. A personal computer and smartphone are the key components for user identification and authentication, whereby a Wi-Fi network role is to gel and harmonize the whole solution with the implementation of a 3D facial recognition application and a database. During the registration process the communication channel between the personal computer and smartphone was established whereby a network has retrieved the device information and stored it temporarily. The system shall use the channel to forward the response request for the user to launch a 3D facial recognition application on the smartphone. Then enable a database to retrieve, map, process and store information gathered from both devices for in future when a registered user login with his or her personal computer to access a patient electronic health record via the URL.

In Fig. 1, the high-level system overview illustrates how the solution should work for user identification and authentication. A user login with his or her personal computer, and then a network retrieves the device information temporarily for a database to perform user match for identification and authentication. Then if a device is registered already, a database will respond with a query for the web server to ask for a launching of the 3D

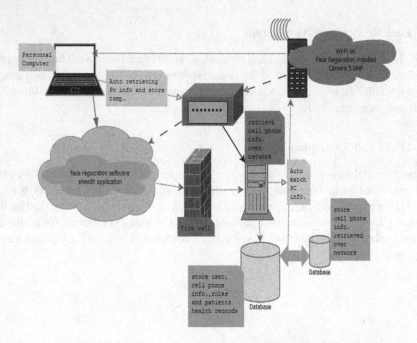

Fig. 1. Proposed system architecture and interactions

facial recognition application for authentication. If it's a new device then it means a new registration process.

5 Conclusions

This paper proposed the integrated multi-authentication processes into a single login procedure for e-health system. The system framework includes the popularity usage of computer networking, 3D face recognition technologies and smartphone device for a secure login. Integrated multi- factor authentication includes Wi-Fi for mobile device detection and face recognition pair as well as username and password when necessary. The proposed security framework can overcome the vulnerability of a traditional authentication process in developing countries. The idea of this security framework system is to leverage the mobile device as a personal and unique identifier for each user. The system brings many advantages in improving the security of the secure authentication and it is efficient, affordable and easy to implement in developing countries.

Appendix: Acronyms and Definitions

1. E-health- is an electronic patient health record system used to store and help in centralizing the individual's medical history.
2. Wi-Fi- a local area network that uses high frequency radio signals to transmit and receive data over distances of a few hundred feet; uses Ethernet protocol.
3. MAC- a media access control address is a unique identifier assigned to network interfaces for communications.
4. IMEI- a unique, number to identify mobile phones and satellite phones.
5. Smartphone- is a mobile phone with an advanced mobile operating system which combines features of a personal computer operating system with other features useful for mobile.
6. 3D facial recognition- is technique that uses 3D sensors to capture information about the shape of a face.
7. Drs- General health practitioners.
8. Specialist- a doctor highly skilled in a specific and restricted field of medicine.
9. Nurse- a person who is qualified to treat certain medical conditions without the direct supervision of a doctor.
10. Pharmacist- member of the health care team directly involved with patient care and dispense medicines.
11. URL- Uniform Resource Locator is a protocol for specifying addresses on the Internet.

References

1. Jacob, J., Agrawal, V.: Privacy in electronic health record systems – consumer's perspective (2003)
2. Barrows, J.R.C., Clayton, P.D.: Privacy, confidentiality, and electronic medical records. J. Am. Med. Inform. Assoc. 3(2), 139–148 (1996)
3. Papoutsi, C., Reed, J.E., Marston, C., Lewis, R., Majeed, A., Bell, D.: Patient and public views about the security and privacy of Electronic Health Records (EHRs) in the UK: results from a mixed methods study, October 2015
4. Crosman, C.P.: Biometric Tipping Point: USAA Deploys Face, Voice Recognition, February 2015. http://www.americanbanker.com/news/bank-technology/biometric-tipping-point-usaa-deploys-face-voice-recognition-1072509-1.html
5. PR Newswire: ZoOm™, The World's First Secure Selfie 3D Authentication App, Announced By FacialNetwork, July 2015. http://www.thestreet.com/story/13212142/1/zoom-the-worlds-first-secure-selfie-3d-authentication-app-announced-by-facialnetwork.html
6. Mirembe, D.P.: Design of a Secure Framework for the Implementation of Telemedicine, eHealth, and Wellness Services (2006)

Investigating TOE Factors Affecting
the Adoption of a Cloud-Based EMR System
in the Free-State, South Africa

Nomabhongo Masana[✉] and Gerald Maina Muriithi

Department of Information Technology, Central University of Technoloy,
Private Bag X20539, Bloemfontein, South Africa
nnomabhongo@gmail.com, gmuriithi@cut.ac.za

Abstract. Paper based medical records face many challenges such as inability of real-time access to patient data, exchange and share medical data, and monitor a patients' health progress. This negatively affects the ability to improve a patients' health and carry out medical research. Adopting electronic medical records (EMR) may help address some issues faced with paper records. However, standalone EMR systems may not fully mitigate some issues with paper records due to lack of real-time access to patient data. Cloud Computing presents cost-effective ways of integrating EMR systems together for different health institutions to share selected patient data. However, the extent to which South African health facilities are ready to adopt cloud based EMR, and the nature of patient data that can be shared on the cloud remains unclear. This study investigates the viability of a cloud based EMR for health institutions in the Free State province of South Africa.

Keywords: Adoption · Cloud-Based · Cloud computing · EMR · HealthCare · TOE framework

1 Introduction

Majority of health institutions (especially those in developing countries) still use paper-based medical records [1]. Paper-based medical records face many challenges, including the inability to get real time access to patient data when needed, inability to exchange and share medical data among health institutions, difficulties in compiling accurate medical reports, and in monitoring patient health progress [2]. In addition, paper-based medical records are often difficult to use for medical research and problematic when used for clinical studies [2]. In a recent study [3], it was found that inadequate record keeping is a major obstacle in doing archival research in a rural community in South Africa. Adopting new technologies, such as an Electronic Medical Record (EMR) system, may address some of the challenges facing paper-based records [4]. Although EMRs may help resolve some of the problems with paper-based medical records, if the EMR systems are not linked or integrated, the problem of real-time accessibility and exchange of patient data remains unresolved.

© ICST Institute for Computer Sciences, Social Informatics and Telecommunications Engineering 2018
F. Belqasmi et al. (Eds.): AFRICATEK 2017, LNICST 206, pp. 233–238, 2018.
https://doi.org/10.1007/978-3-319-67837-5_23

The emerging cloud-computing model, which leverages the Internet to allow the sharing of IT resources as online services, may offer a cost effective solution of integrating diverse EMR systems. Cloud computing is a model that offers ubiquitous access to the network in a convenient way with minimal management effort [5]. Furthermore, most managers and experts believe that cloud computing may improve health care services and benefit medical research and reduce costs associated with setting up a shared EMR infrastructure [6]. Integrating EMR systems with the cloud enables the sharing and exchange of selected medical data among the different healthcare facilities [7]. Despite the benefits of using cloud computing such as lower costs, faster rollout and anytime, anywhere access, implementing a cloud-based EMR platform faces several challenges, and key among them is data security risks. Adopting cloud-based EMR, innovative as it is, requires thorough evaluation before deciding whether it is viable, and if viable what patient data to move to the cloud and what security provisions to put in place [6]. The path to cloud-based EMR is likely to differ from one country (or even one region) to the other based on the prevailing regulatory framework and state of readiness.

The purpose of this study is twofold. First, assess the current state of use of EMR systems within the Free State (FS) province of South Africa (RSA). Secondly, determine the extent to which health facilities (both public and private) are ready to embrace cloud-based EMR in which selected patient data is made shareable among participating institutions. In determining this, a set of factors that influences or impedes the adoption of cloud-based EMR will be evaluated. The study will be anchored on the Technology-Organization-Environment (TOE) framework, an organizational level framework that describes key elements which influences a firms' decision to adopt an innovation [8–11]. The key deliverable of this study is a framework that can guide the adoption of a cloud-based EMR system for the Free State province.

The study will target public and private clinics and hospitals drawn from the Free-State province of South Africa. The results obtained from this study will be used to propose a model for adopting cloud based EMR in the Free State province.

2   Literature Review

2.1   Cloud Computing and Cloud EMR

The National Institute of Standards and Technology (NIST) defines cloud computing as *"a model for enabling ubiquitous, convenient, on-demand network access to a shared pool of configurable computing resources (e.g. networks, servers, storage, applications, and services) that can be rapidly provisioned and released with minimal management effort or service provider interaction"* [5]. The cloud can help break the barriers to the adoption of EMR in resource-poor areas, removing the need for building a local infrastructure (which includes including a server, network, security, maintenance and power supply) for each clinic, and having only one server used to cater for all the clinics [12]. Integrating EMR with the Internet provides flexibility in terms of *"transferability of information, greater communication among doctors, and improvement in quality of care"* [13]. Getting the right information at the right time when it is needed saves lives [14]. Due to its improved accessibility, storing medical data in the cloud enables physicians and medical staff to collaborate with each other for medical research in order to improve and offer better quality healthcare services to people [15, 16]. Cloud-based medical record systems are much better, faster and easier to access than traditional sever-based storage systems, are more cost-effective, more scalable and results in increased productivity [17]. However, adopting a cloud-based EMR requires careful consideration in the face of challenges such as security fears, complexity of integration among other issues.

2.2   TOE Framework

The TOE framework is an organizational level theory that explains the elements which influences a firms' decision on the adoption of an innovation [18]. These elements are the technological context, organizational context and environmental context [8, 10]. Technological context considers both the existing technologies and technologies that can be purchased or added to the existing ones for improvement of the firm. Organizational context refers to the organization's resources, which includes how the employees are structured, communication methods, the size/scope of the firm and managerial structures. Environmental context refers to the structure of the industry, consisting of government, community, competitors and the availability of service provider or suppliers [8, 9, 11]. The figure below illustrates the TOE framework developed by Tornatzky and Fleischer [18] (Fig. 1).

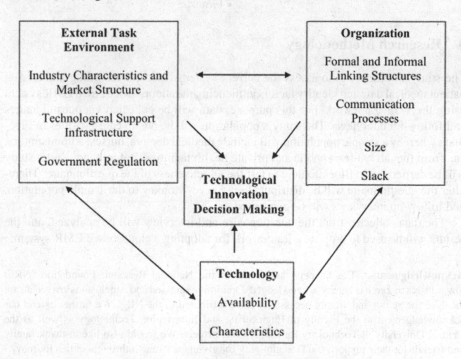

Fig. 1. Technology-Organization-Environment (TOE) framework.

Since we consider cloud EMR as an innovative approach that is not yet widely deployed, employing the TOE framework allows us to consider the most relevant factors when assessing its adoption. The use of the TOE framework is widely supported and has been utilized in existing literature which addressed the adoption of innovative technologies and models [19–21]. The table below presents a summary of some studies that relied on the TOE framework (Table 1).

Table 1. TOE studies on cloud computing adoption.

Preliminary studies on TOE framework			
Source/Study	Technological factors	Organizational factors	Environmental factors
Assessing a new IT service model, cloud computing [19]	• Perceived benefits • Perceived barriers	• Organizational learning capacity • Organizational IT capability	• Competitive pressure • Expectation of network dominance
TOE drivers for cloud transformation: direct or trust-mediated? [20]	• Reliability • Information security	• Size • International scope • IT competence • Entrepreneurship	• Institutional pressure • Structure assurance • Vendor scarcity
Cloud computing adoption by firms [21]	• Technology readiness	• Global scope • Top Management support • Firm size	• Competitive pressure • Regulatory support

3   Research Methodology

The study's objective is to assess the current systems used for recording and storing patient medical data and identify factors influencing the adoption of a cloud EMR system using the TOE framework. For this purpose, data will be collected via questionnaires and follow-up interviews. The study's population will be health care facilities in Free-State whereby a sample population will include medical doctors, nurses, administrators, etc. from (not all but few) public and private health facilities. Beforehand, a pilot study will be carried out in Bloemfontein to test the effectiveness of the questionnaire. Thereafter the questionnaire will be distributed via SurveyMonkey to the sample population, and follow-up interviews will be conducted.

The data collected from the questionnaire and interview will be analyzed, and the results will be used to propose a framework for adopting a cloud-based EMR system.

Acknowledgments.   The financial assistance of the National Research Foundation (NRF) towards this research is hereby acknowledged. Opinions expressed and conclusions arrived at, are those of the author and are not necessarily to be attributed to the NRF. We further extend our acknowledgement to the Faculty of Engineering and Information Technology as well as the Central University of Technology for funding this project. We would also like to thank family and friends for their support, and God almighty for giving us strength throughout this journey.

References

1. Fraser, H.S.F., Allen, C., Bailey, C., Douglas, G., Shin, S., Blaya, J.: Information systems for patient follow-up and chronic management of HIV and tuberculosis: a life-saving technology in resource-poor area. J. Med. Internet Res. **9**, e29 (2007)
2. Fenz, S., Heurix, J., Nubauer, T.: Recognition and privacy preservation of paper-based health records. In: Quality of Life Through Quality of Information, Pisa (2012)
3. Wegner, L., Rhoda, A.: Missing medical records: An obstacle to archival survey-research in a rural community in South Africa. SA J. Philos. **69**, 15–19 (2013)
4. Pourasghar, F., Malekafzali, H., Kazemi, A., Ellenius, J., Fors, U.: What they fill in today, may not be useful tomorrow: Lessons learned from studying Medical Records at the Women hospital in Tabriz, Iran. BMC Public Health. **8**, 139–145 (2008)
5. Hogan, M., Sokol, A.: NIST Cloud Computing Standards Roadmap. Report, National Institute of Standards and Technology Roadmap Working Group (2013)
6. Kuo, A.M.-H.: Opportunities and challenges of cloud computing to improve health care services. J. Med. Internet Res. **13**, 1–15 (2011)
7. Haskewa, J., Rø, G., Saitoc, K., Tuner, K., Odhiambo, G., Wamae, A., Sharif, S., Sugishita, T.: Implementation of a cloud-based electronic medical record for maternal and child health in rural Kenya. Int. J. Med. Inform. **84**, 349–354 (2015)
8. Baker, J.: The technology-organization-environment framework. In: Dwivedi, Y.K., et al. (eds.) Information Systems Theory: Explaining and Predicting Our Digital Society. Springer, Heidelberg (2011)
9. Angeles, R.: Using the technology-organization-environment framework for analyzing nike's "Considered Index" green initiative, a decision support system-driven system. J. Manage. Sustain. **4**, 96–113 (2014)
10. Oliveira, T., Martins, M.: Literature review of information technology adoption models at firm level. Electron. J. Inf. Syst. Eval. **14**, 110–121 (2011)
11. Safari, F., Safari, N., Hasanzade, A.: The adoption of software-as-a-service(SaaS): ranking the determinants. J. Enterp. Inf. Manage. **28**, 400–422 (2015)
12. Haskew, J., Rø, G., Turner, K., Kimanga, D., Sirego, M., Sharif, S.: Implementation of a cloud-based electronic medical record to reduce gaps in the HIV treatment continuum in rural Kenya. PLoS ONE **10**, 1–10 (2015)
13. Weeks, R.: Electronic medical records: Managing the transformation from a paper-based to an electronic system. J. Contemp. Manage. **10**, 135–155 (2013)
14. Lupse, O.-S., Stoicu-Tivadar, V.: Cloud computing and interoperability in healthcare information systems. In: The First International Conference on Intelligent Systems and Applications (2012)
15. Yu, H.-J., Lai, H.-S., Chen, K.-H., Chou, H.-C., Wu, J.-M., Dorjgochoo, S., Mendjargal, A., Altangerel, E., Tien, Y.-W., Hsueh, C.-W., Lai, F.: A sharable cloud-based pancreaticoduodenectomy collaborative database for physicians: Emphasis on security and clinical rule supporting. Comput. Method Programs Biomed. **3**, 488–497 (2013)
16. Singh, V.J., Singh, D.P., Bansal, K.L.: Proposed architecture: cloud based medical information retrieval network. Int. J. Comput. Sci. Eng. Technol. **4**, 485–496 (2013)
17. Gupta, A.K., Mann, K.S.: Sharing of medical information on cloud platform-a review. IOSR J. Comput. Eng. **16**, 08–11 (2014)
18. Tornatzky, L.G., Fleischer, M., Chakrabarti, A.K.: The Process of Technological Innovation. Lexington Books, Lexington (1990)

19. Son, I., Lee, D.: Assessing a new IT service model, cloud computing. In: Pacific Asia Conference on Information Systems (PACIS) (2011)
20. Li, M., Zhao, D., Yu, Y.: TOE drivers for cloud transformation: direct or trust-mediated? Asia Pac. J. Mark. Logistics **27**, 226–248 (2015)
21. Espadanal, M., Oliveira, T.: Cloud computing adoption by firms. In: Mediterranean Conference on Information Systems (2012)

Author Index

Achtaich, Asmaa 57
Al Taei, May 120
Aldwairi, Monther 181
Alfandi, Omar 3, 120, 171
Al-Obeidat, Feras 110
Alolama, Abdulhakim 181
AlRoum, Khalifa 181
Amezzane, Ilham 214
Asal, Rasool 159
Ater Kranov, Ashley 220

Bah, Slimane 22, 33
Bakhouya, Mohamed 214
Bauld Wallace, Julie 220
Beachboard, John 3
Belo, Orlando 79
Benkaouz, Yahya 67
Bentahar, Jamal 129, 140
Bouguila, Nizar 192
Bouhaddioui, Chafik 99
Boukhris, Yness 205

Cimato, Stelvio 159

Damiani, Ernesto 159
Danaher, Maurice 220
Darqaoui, Mohamed 33
Driouache, Saida 12
Dssouli, Rachida 99, 129, 140
Duarte, Duarte 79

El Aroussi, Mohammed 214
El Barachi, May 181
Elgraini, Belhaj 22
El-Kassabi, Hadeel 99
Elqortobi, Mounia 129
Erradi, Mohammed 67

Fakhri, Youssef 214
Frati, Fulvio 159

Houngbo, Perpetus Jacques 159
Hounsou, Joël T. 159
Hughes, Danny 45

Jabir, Raja 171
Jamali, Abdellah 12

Kafeza, Eleanna 110, 120
Kalake, Lesole 226
Kamel, Rami 181
Kesserwan, Nader 140

Lawrence, Piers W. 45

Madani, Mohamed Amine 67
Masana, Nomabhongo 233
Mazo, Raul 57
Merai, Mehdi 89
Muriithi, Gerald Maina 233

Naja, Najib 12

Phippard, Trisha M. 45

Ramachandran, Gowri Sankar 45
RB, Jagadeesha 3
Riyahi, Amina 22
Roudies, Ounsa 57

Salinesi, Camille 57
Sebgui, Marouane 22, 33
Serhani, Mohamed Adel 99
Shehada, Dina 159
Shoepp, Kevin 220
Singh, Jai Puneet 192
Souissi, Nissrine 57
Spencer, Bruce 110

Yeun, Chan Yeob 159
Yoshida, Chika 226
Yu, Jia Yuan 89

Printed in the United States
by Baker & Taylor Publisher

Printed in the United States
By Bookmasters